Hawai'i
Regional
Cuisine

FOOD IN ASIA AND THE PACIFIC

Series Editors: Christine R. Yano and Robert Ji-Song Ku

This series showcases new works focused on food in the Asia-Pacific region and its diasporic iterations, highlighting the commonalities that the area and cultures might bring to the subject. Books in this series are disciplinarily diverse, drawing from the fields of geography, sociology, anthropology, history, globalization studies, gender studies, science and technology studies, development studies, ethnic studies, and cultural studies. The Asia-Pacific region evokes particular global relationships and domestic infrastructures—center-periphery, postcolonialism, imperialisms, and politicized imaginaries. The goal of the series is to bring food to bear in considering these relationships and infrastructures. We see a regional focus—including the inherent mobility of transnational flows, migration, and global capitalism therein—as productive elements, rather than as reifying limitations. By bringing together books that have a general topic (food) and an area focus (Asia-Pacific), the series locates mobility itself as the framework from which scholarship may enrich our understanding of this complexly globalized world.

Hawai'i Regional Cuisine

THE FOOD MOVEMENT THAT CHANGED THE WAY HAWAI'I EATS

Samuel Hideo Yamashita

University of Hawai'i Press   Honolulu

24 23 22 21 20 19   6 5 4 3 2 1

Library of Congress Cataloging-in-Publication Data

Names: Yamashita, Samuel Hideo, author.
Title: Hawai'i regional cuisine : the food movement that changed the way
    Hawai'i eats / Samuel Hideo Yamashita.
Other titles: Food in Asia and the Pacific.
Description: Honolulu : University of Hawai'i Press, [2019] | Series: Food in
    Asia and the Pacific | Includes bibliographical references and index.
Identifiers: LCCN 2018041489| ISBN 9780824877453 (cloth ; alk. paper) |
    ISBN   9780824879723 (pbk. ; alk. paper)
Subjects: LCSH: Cooking—Hawaii. | Hawaiian cooking.
Classification: LCC TX724.5.H3 Y295 2019 | DDC 641.59969—dc23
LC record available at https://lccn.loc.gov/2018041489

Cover art: (Front) The twelve founding Hawaii Regional Cuisine chefs.
Courtesy of Mark Ellman. (Back) Salad with warabi fern, kamaboko,
tomatoes, onions, sesame oil, and oyster sauce. Leigh Anne Meeks/
Shutterstock.com

To my brother, David

Contents

Preface   *ix*

1 Origins   1
2 Development   24
3 Cuisine   57
4 Successors   86
5 Legacy   117

Glossary   *131*
Notes   *139*
Selected Bibliography   *163*
Index   *173*

Preface

This book began with a discovery. In August 1992, my wife and I were vacationing on the Big Island, and we decided to have dinner at the CanoeHouse restaurant at the Mauna Lani Resort on the Kohala coast. We arrived at dusk and were quickly ushered to a table near the ocean, where we watched twilight give way to darkness. At some point, the candle on our table was lit, and it was then that I noticed something I had never seen in a fine-dining establishment in the islands: on one side of the table were a bottle of shoyu and a bottle of what is called "chili pepper water." When I was growing up in the islands, these condiments were fixtures in the homes of many locals but were never found in the best restaurants. When I asked the waitress about this, she said, "Oh, we have a new chef, Alan Wong, and this is his idea." "Interesting," I thought. Now, twenty-six years later, I have written a book, *Hawai'i Regional Cuisine: The Food Movement That Changed the Way Hawai'i Eats*, that explains the significance of the shoyu and chili pepper water on the table at CanoeHouse.

I spent six years (2009–2015) interviewing chefs, food writers, farmers, ranchers, fishermen, aquaculturists, coffee growers, culinary educators, and others involved in some way with the Hawai'i Regional Cuisine (HRC) movement. I interviewed Wanda Adams, Kevin Chong, Sam Choy, Tane Datta, Mark Ellman, Amy Ferguson, Hiroshi Fukui, Beverly Gannon, John Heckathorn, Kurt Hirabara, Pam Hirabara, Edward Kenney, Derek Kurisu, Andrew Le, Frank Leake, Erin Lee, Gary Maunakea-Forth, George Mavrothalassitis, Peter Merriman, John Morton, Dan Nakasone, Joan Namkoong, Conrad Nonaka, Dean Okimoto, Edward Sakamoto, Gladys Sato, Sheldon Simeon, Russell Siu, David Sumida, Fern Tomisato Yoshida, Joe Wilson, Alan Wong, and Roy Yamaguchi. Each interview lasted from

Chili pepper water and shoyu cruets at Alan Wong's. Courtesy of Alan Wong's.

thirty to ninety minutes. I am grateful to everyone who made time to meet with me and to answer my questions, the good ones as well as the uninformed and foolish ones. I could not have written this book without these interviews, but sadly, John Heckathorn, Kurt Hirabara, and Conrad Nonaka died before I finished. I also would like to thank David Yamashita, Warren Osako, Kepā Maly, Kurt Matsumoto, and Alberta De Jetley for sharing information about the brief history of Hawai'i Regional Cuisine on Lāna'i. Dara Fukuhara, Nicole Ng, Marylee Sakas, and Tony Novak-Clifford helped me get some of the photographs of HRC chefs and restaurants. Leigh Ito helped me in so many ways that I can't begin to remember all of them.

I am deeply indebted to the many librarians who helped me gather material for this book. Joan Hori, Dore Minatodani, and Jodie Mattos, the librarians in the Hawaiian Collection at Hamilton Library at the University of Hawai'i at Mānoa, were especially helpful. At the Hawai'i State Public Library, Shelly Brown brought out a file on Honolulu restaurants that was an unexpected treasure trove, and Kathryn Arinaga helped me find information that I could not find on my own. At the State of Hawai'i Archive, Melissa Shimonishi and Troy Kimura facilitated my search for photographs for my book; the librarians at the Los Angeles Public Library guided my searches for material that I needed to cite correctly; and the staff of the

Inter-Library Loan Office of Honnold/Mudd Library at the Claremont Colleges helped me retrieve materials not in our collection.

The ample resources of these several libraries enabled me to collect nearly everything written about the HRC movement: articles in local newspapers and local magazines as well as national newspapers and magazines such as the *New York Times, Los Angeles Times, Chicago Tribune, Gourmet, Bon Appétit, Food & Wine, Travel & Leisure, Esquire, Condé-Nast Traveler,* and *Wine Spectator.* I also bought all the cookbooks the HRC chefs published between 1991 and 2016. In the process of doing this, I may have amassed the largest and most complete archive of material on Hawai'i Regional Cuisine.

I had several opportunities to present parts of this manuscript to informed audiences both in this country and abroad. In 2011, Madeline Hsu, a former student of mine and a fine historian of Asian America, organized a panel on Asian American food at the annual meeting of the Association for Asian American Studies and invited me to join the panel. I presented there a paper on the origins and development of the HRC movement titled "The Postcolonial Significance of Hawai'i Regional Cuisine," which was later published in *Eating Asian America: A Food Studies Reader* (New York University Press, 2013), edited by Robert Ku, Anita Mannur, and Martin Manalansan IV. I also presented "The Strange Tale of the *Loco Moco*" at Pomona College in 2013 and the University of Tokyo in January 2015.

I owe a special debt to Robert Ku, who invited me to consider submitting this book for the Food in Asia and the Pacific series published by the University of Hawai'i Press, for which he and Christine Yano are the series editors.

I want to thank as well those who arranged the funding for my research: the Research Committee at Pomona College and Associate Dean Cynthia Selaissie, who approved my first short research trip to Hawai'i in 2011; and Dean Elizabeth Crighton, who funded a weeklong trip to the islands in July 2015 that allowed me to interview the post-HRC chefs. Dean Audrey Bilger paid for the maps and photographs that appear in this book.

My former students Daniel Allen, Allison Uchima, and Hong Deng Gao performed the thankless task of transcribing my interviews, which enabled me to use them more easily in my research.

Bill Nelson made the maps that appear in the book, and their clarity and precision enhance my account of Hawai'i Regional Cuisine. Finally, I am deeply grateful to those who read different versions of the manuscript that became this book. Michiko Kodama-Nishimoto from the Center for Oral History at the University of Hawaiʻi at Mānoa sent me sources that I had overlooked and carefully read an early version of chapter 1, catching many problems I missed. My colleagues Emily Chao, Angelina Chin, and Joe Jeon gave me their thoughts on the same early version of chapter 1, and my Claremont colleague Hal Barron kindly gave me his thoughts on the manuscript as a whole. My brother, David, recommended recent publications on the islands' food security and sustainability that proved indispensable, and two anonymous readers for the University of Hawaiʻi Press offered helpful suggestions that made this a better book.

As always, I am grateful to my wife, Margaret Barrows Yamashita, who was my companion at a truly uncountable number of dinners at the restaurants of the chefs I discuss in this book and whose professional editor's eye improved the book manuscript in a thousand ways.

Hawai'i Regional Cuisine

1 | Origins

> Eating in Hawaii is like having airline food three times a
> day. Take some olive oil and vinegar with you. That way at
> least you'll be able to pick some wild watercress and have a
> decent salad.
>
> Alice Waters

At first glance, Hawai'i Regional Cuisine, like other American regional cuisines, seems nothing less than a paean to the state's diverse ethnic communities and their foods and to its natural bounties from its air, land, and sea. But given the history of the Hawaiian islands as first an independent kingdom (1795–1893), then a US colony (1898–1959), and finally a state (1959–present), Hawai'i Regional Cuisine has a much larger significance.

Fine dining in Hawai'i was generally assumed to be Continental cuisine, like that usually found at restaurants in Waikīkī. These establishments had long hired French, German, or Swiss chefs with impeccable credentials, who had been trained and apprenticed in Europe and had brought their Continental culinary techniques, values, and traditions to the islands. These chefs' richly sauced dishes echoed classic French cuisine and were consumed with French or, later, California wines. In theory, a fine meal at La Mer, the fabled French restaurant at the Halekulani Hotel in Waikīkī, was no different from a fine meal at La Côte Basque in New York City or La Pyramide in Vienne, France.[1] Crucial here was the long-standing and unassailable dominance of a central and culturally superior culinary idiom

(French cuisine) that originated in Europe and took precedence over all regional and local idioms.[2]

In contrast, because the local food that most of Hawai'i's population ate was not Continental, it was denigrated, overlooked, or, at best, tolerated. Indeed, local food and Continental cuisine were not to be mentioned in the same breath except perhaps ironically, as when one spoke of a "local French restaurant." Local food was denigrated simply because it was what "locals" ate.[3] During the colonial period, a local was someone born, raised, or educated in Hawai'i who was not Caucasian but was a member of either the indigenous Hawaiian population or one of the many groups that had immigrated to the islands to work on the plantations or ranches.[4] Typically, Hawaiians, Chinese, Japanese, Puerto Ricans, Spanish, Portuguese, and Filipinos were regarded as locals. Indeed, at this time, Hawai'i had a rigid "caste system" of racial hierarchies and distinctions, to which the colonial authorities and business elite strictly adhered.[5]

Every aspect of life in the colony was racialized: the inhabitants' political, economic, and social lives, as well as their education, sports, and culture.[6] Well-born members of the Caucasian elite attended Oahu College (known after 1934 as Punahou School) or a mainland (that is, continental United States) boarding school and then were sent away to an Ivy League university. After marrying someone from the local elite or the mainland, they returned to take their place in one of the five major companies, known as the Big Five, spending their free time playing tennis or golf and dining at one of several established Honolulu country clubs and reveling in the benefits of their superiority.[7] Those Caucasians who were not so well born attended one of the English Standard Schools and then the University of Hawai'i.[8] They then entered one of several local companies, where their race entitled them to rise to a managerial or supervisory position.

Those of Hawaiian, Chinese, Japanese, Filipino, Portuguese, Spanish, or Puerto Rican descent, or some combination of these, were locals and thus inferior. Within a century of the arrival of the first Europeans to the islands in 1778, the indigenous population had dropped from between four hundred thousand and one million to forty thousand, owing to both the diseases brought by the Europeans and the profound changes in land tenure, government, religion, and culture carried out at their urging.[9] In 1893, prominent American businessmen engineered the overthrow of the native monarchy and pushed hard for the US annexation of the islands, which took place on July 7, 1898, despite the fierce opposition of the indigenous population.[10] A decade after the islands were annexed, the remnants of the Hawaiian population were in both physical and cultural decline, and Asians were regarded by the Caucasian elite as mere instruments of production, akin to the "cattle of the ranges."[11] The exceptions were Hawaiians from the ali'i (chiefly) class, many of whom had managed to preserve their landholdings and married Caucasians, and locals who had succeeded in business.[12] Most locals went to public elementary schools through the eighth grade and then started working at age fifteen, joining the large pool of plantation, factory, or dock workers. Some, though, were lucky enough to be sent to one of the four other private schools in Honolulu: 'Iolani School, Mid-Pacific Institute, Kamehameha Schools, or the College of St. Louis. Kamehameha was open only to Hawaiians, and although the others were open to all groups, 'Iolani attracted many Chinese, Mid-Pacific many Japanese, and St. Louis a combination of Hawaiian, Portuguese, and Chinese.[13] Many private school graduates attended the University of Hawai'i, and after graduating, they became teachers or entered family businesses or local companies, with a good chance of rising to a managerial position. A small number attended professional schools on the mainland, and some Hawaiians and Portuguese even rose to supervisory positions on plantations.[14]

Race mattered politically, too. In 1917, the ethnic breakdown of Hawai'i's population of 228,771 was Caucasian, 16,042; Chinese, 21,954; Filipino, 16,898; Hawaiian/part-Hawaiian, 39,104; Japanese, 97,000; Portuguese, 23,753; Puerto Rican, 5,187; Spanish, 3,577; and other, 5,254.[15] Even though Caucasians made up only 7 percent of the colony's population, they nonetheless dominated the other 93 percent and were supported in doing so by the 13,249 American soldiers and sailors stationed in the islands.[16] Not surprisingly, as the number of servicemen increased, so, too, did the interracial tension. Officers responded by sending their children to private schools in Honolulu, and enlisted men got into fights with locals, often over women.[17] But even when large numbers of Hawaiians and immigrant children gained the right to vote, and thus the ability to wield political power, many nineteenth-century notions of Caucasian superiority persisted well into the 1950s.[18]

Caucasians and locals met as equals only on the colony's playing fields, as members of a high school team or in one of the racialized sports leagues. For example, the Hawai'i Major League consisted of single-ethnicity baseball teams: the Wanderers were the Caucasian team; the Chinese, or the Chinese Tigers, were the Chinese team; the Rising Suns (Asahi) were the

Annexation, August 12, 1898. Hawaiʻi State Archive.

Japanese team; the Braves were the Portuguese team; and Filipinos formed a team later, called "the Filipinos." To protect the league's racialized nature, each team was allowed to have only two players of a different ethnicity.[19]

Colonial Hawaiʻi's racial and class hierarchies also had long shaped the "food supply, culinary treatments and habits of consumption."[20] In the 1800s, Caucasians continued to eat the food they always had, but with locally sourced meat, fish, shellfish, fowl, vegetables, fruit, and dairy products.[21] Their beef, mutton, pork, and poultry came from one of the many local ranches, and indeed, local meat was more highly regarded than meat packed in ice and shipped from the mainland. Their fish and shellfish were also locally caught. One observer noted that "Hawaiian mullet, boiled, baked or fried, approaches in flavor the blue fish of the Atlantic coast." Central Union Church's *Hawaiian Cook Book*, compiled in 1918 by the Woman's Society of Central Union Church, even included a guide to local fish that indicated when a particular fish was available and how it might be cooked. For example, mahimahi (dolphinfish) was caught year-round and could be used in "chowder, fried in deep fat, scalloped, [or made into] fish jelly."[22] Also available were locally grown tomatoes, corn, beans, cauliflower, cucumbers, carrots, turnips, potatoes, and artichokes. Caucasians even ate taro, regarding it as "far ahead of the potato in nutrients," and enjoyed local fruits such as breadfruit, guava, and pohā berries.[23] That Caucasians discovered these staples of the Hawaiian diet is hardly surprising because, as historian David Stannard observed, "[t]he foods and health habits of the Hawaiians were far more salubrious than those of their European contemporaries and were even superior to those of modern Americans in their diets' nutritional value and relative lack of saturated fat, cholesterol, sugar and sodium—and, of course, in the absence from their lives of alcohol and tobacco."[24] In time, even well-to-do local businessmen began to adopt the Caucasians' diet, although they continued to eat rice and to have their meals "cooked and served in semi-American style."

Most immigrants, however, still preferred to eat the foods to which they were accustomed.[25] Accordingly, Portuguese baked bread as they did in the old country, and Chinese, Japanese, and Filipinos made rice the center of their meal, supplementing it with local fish, pork, chicken, duck, and home-grown vegetables when they were available. Those who lived near towns or cities such as Honolulu, Līhuʻe, Wailuku, or Hilo could buy locally made tofu, miso, shoyu (soy sauce), sausages, fish sauce (bagoong), and even noodles. Hawaiians, and part-Hawaiians, too, adhered to their traditional diet, eating poi, catching fish, and gathering seaweed (limu) at nearby beaches.[26]

Hawaiʻi's First Restaurants

The first restaurant in the islands, Warren House, opened in 1819 at the corner of Hotel and Bethel Streets in Honolulu. The second restaurant was Butler's Coffee House, nearby in Warren Square, which opened in 1836.[27] Most of the restaurants established between 1850 and 1900 were owned by residents of Chinese descent. Some were a combination of a bakery and a coffee shop, like Po Hee Hong's in Hanapēpē, Kauaʻi; several were grocery or dry goods stores that included canteens, as was the case with Hew's Store and Restaurant in Pāʻia, Maui; and a few were saloons that also served food.[28] Since most of their customers were not Chinese, these restaurants served Hawaiian and Western as well as Chinese fare.

In the late 1800s, Honolulu had two imposing Chinese restaurants in Chinatown: Wo Fat opened in 1882 and Sun Yun Woo in 1892. Both served Cantonese food.[29]

Beginning in the 1920s, new Honolulu restaurants catered to both the local population and servicemen stationed on Oʻahu. The first of these, the American Café, opened in 1923.[30] Sakazo Fujika, an immigrant from Hiroshima, started the Diamond Ice Cream Parlor at the eastern end of Kalākaua Avenue, which served chili con carne, hamburger steak, beef stew, and pies. Later, Fujika renamed his restaurant the Unique Lunch Room and added to his menu such Hawaiian dishes as laulau, lomilomi salmon, and pipi kaula.[31] In 1927, George C. Knapp and Elwood L. Christiansen opened the first drive-in restaurant in Hawaiʻi at the corner of Kalākaua Avenue and Ala Wai Boulevard on the edge of Waikīkī.[32] In 1929, Pang Yat Chong opened a Chinese restaurant, Lau Yee Chai, in Waikīkī, which, with its beautiful and well-decorated interior, attracted both locals and tourists.[33] In the 1930s, more restaurants opened in Honolulu and its environs, and like the American Café, many were owned and operated by the children of Japanese immigrants from the Okinawan community of Oroku.[34] In 1939, brothers Spencer and Clifton Weaver opened the Swanky Franky hot dog stands, and from this modest beginning, they created a veritable restaurant empire of Spencecliff restaurants, which by 1987 numbered twenty-three on Oʻahu and Maui.[35] After World War II, when people dined out more often, they usually went to a Spencecliff or one of the many Okinawan-run restaurants that opened in the 1940s and 1950s. By the 1960s, the top fine-dining choices were in Waikīkī: Canlis, a Spencecliff restaurant; Michel's, a French restaurant; and P. Y. Chong's Lau Yee Chai.[36]

Besides the distinctions between fine dining and local restaurants, the other peculiarity of the colony's culinary and gastronomic life was that much of the food was imported, although the best fine-dining establishments did serve locally sourced foods. A menu from the Alexander Young Hotel, dated February 28, 1928, lists Baked Island Pond Mullet, Normandy Pommes Hollandaise, Fresh Island String Beans, and Hawaiian Banana Fritters. Two decades later, Richard Kimball, the owner of the Halekulani Hotel, took great pride in serving locally caught fish and locally grown vegetables and fruit. But his kitchens served mahimahi from local waters that had been frozen after being cleaned and filleted.[37] Even Fisherman's Wharf, famous for its seafood, served frozen fish caught elsewhere.[38] In fact, much of what was served, even in the top restaurants, was imported, and

Lau Yee Chai (exterior). Courtesy of Pan Pacific Press.

this was true especially of meat but also vegetables,[39] continuing into the 1960s, 1970s, and through the 1980s. This was not so remarkable, though, for in the 1970s, "even the white-tablecloth French restaurants . . . in San Francisco," according to David Kamp, "were using frozen steaks and pre-butchered poultry."[40]

Lau Yee Chai (interior). Courtesy of Pan Pacific Press.

The local population, as well, ate both local and imported foods, as they could not afford to do otherwise. Most local families ate fish that they caught themselves or were given; chicken, pigs, rabbits, and ducks that they raised; vegetables that they grew or bought; and fruit that they picked. Even their poi, tofu, miso, shoyu, dried shrimp, fish sauce, sausages, and noodles were made locally. In addition, the plantation stores always stocked bags of rice and canned goods, and most families kept on hand a small supply of canned corned beef, luncheon meat, vienna sausage, tuna, and vegetables, even though they were relatively expensive.[41] Of course, because canned foods were "American," their consumption in the islands would have been applauded by reformers on the mainland who worked to wean immigrants away from their traditional diets.[42]

The relationship of fine dining and local food before Hawai'i became a state in 1959 thus cannot be understood apart from the racialized nature of life in the colony. It explains why Caucasians and locals ate what they did and the distinction between "fine dining" and "local food," as well as Hawai'i's dependence on imported food and canned goods.

The Broader Colonial Context

The territory of Hawai'i was not exceptional, and what happened in the islands after annexation had also happened in many other places. Imperialism quickly dominated vast swatches of the world. It began slowly in the 1600s with the Spanish, who established the first colonies in South America, the Caribbean, and the Philippines, and continued at a faster pace in the 1800s with the British, French, Dutch, Americans, Germans, and Japanese creating their own colonies in South America, Africa, Asia, and the Pacific. Driving the nineteenth-century acquisitions was a new, global capitalism and, later, the Industrial Revolution with its ever growing need for markets for manufactured goods. Classical Liberalism, an eighteenth-century conception of political economy, and, later, Social Darwinism offered a rationalization for these changes imposed by the colonial powers, and advances in communication, transportation, and military technology supported and enabled the execution of their vision of the world.

Besides dominating their newly acquired territories politically, militarily, and economically, these powers killed much of the indigenous population in the process of bringing them firmly under their control, although many more were killed by the diseases brought by the Westerners and the impact of their presence. Historian Stannard studied this genocidal process in the Pacific and along its rim and calculated the percentage of indigenes in each area who died in the century after Western contact:

Guatemala, 82 percent (1511–1611)
Nicaragua, 99 percent (1522–1582)
Mexico, 95–96 percent (1511–1586)
Peru, 88 percent (1770–1820)
Southeastern Australia, 94–96 percent (1788–1848)
Marquesas, 96 percent (1830–1900)
Tahiti, 86–90 percent[43]

In New Zealand, the figures are comparable—a 75 percent decline within a century—but resulted as well from intense fighting among the Maori, the indigenous population.[44] When the United States annexed the Philippines in 1898, there was considerable popular resistance, with conflict breaking out two days before the US Senate ratified the annexation treaty. The ensuing Philippine-American war lasted for three years and resulted in the deaths of up to 220,000 Filipinos: 16,000 to 20,000 combatants and 200,000 civilians.[45]

To stabilize and perpetuate their dominance, the colonizers did what modern states had begun to do after the Enlightenment. They declared the spaces they conquered *terra nullis* and carefully defined and closed these spaces; they recorded and confirmed transactions like the sale of property; they counted and classified their populations; they designated some actions as "legitimate" and others as "illegitimate"; they fostered the belief in how things are and ought to be; and they made all of this official. They also introduced Western forms of knowledge, studied and recorded the local languages, and composed the first grammars and dictionaries. The creation of colonial forms of knowledge also required that a "past" be recovered (that is, created) and a "history" written, one that told the story of progress from an earlier, barbaric, time to the civilized present. Finally, the colonizers insisted on not only separating themselves from their subjects but also elevating themselves above them, a distinction based formally on race and ethnicity. All this was carried out according to instructions from the metropoles in the home country.[46] In many ways, then, the territory of Hawai'i was a textbook case of colonization.

The colonial authorities apparently also did the same thing with food. Zilkia Janer analyzed how the Spanish colonizers did this in Mesoamerica beginning in the sixteenth century: they brought new foods, new dishes, and new food practices, and they introduced cabbage and aromatic herbs, the consumption of bread and beef, and the place of fasting in the Catholic calendar. They also brought foods from other Spanish colonies, including tomatoes, potatoes, okra, garlic, rice, onions, lettuce, cucumbers, and carrots.[47] In time, the imports quickly displaced indigenous foods such as maize, and chilis were viewed with suspicion and avoided. But one native plant, cacao, which produces seeds that are processed into chocolate, was eventually accepted.

The predictable result of these changes was what Janer calls a "new culinary culture" that "authorized Spanish culinary practices" and denigrated local foodways. Not surprisingly, the colonization of food in Mesoamerica created a hierarchy of cuisines: as "the culinary expression of European modernity-rationality," French cuisine was regarded as superior, and "indigenous and other culinary knowledges" were inferior. But even though colonial chefs used exclusively French culinary techniques, they did avail themselves of indigenous vegetables and fruits when necessary.[48]

The same thing happened in the Hawaiian islands, but initially not in the expected way. In the closing years of the republic, David Kalākaua (1836–1891), chamberlain to King Kamehameha V, hired Robert von Oehlhoffen, who had come to the islands as "a cook on a sailing vessel."[49] The German proved to be an excellent choice: he oversaw elaborate French dinners prepared for Kalākaua that were described by one contemporary as "a triumph of taste and art."[50] When the new Hawaiian Hotel opened across the street from 'Iolani Palace in Honolulu in February 1872, von Oehlhoffen was hired as the chef de cuisine, and he did not disappoint. One of his admirers was Isabella Bird (1831–1904), an intrepid Englishwoman famous for her accounts of her trips to the islands as well as to China, Japan, Korea, Tibet, and Central Asia.[51] Another admirer was Kalākaua, who became king in 1874. At one point, von Oehlhoffen prepared a dinner honoring the king that

> for the first course [consisted of] a Windsor soup (calf's feet and chin of veal boiled and thickened with rice flour) with a julienne garnish. The fish course featured Uhu à la Cardinale and mullet with a hollandaise sauce, accompanied by a boiled potato. Anchovies were then served as an hors d'oeuvre.
>
> Preceded by plovers on toast, a roast of spring lamb with mint sauce was next, accompanied by potatoes à la Figaro and a salmy (salmigondis) of wild ducks. The entrees were Epigrams of Chicken (presumably breaded and lightly fried in butter) served with stewed tomatoes and followed by a Calf's Brain à la Viroli. Next came a serving of asparagus followed by a salad of Chicken Mayonnaise (probably decorated with capers, small-pitted olives, anchovy fillets, and quartered hard-boiled eggs), plain lettuce, and cheese.
>
> For dessert, von Oehlhoffen served Cabinet Pudding (egg custard poured over alternate layers of Lady's Fingers soaked in rum or a liqueur, and raisins and crystallized fruit, soaked in rum and baked in an oven for forty-five minutes), confectionery and fruits. The dinner concluded with the serving of Caffe Puss (pousse café), carefully poured layers of ice cold, colorful liqueurs, the order determined by the weight of the liqueur, the heaviest (most sugar) at the bottom and working up to the lightest (most alcohol), topped with heavy cream.[52]

Von Oehlhoffen's importance to Kalākaua is not surprising. French cuisine was, as food historian Rachel Laudan pointed out, "the preferred cuisine of monarchies" in Europe as well as in Asia.[53]

After the United States overthrew the Hawaiian monarchy and annexed the islands in 1898, a new culinary hierarchy was established. French cuisine was replaced by an American cuisine that was inspired more by a tradition of home cooking transmitted within families from the mainland than by a French *cuisine classique*. This American cuisine, favored as it was by the colony's ruling elite, was elevated above local food, which continued to be the food of the territory's non-Caucasian subjects, the food of the colonial "other." The *Hawaiian Cook Book*, compiled by the Woman's Society of Central Union Church beginning in 1882, leaves little doubt whose foods were acceptable and whose were not. Most of the recipes in the *Hawaiian Cook Book* were contributed by the leading families of the colony—the Alexanders, Athertons, Damons, Dillinghams, Judds, and McCullys—and most were old American standbys such as soups, chowders, sauces, fish balls, croquettes, meat pies, stews, creamed vegetables, cakes, and cookies. Also included were detailed instructions for "A Hawaiian Feast—'Ahaaina,' or More Commonly Called 'Luau'" and recipes for taro (H. kalo) dishes, "Baked Hee, or Squid," haupia, kūlolo, and several made with seaweed.[54] Interestingly, recipes for South Asian dishes ("Mulligatawny Soup" and "Fish Moultee") and condiments ("Tomato Chutney" and "Tamarind Chutney") also found their way into the cookbook and always were identified as "Indian recipes."[55] As Willa Tanabe pointed out, the preponderance of American dishes in the *Hawaiian Cook Book* was true of other cookbooks published in the islands before World War II, such as *Helen Alexander's Hawaiian Cook Book* (1938), which contained chapters titled "Hawaiian Dishes for Lunch or Dinner" and "Oriental Dishes."[56] In both cookbooks, however, the dominance of Euro-American dishes is conspicuous. Race and ethnicity clearly mattered in the colony's culinary life.

The sharp distinction between Euro-American cuisine and local food survived into the post–World War II period. The arrival of European chefs schooled in *cuisine classique* reintroduced French cuisine and reaffirmed the culinary hierarchy. Nothing confirmed this as well as the existence for many years of two modern professional organizations for chefs—one for those with European training and the other for locally trained chefs.

The Chefs de Cuisine consisted almost entirely of Europeans and was affiliated with the American Culinary Federation, the "leading professional culinary association in twentieth-century America."[57] Its members held the head position or that of the executive chef at a hotel restaurant.[58] Wallace Takara, the son of Okinawan immigrants, got a job in the kitchen at the

HAWAIIAN COOK BOOK

COMPILED BY THE

LADIES' SOCIETY

OF

CENTRAL UNION CHURCH

———

"Now good digestion wait on appetite
And health on both."

—Macbeth III, IV

———

FIFTH EDITION
REVISED AND ENLARGED

———

HONOLULU:
HAWAIIAN GAZETTE CO., LTD.
1909

Cover of the *Hawaiian Cook Book*. Author's collection.

Royal Hawaiian Hotel in 1935, the leading hotel of its day in Waikīkī. When asked years later who the head chefs were at the time, he answered, "Da kine French" (those who were French) who came from Europe.[59]

The Professional Chefs of Hawaii, the other organization, was mainly for "locally grown chefs," chefs who worked under the European chefs, were trained by them, or owned their own restaurants. Gladys Sato, a pioneering culinary arts instructor on Oʻahu, remembered that "each [group] tried to outdo the other," and although they had similar goals and interests, "they never did things together," a revealing observation.[60] This arrangement became "the tradition in Hawaiʻi," according to Fern Tomisato Yoshida, another longtime culinary arts instructor.[61]

Chef Sam Choy remembered the "time in the early '70s when Hawaiʻi was dominated by European chefs." He grew up in a Hawaiian Chinese family in Lāʻie, on the windward side of Oʻahu, and learned to cook at home and at the luaus his father staged for a local church. Early in his career, in the late 1980s, Choy worked as the executive chef at the Kona Hilton Beach and Tennis Club on the island of Hawaiʻi. "I learned a great deal from them, and I owe them a lot," Choy admitted, but he also recalled their contempt for local food. "Once, in the '70s, when I was just starting out in the business, I remember cooking up a simple dish of chow fun for the workers at the hotel, preparing it just as my dad taught me; cut up the ham and char siu, slice all of the vegetables—carrots, julienne celery, some onions, bean sprouts, and chives—cook it with sesame seed oil. Well, everybody loved it, except the European chefs. They said, 'I would *never* eat that—the vegetables are raw.'"[62] In Choy's retelling, the disapproving voice of the European chef ("I would *never* eat that") conveys an utter contempt for local food. Also apparent is the clear separation of fine dining and local food, as well as of the chefs who prepared each. It is not surprising that when Choy was asked in 1989 what trends in the hotel industry bothered him, he pointed to the "import of so many European chefs." "Why do we have to import so many European chefs?" he asked. What made it even worse, he continued, was that they shamelessly borrowed from the very culinary traditions they seemed to despise. As he put it, "Many of them sneak our recipes, add a little garnish here and there, and call them their own."[63] Choy's complaint is an excellent example of what food scholar Krishnendu Ray called ethnic chefs "talking back and telling us what they think."[64] The European chefs' appropriation of local cuisine also echoes what colonial chefs in Mesoamerica and Hawai'i's colonial rulers did even while they were denigrating the local culinary culture.

The August 1991 Meeting

On August 27, 1991, fine dining in Hawai'i began to change. Fourteen chefs based in Hawai'i gathered at the Maui Prince Hotel in the resort town of Wailea on the southeastern side of the island of Maui.[65] They were meeting for what was grandly called the "First Hawaiian Culinary Symposium," the idea of three chefs—Roger Dikon, Peter Merriman, and Alan Wong.[66] They earlier had flown to Kaua'i to cook together and celebrate Jean-Marie Josselin's birthday at his new restaurant, A Pacific Café. While they were there, they talked about finding a way to meet more often. Merriman remembered that he and other chefs often visited one another's restaurants, that he would "fly to Roy's [Roy Yamaguchi, the founder of Roy's Restaurants] place and cook for a night and fly home. What it really entailed was that you'd fly in there midday and you'd cook your ass off; you had to cook dinner for 150 people that night, go out and have a few beers, and then fly back to your restaurant in the morning." Merriman continued, "I realized that we were at a disadvantage because we were islands . . . 'cause in cities guys can meet at one particular bar. Chefs often do that."[67] Although he then was relatively young, he had watched chefs interact in this way when he worked in restaurants on the East Coast and in Europe.

Dikon, Merriman, and Wong all had lived and worked elsewhere. Merriman was a graduate of the University of Pennsylvania and had been trained and had worked on the East Coast and in Germany before he was hired as a *saucier* at the Mauna Lani Bay Hotel in 1983.[68] Dikon had moved to Hawai'i from Florida in 1978, and Wong had returned to the islands in 1986 after five years of training on the East Coast, including three years at New York City's iconic French restaurant Lutèce, the "best and most expensive French restaurant" of its day.[69]

Dikon offered his hotel, the Maui Prince, as a meeting place, and Merriman suggested calling the gathering a "symposium," a word whose meaning he later confessed he was not sure of at the time. He knew that the word meant "a place where there was a lot of eating and drinking," and he thought, "That's for us."[70] Twelve other chefs attended the meeting.

John Farnsworth was the group's most distinguished and senior chef. A native of Connecticut, he had graduated with honors from the Culinary Institute of America (CIA) in 1975 and had worked for fourteen years at resorts in the Caribbean. In 1988, he was invited to become the chef at two new resorts scheduled to open in the spring of 1990 on the island of Lānaʻi. He was told that the plan was to have the restaurants at the resorts serve food raised or harvested on the island. "When I got the offer," Farnsworth later remembered, "I thought I had died and gone to heaven." The Lodge at Koele opened in April 1990, and the Manele Bay Hotel a month later. As promised, Farnsworth got a farm, a ten-acre plot located six miles from the resorts. He also had a greenhouse that was half the size of a football field, a pig farm, a henhouse, and a fruit-tree orchard. "I always wanted to harvest vegetables in the morning and serve them for dinner that night. Now I can. All I have to do is walk through the garden and see what's at its peak of maturity and flavor. Then it's in my kitchen and on guests' tables." The August 1991 issue of *Food & Wine* had named him one of the country's best new chefs, so his star as a chef was clearly rising when he took the job on Lānaʻi.[71]

Roy Yamaguchi was the other star of the group. After graduating from the Culinary Institute of America in 1976, he worked in Los Angeles for nearly a decade, first at L'Escoffier in Beverly Hills and then briefly at Michael's, whose chef-owner, Michael McCarty, became known for his newer California version of French cuisine.[72] Yamaguchi ended up at L'Ermitage, the city's best French restaurant, working under Jean Bertranou. Besides being a superb chef, Bertranou recognized early on the relevance of nouvelle cuisine in a state where, as David Kamp put it, "quality ingredients were easier to come by." After Bertranou died in 1980, Yamaguchi worked for a short time at Le Gourmet, a French restaurant in the Sheraton Plaza La Reina near the Los Angeles International Airport. Finally, in 1984, Yamaguchi opened his own restaurant, 385 North, in West Hollywood, and later that year, the California Restaurant Writers Association named him California Chef of the Year. The food magazine *Bon Appétit* featured Yamaguchi in its June 1988 issue, and four months later he moved to Hawaiʻi to open Roy's in a suburb of Honolulu.[73] Besides being the "rock star" of the group, as a fellow chef put it, Yamaguchi also brought firsthand experience with what came to be called "California Cuisine."[74]

Of the fourteen chefs who gathered at the Maui Prince, Sam Choy may have had the clearest vision of what they were about to do. In his cookbook

Sam Choy's Cuisine Hawaii (1990), he already had coined the term "Cuisine Hawaii" and offered an early statement of the philosophy that the group would soon adopt. Choy described what he called "Cuisine Hawaii" as "home-grown ingredients dressed up in gourmet fashion."[75]

> It's the best of what we've cultivated here for generations served in creative presentations. Cuisine Hawaii calls heavily upon the specialties of each island. For example: Puna papaya and Puako limes from the Big Island of Hawaii, onions and tomatoes from Maui, lamb from the privately-owned island of Niihau, beef raised on the Big Island's Parker Ranch, Kilauea guava from Kauai, potatoes and macadamia nuts from Molokai, and on Oahu, shrimp and prawns from Kahuku and lettuce from Manoa. The shopping list never ends! To me, Cuisine Hawaii means the best possible blend of freshness and creativity. It's a unique style inspired by the beauty of my homeland.[76]

Rhetorically, Choy was a step ahead of the rest of the group when they met in August 1991. But this is not surprising, since he was the oldest of the group.

The twelve founding HRC chefs. Courtesy of Mark Ellman.

Most of the fourteen chefs could not have anticipated what was about to happen, and none could have known what impact their August 1991 meeting would have on the fine-dining scene and much else in Hawai'i. Indeed, most of them were only in their early thirties and trying to survive in a notoriously demanding business. By this time, eight were chefs at major hotel restaurants, and five had their own restaurants. Nearly all were products of local, mainland, or European culinary schools, and most had apprenticed and trained at leading restaurants in the United States and Europe.[77] The exception was Mark Ellman, who was self-taught and had worked as a personal chef for celebrities before Longhi's, an Italian restaurant on Maui, hired him in 1985.[78]

At the August 1991 meeting, the chefs discussed the unhappy state of fine dining in the islands. Of special concern was their restaurants' continuing reliance on imported fish, meat, and vegetables.[79] Dikon recalled that when he worked at the Kapalua Bay Hotel on Maui (from 1978 to 1986), only a quarter of the vegetables and fruits served at the hotel's restaurants was grown locally.[80] Josselin, who came to Hawai'i in 1984 from Paris via New Orleans to cook at the Hotel Hana Maui, remembered, "I was in shock. It was so isolated. I was given frozen and canned food to cook with; it was like being in a professional kitchen twenty-five years ago."[81] Amy Ferguson, a native of Dallas who was hired as the food and beverage director at the Kona Village Resort in 1985, agreed. "Old World chefs were running the kitchen and preparing continental cuisine. Sometimes they even cooked with frozen produce."[82] She wondered why "they were serving Scandinavian buffets instead of [the] foods of Hawai'i."[83]

Several members of the group talked about what they had done to remedy the problem. Dikon began to frequent local swap meets and would return with "as much local produce as he could carry."[84] He also started growing his own vegetables in an eight-hundred-square-foot garden.[85] In 1980, Gary Strehl, a chef at the Maui Prince, arranged with other Maui chefs to have a farmers' cooperative grow "specialty items" for them.[86] Merriman remembered seeing gardeners trimming the coconut trees on the grounds of the Mauna Lani Hotel and wondered what was being done with the coconuts. When he found out that they were thrown away, he asked the gardeners if he could have the ones they cut down, and when they agreed, he had them delivered to farmers in Kealakekua, who husked them. The coconut meat was then brought to Merriman in a laundry truck that made a daily trip between the Mauna Lani and Kona.[87] In 1986, Philippe Padovani, the

new chef at La Mer, the premier French restaurant in Hawai'i, quickly discovered fresh vegetables and fish at the markets in Honolulu's Chinatown,[88]
and of course, Farnsworth had been cooking for just over a year with what
his resort's Lāna'i farms and orchard produced and what the local waters
offered in the way of fresh seafood.[89]

These stories, and others like them, raise the obvious questions: Why
weren't these chefs already using locally grown tomatoes? Why weren't
they serving lamb or beef raised on local ranches? Why weren't they avail-
ing themselves of the islands' locally caught fish? Farnsworth's experience and the Maui chefs' success in making their own arrangements with
farmers and the local produce and fish markets already suggested possible

Peter Merriman. Courtesy of Marylee Sakas.

solutions. At the end of their first meeting, the chefs agreed to investigate buying directly from local farmers, ranchers, and fishermen and to meet again soon.

Twelve of the original fourteen chefs met again six weeks later, this time on the Big Island. According to Merriman, "We literally loaded these chefs on a bus and took them from farm to farm. Because they didn't know farms existed. I'm not gonna name names, but some of the chefs were Big Island chefs, and I'm taking them on their island, saying, 'Look, here's a farm.'"[90] Looking back, Merriman acknowledged that the key issue was finding farmers willing to grow what the chefs needed and wanted. In the old days, he recalled, chefs would work through their hotel delivery departments and simply look for the lowest price. Accordingly, most of what they bought was imported.[91] For this to change, they had to start thinking "far outside the box."

The idea of chefs establishing relationships with local farmers was brilliant but proved difficult to put into practice. Merriman's experience on the Big Island was typical. After he and his wife, Vicki, opened Merriman's in December 1988, their first problem was finding farmers willing to grow produce for them. In addition, many of those who offered their services had never farmed before. The Merrimans were saved by Tane Datta, a farmer who had been at the 1991 meeting with his wife, Maureen. Datta was a recent graduate of Guilford College in Greensboro, North Carolina, with degrees in geology, environmental studies, and alternative energy, and he had been farming on the Big Island since 1979.[92] He and Merriman looked over his seed catalogs, with Merriman marking the things he wanted. Datta then worked with the farmers who wanted to grow for Merriman's restaurant, assigning crops to each of them and suggesting where and at what elevation they could grow them. Their plots were tiny—some only six by forty feet—and they used French intensive-gardening techniques.[93]

On O'ahu, Yamaguchi developed a relationship with Dean Okimoto, a young local farmer in Waimānalo. Okimoto had graduated from the University of Redlands, in California, in 1983 with a degree in political science and, before leaving to go to law school, was working on his father's farm, growing lettuce hydroponically. It was a very small operation, involving only three people, and Okimoto says they were on the verge of giving up when he met Yamaguchi. But Yamaguchi advised him, "Don't quit. We'll buy herbs from you, and I want you to start growing other things." Okimoto thus became Yamaguchi's go-to farmer, growing whatever he needed. Yamaguchi then began taking Okimoto along on his demonstrations at Liberty House, a big department store in Honolulu. He would say, "Come with me . . . and you can explain the different greens," Okimoto remembers. "Every time we did this, I'd get five or six calls from restaurants. That's how our business started growing."[94]

Because the new arrangements had not yet been tested in the islands, the farmers had to be willing to take risks. This was the chefs' second problem. Merriman recalled that he found a farmer willing to grow vine-ripened tomatoes for his restaurant, a rarity in those days. Or more precisely, he found a farmer who grew something other than tomatoes but who was willing to try growing them. Her name was Erin Lee, and she showed up one day at his restaurant with herbs.

> So Erin comes in, and she's got herbs. I'm talking to her . . . she's a very intelligent woman, and I think, "This lady's got it going on." So I tell her, we've got enough herbs. What we really would need are vine-ripened tomatoes. At the time, everybody knew you couldn't grow vine-ripened tomatoes because of the fruit flies. That was a known fact. . . . So anyway, 120 days later, here comes Erin back in my kitchen with vine-ripened tomatoes. What she figured out was that if she moved to a high-enough elevation, the fruit flies wouldn't come up there. But it was always raining up there. So she put plastic over her tomatoes and irrigated. So she went to the wet side of Waimea and put in irrigation. . . . The point is that very few people go to the wet side and irrigate. She had the brains to do that. So she was selling tomatoes to us for a number of years.[95]

The other farmers on the Big Island finally adopted Lee's model. Many of them had grown flowers until South American growers took over their markets with the help of FedEx.[96] This is an example of how globalizing economic forces in North and South America and a transnational firm—in this case, FedEx—affected a local economy on an island in the middle of the Pacific.

The chefs' third problem, according to Merriman, was that forging relationships with local producers took a lot of time. An example is how he began working with Herbert M. "Monty" Richards, a well-known local rancher who raised lambs on the Big Island. "He tried to sell us some lamb, and it was frozen, and I said we really want to get fresh lamb. He said the only way you could do that would be if you bought the whole animal. I said, OK, we'll do it. That's how we got that tradition, which is now one of our signatures, of a different lamb dish every day. Now it's becoming famous: snout-to-tail is the concept. I laugh about this. Yeah, snout-to-tail is the latest thing. People are using the whole animal, whole animal contact." Merriman worked with Edwards for twenty years and continually gave him feedback on the lambs—whether they were too small, their meat too dry, not fatty enough, and so forth.[97]

Merriman's experiences were typical. All of the chefs had to work hard to realize their collective vision of this new regional cuisine: it meant seeking out farmers, fishermen, and ranchers willing to supply them with locally grown vegetables, locally caught seafood, and locally raised meat. In time, each chef had a stable of producers, which grew over time. Most important, they had taken a big first step, one that had lasting implications for the restaurant world in the islands.

Conclusions

The chefs' agreement to buy local was revolutionary. It both called into question how they had viewed their own culinary productions and became a new way of looking at food and their relationship with the land and sea and with those who worked the land and who fished in local waters. This agreement also meant not relying solely on the big wholesalers that supplied restaurants and hotels: the Suisan Company and Armstrong Produce. Instead, in 1991, the chefs were imagining an entirely new foodscape.

In addition, the August 1991 meeting led to the acceptance of the term "Hawai'i Regional Cuisine." The group had considered "Hawaiian Regional Cuisine," but Sam Choy, the only part-Hawaiian in the group, reminded them that the descriptor "Hawaiian" refers to the indigenous cuisine and could not be appropriated.[98] After much discussion, the chefs settled on "Hawai'i Regional Cuisine (HRC)," which emerged just as regional cuisines in other parts of the country were gaining recognition.[99] Merriman may have been the first chef in the group to use the term "regional cuisine." He says he first used it in 1985 when he was interviewed for the position of head chef at the new Gallery Restaurant at the Mauna Lani Resort on the Big Island.[100] After he got the job, he remembers thinking, "Oh, crap. Now I've gotta invent that thing."[101] An article on the food scene in the islands that appeared in 1991 begins by quoting Merriman: "The changes I've seen since I came to Hawaii in 1983 are incredible. At that time, everybody was using frozen food and trying to emulate Europe; now, everything's got to be fresh and there's a blending of Pacific cultures that I don't think you see anyplace else. It's a new *regional cuisine*."[102] The HRC group's decision to identify what it was doing as "Hawai'i Regional Cuisine" was a smart one because that gave the chefs a brand and linked them to similar developments in the restaurant world on the mainland. It also explains why several of the HRC chefs emerged later as celebrity chefs with a national and, eventually, global standing.

The emergence of Hawai'i Regional Cuisine was revolutionary in a third way. The presence of Choy, Wong, and Yamaguchi at that first meeting represented a frontal challenge to the long-standing racial hierarchies that had elevated Caucasian chefs who had come to the islands from Europe and the mainland and had subordinated non-Caucasians. Although not openly discussed at the August 1991 meeting or at subsequent gatherings, Hawai'i Regional Cuisine nonetheless began to change the face of the kitchens at fine-dining establishments in the islands and to undo the racial hierarchies that had governed the restaurant world there since the 1890s. This opened the way for other local men and women of color who aspired to follow the path blazed by Choy, Wong, and Yamaguchi and who dared to cook *their* food.[103]

This demographic change coincided with two other important developments in the American restaurant world. The first was the emergence of the nouvelle cuisine in France, which challenged the culinary hegemony of classical French cuisine and inspired several new regional cuisines in the United States. The second saw Japanese cuisine, formerly an "ethnic cuisine," moving from the confines of that category and becoming a "foreign cuisine" that even began to rival French cuisine.[104]

Finally, the very existence of "Hawai'i Regional Cuisine" gave the lie to Waters' often-quoted advice to her Hawai'i-bound friend.

2 | Development

A restaurant world focuses on production of a more or less well-defined culinary product and coheres through networks of individuals.

Patricia Ferguson, *Accounting for Taste*

How did the Hawai'i Regional Cuisine movement fare after the founding meeting in August 1991? At first, the new regional cuisine did not attract much attention in the islands, but it did begin to affect the lives and careers of the HRC chefs in several ways. First, the new movement gave them and their locavoric philosophy greater visibility in the islands and generated interest in what they were doing at their restaurants. Second, it brought fine dining in the islands in line with the "food revolution" taking place on the mainland and with the emerging regional cuisines. It also encouraged national food writers and journalists who had been following the careers of several of the HRC chefs to write about what members of the group were doing in their restaurants and in their communities.[1] Third, the new regional cuisine movement brought the HRC chefs opportunities to win national culinary awards and to make appearances on the emerging food television scene. Finally, the HRC chefs became part of a widening network of celebrity chefs on the mainland and in Europe and Asia. Their locavoric philosophy, media exposure, awards, and new relationships with other celebrity chefs signaled their entry into what might be called a national restaurant world.[2] In time, several of the HRC chefs gained true celebrity, and most enjoyed new material success, but several also made missteps and even failed, and the two chefs who never opened their own restaurants eventually moved away.

The First Stage, August 1991 to December 1994

The first stage in the development of Hawai'i Regional Cuisine began with the founding meeting in 1991 and lasted until the end of 1994. This is when the movement found its footing. At this time, the local media in the islands usually featured chefs who opened new restaurants, moved from one hotel restaurant to another, offered a new or special menu, cooked at a benefit dinner, or won an award of some kind. In August 1991, seven of the original fourteen HRC chefs were at the state's top hotel restaurants and thus were often in the news. George Mavrothalassitis was at La Mer at the Halekulani Hotel in Waikīkī, arguably the best French restaurant in the islands. John Farnsworth was at both the Lodge at Koele and the Manele Bay Hotel on Lāna'i; Gary Strehl was at the Hawaii Prince Hotel in Waikīkī; Alan Wong was at the CanoeHouse Restaurant at the Mauna Lani Resort on the Big Island; and Roger Dikon was at the Prince Court at the Maui Prince Hotel. Amy Ferguson had been at the Hotel Hana Maui but then moved to the Ritz-Carlton Mauna Lani Hotel on the Big Island, and Philippe Padovani was hired by the Manele Bay Hotel on Lāna'i after Farnsworth left the islands to take a job in Connecticut in 1992.

At the time of the August 1991 meeting, six of the other HRC chefs already had their own restaurants. Sam Choy opened Kaloko in 1981, as well as Sam Choy's Diner and Sam Choy's Restaurant and Catering in 1990 in Kona on the Big Island. Mark and Judy Ellman opened Avalon in Lahaina on the island of Maui in 1987, and Beverly Gannon opened Hali'imaile General Store in Makawao on Maui in October 1988.[3] Peter and Vicki Merriman opened Merriman's in Waimea on the Big Island three days before Christmas in 1988, and a day later, Roy Yamaguchi opened Roy's in Hawai'i Kai, a suburb east of Honolulu. In 1990, Jean-Marie Josselin opened A Pacific Café in a strip mall in the small town of Kapa'a on the island of Kaua'i.

The locations of five of these seven restaurants appear to have been carefully thought out. Avalon was in downtown Lahaina, a major tourist destination, and A Pacific Café was less than a mile away from the Coco Palms hotel complex on Kaua'i. Clearly, both restaurants were targeting tourists.

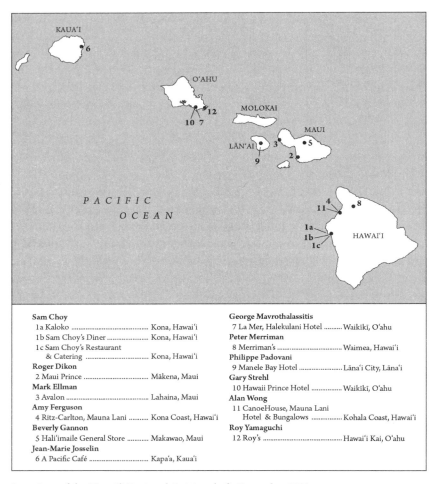

Locations of the Hawai'i Regional Cuisine chefs, December 1991.

In contrast, the five other HRC chefs who opened restaurants chose to locate them away from the hotels and resorts, which suggests that they were targeting not just tourists but also local diners. When Choy opened his restaurants in Kona, he clearly envisioned a mixed clientele of locals and tourists. Roy's was in Hawai'i Kai, a suburb nine miles east of Waikīkī, to target a specific clientele. But Hali'imaile General Store was located upcountry, and Merriman's was more than ten miles from the closest resort.

Each chef had his or her reasons for choosing these locations. For example, Yamaguchi's understanding of Honolulu's fine-dining scene and the culinary life of its multiethnic community shaped his decision:

> I took an offer on a restaurant space in the Honolulu suburb of Hawaiʻi Kai, overlooking the wide, sandy Maunalua Bay beneath Koko Head. And so, in 1988, I opened Roy's, a 170-seat, two-level restaurant with an open kitchen. I was only too happy to renew my acquaintance with island life. But beyond that, Hawaii seemed like an ideal place to further develop my Euro-Asian style, not only because of its location at the crossroads of the Pacific Rim but also because of its unique and wonderful cultural mix. I was more interested in the resident population than the ephemeral tourist trade (although I wanted to appeal to that, too), and I recognized that people here were used to Asian flavors. Most of the hotels and a majority of the independent restaurants in Honolulu served French and European food, so I figured my style of cooking just might work. In addition, I believed my food represented a cutting-edge approach to Pacific Rim cuisine, which was one element lacking in Hawaii's restaurant scene at the time.

He continued, "My aim was to serve exciting, innovative, fun food of the highest quality in an elegant yet casual atmosphere, and at affordable prices. Fortunately, this approach struck a chord in Honolulu, and our local clientele became wonderfully loyal."[4] Yamaguchi's target was a "local clientele."

Gannon claimed that the location of Haliʻimaile General Store in Makawao was less part of a grand design than an accident. She explained the upcountry location of her restaurant:

> It was Christmastime 1987 when we heard that the Haliʻimaile General Store was going to be available for rent. We thought it would work perfectly as a combination gourmet take-out deli, catering headquarters, and general store, with a few tables where people could snack while they were waiting for their take-out order. After almost six months of negotiations, we finally signed the lease. Everyone thought we were crazy, opening a place, literally, in the middle of a thousand-acre pineapple plantation. But remember, we weren't opening a restaurant. We just needed a great space from which to run our catering operation.[5]

When the she opened Haliʻimaile General Store on October 14, 1988, Gannon was surprised to find "a hundred people waiting to get in. We had five or six tables, maybe thirty chairs, no wait staff, and everyone who came in the door asked, 'Where do we sit?' Hali'imaile General Store is a restaurant, in large part, because that's what our customers wanted it to be."[6] But the truth is that the Gannons saw that Makawao was attracting well-to-do residents and believed that the restaurant "had a good shot at being successful." They were right: the restaurant grossed $100,000 a month in its first six months.[7]

Merriman's choice of Waimea for his eponymous restaurant almost proved fatal.[8] He had considered locations in Honolulu, the Kohala coast of the Big Island, and Napa Valley in California but chose Waimea, a sleepy ranching town in the Kohala district, largely because opportunity beckoned there. Robert Chaucer, a vice president for C & H Properties and a real estate developer, was planning to expand the Opelo Plaza in downtown Waimea, and he wondered whether Merriman would be interested in opening a restaurant there. He was, and with help from Stanley Monsef, a local businessman, Merriman's opened two years later, on December 22, 1988. Later, Merriman admitted that he had misjudged the local market. Waimea "is a very remote place, and financially I'm worse off here than I thought I would be. So if I had the chance to do it over again, I probably would go to an urban location."[9] In fact, early in 1989, Merriman's monthly revenue had

Hali'imaile General Store. Courtesy of Beverly Gannon.

Merriman's. Courtesy of Marylee Sakas.

fallen so precipitously that he had to borrow from his partner. What saved his restaurant were positive reviews in two major American newspapers. The first was in the *Los Angeles Times*, and it described Merriman as the "chief exponent" of "an emerging Hawaiian cuisine that combines innovative techniques with the best of locally produced ingredients." The second review was in the *New York Times*.[10] Those reviews alone enticed more and more tourists to dine at Merriman's, beginning in the summer of 1989. Two years later, an even more glowing review appeared in the *New York Times*.[11] Merriman is quick to admit that "tourists are the ones who put us in the black."[12] For Gannon and Merriman, although the decision to locate their restaurants away from the resorts and tourist hotels caused some problems initially, it paid off over the long term, as they attracted local and national media attention and gained loyal clienteles.

Several local food writers were quick to see that the HRC chefs were trying to do what was being done on the mainland, namely, to create a regional cuisine. In June 1989, one local journalist pointed out that Dikon, the chef at the Maui Prince Hotel's Prince Court restaurant, was doing what the practitioners of regional cuisines on the mainland already were doing: "Roger Dikon of [the] Maui Prince Hotel's Prince Court has taken the national passion for American regional cuisine and incorporated Island flavors and the freshest local products to create delicious meals."[13]

The regional cuisine movement on the mainland began in 1971 when Alice Waters opened Chez Panisse in Berkeley, California, and the movement gained speed in the 1980s, generating what came to be known as California Cuisine and inspiring an East Coast version, the New American Cuisine.[14] Wanda Adams, a food writer at the *Honolulu Advertiser*, was aware of these developments and highlighted Merriman's insistence on using only the freshest local produce. She noted that he got butter from Nāʻālehu, corn from Pāhoa, goat cheese from Puna, lamb from Kahuā, snow peas from Volcano, strawberries from Lālāmilo, and tomatoes from Puʻukapu; and that his philosophy was "just gather what's around and serve it. And don't get in its way."[15] Two months later, Catherine Enomoto, writing for the *Honolulu Star-Bulletin*, quoted Strehl, who described what he was doing at the Prince Court: "We set up the Prince Court at the Maui Prince with that new Hawaiian regional theme. It became really popular."[16] Adams, Enomoto, and the unidentified local journalist were the first to discern that Dikon, Merriman, and Strehl were trying to create a local regional cuisine at their restaurants even before the chefs announced the advent of Hawaiʻi Regional Cuisine. The importance of this recognition cannot be overstated.

Not all of Hawaiʻi's food writers were so perceptive. *Honolulu Magazine*'s new food critic, John Heckathorn, a former English professor at the University of Hawaiʻi at Mānoa, panned both Avalon and Haliʻimaile General Store, completely missing the novelty of what Mark Ellman and Gannon were doing. Writing about Avalon, he observed:

> Lahaina's Avalon Restaurant is well-known even on Oʻahu. I went with great expectations of enjoying what Avalon calls "Pacific Basin" cuisine. Ordering from Avalon's menu is like being able to order at a whole range of Oʻahu restaurants all at once. There's rice paper shrimp rolls (like A Little Bit of Saigon), sateh—the chicken sticks (like Keo's)—crab in black bean sauce (like Kirin) and whole steamed ʻōpakapaka with a choice of Asian sauces (like King Tsin).
>
> Since Maui doesn't have any of those restaurants, I suppose it needs a place like Avalon. But Avalon is not a Roy's: It is not refining and re-defining Asian-Pacific food. It simply does a pretty good job on some pretty

standard items. The Thai chicken salad was fine, as were the sateh sticks, but you could have gotten better shrimp rolls with peanut sauce at any Ba-Le Sandwich shop on Oʻahu.

That doesn't mean Avalon's a terrible restaurant. It's an attractive place, stuffed with interesting art. The service is crisp and professional—no one wanted to see my pen here. The wine list is well chosen and—for Maui—reasonably priced. (I bought a Chateauneuf-du-Pape, Vieux Telegraphes stood up pretty well against the food.) Prices aren't bad: You could have a nice dinner for two here for $60 to $70 if you went easy on the wine.

And the most original dish on the menu was the tastiest: sugar snap peas, done up jade green in a wok with Szechuan spices. Shows you what Avalon could do if it went to work on the details.[17]

Besides being unkind, this review reeks of Oʻahu-centrism.

In the same review, Heckathorn also wrote about Haliʻimaile General Store and was even more dismissive. "The food at Haliʻimaile was ambitious, but ambition is not enough. In food, as in writing, it's the details that matter. And here, the details were all wrong. There was an imaginative fresh vegetable torte, for instance. But the veggies were limp and lifeless, the broccoli having turned that dull shade of olive green it gets when it's been overcooked. The puff pastry surrounding it all was soggy and heavy." He closed his review of Gannon's new restaurant with a cutting rhetorical coup de grâce that strangely echoed Waters' famous dismissal of haute cuisine in the islands: "the best thing about Haliʻimaile is the location. It's a nice drive Upcountry."[18] This was hardly a promising reception. Later, Heckathorn did come to understand what the HRC chefs were trying to do and became one of their staunchest advocates, writing positive reviews of their restaurants and commentaries on why what they were doing was so important. But he was not in their corner in the spring of 1991.

At the outset, local television was kinder to the HRC chefs. Choy was the first of the group to appear, in a commercial using electric appliances to cook his specialties.[19] Then in November 1992, Melanie Kosaka, a young television producer, proposed a new show to be aired on public television that would feature Yamaguchi. Although Kosaka had been educated in California, she was born and raised in Hawaiʻi, which may explain her interest in Yamaguchi and his cooking. Thirteen episodes of *Hawaii Cooks with Roy Yamaguchi* were filmed.[20] Each had the obligatory cooking-in-the-kitchen segment, a fixture on such programs since Julia Child's *The French*

Chef, but it also included visits to the farmers, ranchers, cheese makers, and fishermen whose products Yamaguchi used in his cooking. Kosaka even did segments on local artists. When the program first aired on October 26, 1993, neither Kosaka nor Yamaguchi could have imagined that it would begin his transformation into a celebrity chef. Nor could they have predicted what it also would do for the careers of the other HRC chefs and how it would help them gain a place in the national restaurant world on the mainland.

Food television had begun to catch on in the 1990s. Although the first food programs had aired on television in 1946, they failed to command the kinds of audiences they do today. These early programs include *The Queen Was in the Kitchen* (1945), *Elsie Presents James Beard in "I Love to Eat"* (1946), *Chef Milani* (1949), *To the Queen's Table* (1948–1949), *Joyce Chen Cooks* (1966), *The Galloping Gourmet* (1969), *What's Cooking* (1975), *The Frugal Gourmet* (1980s), and Bob Lape's reports on chefs and restaurants in New York.[21] Of course, it was Child's *The French Chef,* produced in Cambridge, Massachusetts, by the Boston public television station WGBH, that came to define the genre. It ran from February 1963 and the last episode aired in January 1973. The reruns are still popular. Although *The French Chef* helped demystify French cuisine and make it accessible to a larger American audience, it was the creation of the Food Network in April 1993 that enabled the success of food television and brought it to a national audience.[22]

That same year, the Japanese food program *Iron Chef (Ryōri no tetsujin)* began to air in the United States. Like *The French Chef,* the *Iron Chef* series created a new genre: the timed competition between two chefs cooking in a kitchen arena against both each other and the clock. One chef was always from the program's stable of chefs, each of whom specialized in Chinese, French, Italian, or Japanese cuisine. The challenger was initially from a well-known French or Italian restaurant in Japan and, later, from the United States or Europe.[23] The series started on October 10, 1993, and ran until September 24, 1999, with subtitled and, later, dubbed versions aired on the Food Network and the Cooking Channel in the United States and on the Special Broadcasting Service in Australia. *Iron Chef* may mark the beginning of the naturalization of Japanese cuisine and its transformation from an "ethnic cuisine" to a "foreign cuisine." Another popular program, *Top Chef,* first aired in 2006 and is still running. Today, a virtually uncountable number of programs feature chefs of a particular culinary stripe in several different formats. *Hawaii Cooks with Roy Yamaguchi* began airing in the fall of 1993, twenty years after *The French Chef,* just two weeks after *Iron Chef* began to run in the United States, and three weeks before the Food Network went on the air.

Mainland food writers, as well, discovered the HRC chefs. Restaurant critics who wrote for magazines and newspapers with a national readership had been following what several of the HRC chefs were doing at their restaurants long before the official announcement of a new Hawai'i Regional Cuisine in 1991. In fact, the national media recognized several of the HRC chefs long before the local food writers and critics did. Ferguson was one of the first HRC chefs to gain national recognition. In 1987, *Metropolitan Home* described Ferguson, who had begun cooking in Dallas, as one of the "creators of Southwestern Cuisine," and *Esquire* named Baby Routh, the restaurant she opened in Dallas, the number one restaurant in the United States.[24] This was very high praise for a young chef. In 1990, Strehl, the chef at the Maui Prince Hotel's Prince Court, was noticed as well and described as a talented chef on the verge of national recognition. Because of articles like these, Ferguson and Strehl gained a bit of celebrity.[25]

Yamaguchi attracted the most attention. In 1988, the California Restaurant Writers Association named him the best chef in the state, for 385 North, the restaurant he opened in Los Angeles in February 1984. In addition, an article in the June 1988 issue of *Bon Appétit* featured Yamaguchi, calling him a "culinary wunderkind."[26] Later that year, he closed 385 North and moved to Honolulu to open Roy's. Then, exactly two and a half years after that, the first reviews of Roy's appeared in the national media. In June 1991, the Los Angeles food writer Janice Wald Henderson raved in *Bon Appétit* about Yamaguchi's new Hawai'i Kai restaurant, calling a meal there "a gastronomic adventure."[27] Henderson wrote a second review for *Food & Wine* four months later, describing Yamaguchi as the first chef in Honolulu "with a mega-reputation" and calling Roy's "the crown jewel of Honolulu's East-West eateries."[28] Not to be outdone, Mimi Sheraton, former food critic for the *New York Times,* lavished high praise on Roy's and Josselin's A Pacific Café, adding them to her list of "Top Fifty" restaurants in the United States in both 1991 and 1992.[29] If mainland food writers like Henderson and Sheraton immediately understood what the HRC chefs were doing, it was because they were aware of the new Euro-Asian fusion restaurants that had opened in Los Angeles in the 1980s, and it was they who brought Hawai'i Regional Cuisine to the attention of a national audience.

In fact, Hawai'i Regional Cuisine owed much to Los Angeles, for this was where Yamaguchi developed his concept of what he called "Euro-Asian cuisine." In 1979, Michael McCarty opened his restaurant Michael's in Santa Monica. McCarty had spent his junior year in high school in France and then stayed on for ten years, returning to the United States with mastery of French cuisine and full of confidence. When he opened his restaurant, he announced, "We're doing something special here," and "my specials are going to blow your socks off."[30] *Los Angeles Times* food writer Ruth Reichl remembered that moment as the "first heady days of what was to be called California Cuisine," and although McCarty's philosophy was to serve "the best possible ingredients I could buy cooked in the simplest way possible," she explained that "in reality it was nothing more than nouvelle cuisine— served in a nouvelle ambience."[31] Reichl's description of what McCarty was doing as nouvelle cuisine was in fact based on the new, lighter, cuisine that younger French chefs had begun to serve in their restaurants in the 1960s and 1970s, and it had inspired both California Cuisine and the New American Cuisine.[32] Given that such future celebrity chefs as Sally Clarke, Ken Frank, Mark Peel, Nancy Silverton, and Jonathan Waxman passed through the kitchen at Michael's, McCarty's influence is indisputable.

Yamaguchi, too, knew McCarty, as his first jobs in Los Angeles were at the Los Angeles Country Club and at L'Escoffier Room in the Beverly Hilton Hotel. He then worked at Condotierre, a Scandinavian restaurant in Beverly Hills, for two and a half years before he was hired as a line cook at L'Ermitage, where he trained under the brilliant Jean Bertranou and his successor, Michel Blanchet. After Bertranou's death in 1980, Yamaguchi cooked at La Serene in Burbank and Michael's in Santa Monica before moving, in 1981, to Le Gourmet in the Sheraton Plaza La Reina near the Los Angeles International Airport.[33] Although Yamaguchi remembers 1980 as the year he invented "Euro-Asian cuisine," the *Los Angeles Times* food writer David Shaw recalled that the "best dinner" he had in Los Angeles in 1981 was at La Serene and that the "best dinner" he had in 1982 was at Le Gourmet when Yamaguchi was in the kitchen at both restaurants. Interestingly, Shaw described both dinners as "French."[34] Yamaguchi himself says of his time at Le Gourmet, "I had a chance to blossom at Le Gourmet. I could buy top-quality ingredients and have things flown in. It's where I began to mix French and oriental culinary styles." He continues, "I wanted to be different from other chefs. . . . And with my background, it was natural for me to add ginger here and wasabi there. I had no idea I was starting something new."[35]

Two years before Yamaguchi opened 385 North, the French chef Wolfgang Puck opened Spago on Sunset Boulevard in 1982 and then Chinois on Main in Santa Monica a year later.[36] Whereas Spago was a quintessentially "California cuisine" restaurant, whose "feeling . . . is American, with suggestions of Italy and Southern France," Chinois on Main was an explicitly Asian fusion restaurant, offering what Puck described as "the modern application of dining in the Chinese manner."[37] Both restaurants were also part of the new regional cuisine movements that began with Waters and Chez Panisse in Berkeley in 1971. As Puck declared, echoing Waters, "In the name of authenticity and absolute freshness, local products are being used whenever possible, as we learn to depend less and less on imported goods."[38] Both locavorism and fusion had arrived in Los Angeles in the early 1980s.

Yamaguchi's invention of "Euro-Asian cuisine" may have had another inspiration. Several Japanese chefs in Los Angeles had already begun to experiment with fusion cuisine. In 1984, the Tsunoda family, a well-established Japanese hotel and restaurant family that had been in the business since the 1600s, opened La Petite Chaya in Silver Lake in 1984 and then a sister restaurant, Chaya Brasserie, in Beverly Hills later that year. Although they were Japanese, the chefs had trained in France and Italy, and all had started their careers in Japan. Shigefumi Tachibe, who began at the Chaya restaurants in 1984, is typical. He had trained at the Kyushu Cultural Academy (Kyūshū Bunka Gakuin) cooking school in Nagasaki, Japan, and worked first at the Hakata Prince Hotel, which the Tsunoda family owned, and then at their La Marée de Chaya restaurant in Hayama in Kanagawa Prefecture, which served French cuisine.[39] Tachibe and the other chefs at the Chaya restaurants cooked what has been described as "French-Japanese" cuisine, which was initially more "French" but then leaned toward what they termed "healthy cooking."[40] The food at the Chaya restaurants in Los Angeles resembled the nouvelle cuisine that had appeared in France in the 1960s and 1970s, as well as the California Cuisine that Waters and McCarty pioneered in the 1970s and Puck made famous in the 1980s. Finally, Nobuyuki Matsuhisa, a Japanese chef who had been in Los Angeles since 1977, opened Matsuhisa in Beverly Hills in January 1987, less than a mile from Yamaguchi's 385 North.[41] Thus the popularity of Yamaguchi's new "Euro-Asian" cuisine in Los Angeles in the 1980s is not surprising, since fusion was the rage, and this is why what the HRC chefs were doing in the islands in the 1990s made perfect sense to mainland food writers.[42]

The HRC chefs' cookbooks increased their visibility as well. The first was *Sam Choy's Cuisine Hawaii* (1990), a beautifully produced affair that offered recipes by not only Sam Choy but also other local chefs, including four HRC chefs.[43] In 1992, Josselin published *A Taste of Hawaii*, in which he spoke of "a kind of world cooking based on the international array of ethnic cuisines on the Islands."[44] Another example can be traced to Maui resident and impresario Shep Gordon, who had introduced the HRC chefs to Robert Schuster, who in turn "put together a cookbook with Villard Books in New York."[45] As a result, in May 1994, Henderson's *The New Cuisine of Hawaii* appeared, opening with her dramatic "Welcome to the last frontier in American cooking" and continuing, "Dubbed Hawaii Regional Cuisine, this new culinary style is generating a buzz across America, from coast to coast to coast. Its practitioners are young, enthusiastic chefs who are fortunate enough to be cooking with the outstanding quality and almost dizzying variety of ingredients most chefs can only dream about. . . . These ingredients—as well as strong influences of the Chinese, Filipino, Korean, Japanese, Portuguese, Southeast Asian and Hawaiian people who live in our fiftieth state—have propelled these chefs to develop a distinct cooking style found only in Hawaii."[46] These are bold claims. Was Hawai'i really the "last frontier in American cooking"? Was Hawai'i Regional Cuisine really "a distinct culinary style"? Were the HRC chefs' culinary creations really "generating a buzz across America, from coast to coast to coast"?

In September 1994, Yamaguchi published *Pacific Bounty*, which was based on his successful television program. It, too, opens with a bold claim:

> A culinary revolution has taken root in Hawaii. We are a growing legion of chefs who go out of our way to get the plumpest ahi (yellowfin tuna) at the Honolulu fish auction. We get dirt under our fingernails in order to taste sweet upcountry Maui strawberries. We milk floppy-eared Nubian goats on the Big Island to learn how rich Puna goat cheese is made. We monitor the availability of crops from one end of the archipelago to the other, and we urge growers to cultivate products with us in mind.
>
> The result of our efforts is a fresh new cuisine. My colleagues and I are passionately committed to ingredients that have been grown on Hawaii's soil or caught in waters off its shores, and we have been able to translate them into dishes such as green bean salad with Maui onions and Kau

oranges; grilled Lanai venison salad; stirfry of wild mushrooms with Puna goat cheese; and cassoulet of Kahuku shrimp in a lemongrass-basil broth.

Yamaguchi then explained what had sparked this revolution, offering a short history of the HRC movement:

> Our islands have long been ripe for a new cuisine. Through the 1970s and most of the 1980s, Hawaii's menus generally offered foods such as Norwegian salmon, Maine lobster and midwestern beef. Separated from the mainland by thousands of miles, island chefs were forced to settle for ingredients that were canned, packaged or half-ripened. The hotel-building boom of the 1980s brought a new wave of chefs to Hawaii, many to work in the visitor industry, others to start their own restaurants. These young chefs began to seek out food sources in their own backyard. Small-restaurant owners began to talk with farmers; chefs in some of the larger hotels took notice and followed suit, encouraging their staffs to work primarily with Hawaiian produce, fish and livestock. In the early 1990s, chefs started talking about these trends. We opened our address books and shared phone numbers of specialty farms that we had discovered, and our movement gained momentum. We toured neighboring island farms to learn more about their operations, and we networked with growers to keep informed about what they produce.

He closed with a clear statement of the HRC philosophy:

> Our theory is simple: Diners in Hawaii should be able to taste Hawaii. Why eat a flavor-less tomato that has been mass-produced, gassed and shipped from the mainland, when you can have a juicy, vine-ripened tomato from the Big Island? Why eat a fillet of sole frozen two months ago, when you can have a delicate grilled shutome (Hawaii swordfish) caught this morning? In its purest form, Hawaii cuisine provides the palate with the sweetness of our sun, the saltiness of our surf and the richness of our land.
>
> We are not afraid to import international ingredients such as Greek olives, Italian parmesan and French truffles. But to create true Hawaii cuisine, we must turn to the products of Hawaii whenever possible, whether it is Kona yearling beef from Palani Ranch or salad greens from a farmer on Molokai. The growers and fishermen give us a beautiful, flavorful product, and we, in turn, help them build their businesses.[47]

Pacific Bounty contains recipes for dishes created by six HRC chefs and others as well, evidence of the "culinary revolution" that Yamaguchi believed was taking place in the islands. His cookbook reveals, too, that the HRC chefs had enticed not only other chefs to embrace their new vision but also farmers, fishermen, ranchers, and other producers.

Yamaguchi's string of prestigious national awards in the early 1990s suggests that he was not exaggerating when he spoke of a "culinary revolution." In April 1990, he received Chefs in America's Chef of the Year award. Later that fall, Roy's Hawaii Kai appeared on Gayot's list of America's top forty restaurants, and *Restaurant Hospitality*, a food industry magazine, named Roy's first in the Best (Short) Wine List Competition.[48] Several other developments affirmed Henderson's hyperbole when the *Nation's Restaurant News*, another food industry publication, named Yamaguchi to its Fine Dining Hall of Fame in 1992. Then that April, the James Beard Foundation invited him to present his Euro-Asian-Pacific style of cooking at a dinner in the foundation's series Great Regional Chefs.[49] A year later, in March 1993, Yamaguchi was given the James Beard Foundation Award for Best Chef: Pacific Northwest. After just four and a half years at the helm of his new Hawaii Kai restaurant, Yamaguchi had won five of the nation's top culinary awards. In the wake of the Beard award, there were even plans to air *Hawaii Cooks with Roy Yamaguchi* on the mainland that summer.[50] By recognizing Yamaguchi's extraordinary culinary skill and achievements, these awards succeeded in transforming him into a "celebrity chef," and they also drew attention to the larger HRC movement and its vision of a new regional cuisine in the islands.[51]

Evidence that HRC was becoming part of the national restaurant world is not hard to find. In the early 1990s, Yamaguchi was the first of the HRC chefs to join the growing circle of celebrity chefs on the mainland. Then, late in 1991, he invited three leading Los Angeles chefs— Kazuto Matsusaka (Chinois on Main), Matsuhisa (Matsuhisa), and Antonio Tommasi (Locanda Veneta)—to join Josselin and himself in cooking the third anniversary dinner held at Roy's Hawaii Kai on January 28, 1992.[52] A month later, Yamaguchi was a guest chef at the sixth annual Masters of Food and Wine event, held at the Highlands Inn in Carmel, California. The other guest chefs were Roger Vergé (Moulin de Mougins, Mougins, France), Daniel Boulud (Le Cirque, New York City), Joachim Splichal (Patina, Los Angeles), Charlie Trotter (Charlie Trotter's, Chicago), and Jasper White (Jasper's, Boston).[53] Vergé, White, and Splichal were the most eminent of the group. Vergé, one of the architects of the nouvelle cuisine, had a restaurant near Cannes, that had won three Michelin stars. White had won the

Beard Award for Best Chef: Northeast in 1991, and Splichal had won the Beard Award for Best Chef in America in 1991.

The other three chefs present at the Highlands Inn event were about to win Beard awards themselves: Boulud, the Beard Award for Best Chef: New York City; Trotter, the Beard Award for Best Chef: Midwest; and Yamaguchi, the Beard Award for Best Chef: Pacific Northwest. Surely it was no coincidence that three of the Beard Award winners in 1993 were cooking together at the Highlands Inn thirteen months before the awards were announced. Moreover, these three chefs represented two new regional cuisines, the New American Cuisine (Boulud and Trotter), and Hawai'i Regional Cuisine (Yamaguchi).

In 1993, six of the HRC chefs (Choy, Dikon, Ellman, Gannon, Josselin, and Merriman) cooked at Arnold Schwarzenegger's Schatzi on Main in Santa Monica for the "founding dinner of the Planet Hollywood chain." The other chefs taking part were Vergé; Dean Fearing, cofounder of the Southwestern Cuisine movement; and Puck, a practitioner of the California Cuisine and a rising celebrity chef. The HRC chefs were now moving in high culinary circles and hobnobbing with some of the top practitioners of the new regional cuisines and the now not-so-new nouvelle cuisine.

Roy Yamaguchi. Courtesy of Roy's.

Ferguson was the other HRC chef who entered the world of celebrity chefs at this time. In September 1994, Child, the grande dame of American cuisine, invited Ferguson to appear on one of the sixteen episodes of her new program *Cooking with Master Chefs*.[54] Other segments featured Emeril Lagasse (Emeril's, New Orleans), André Soltner (Wong's mentor at Lutèce), Michel Richard (Citrus, Los Angeles), and Waters (Chez Panisse, Berkeley). The fact that Ferguson and Yamaguchi were rubbing shoulders with four of the United States' greatest celebrity chefs (Waters, Soltner, Boulud, and Trotter) and an emerging celebrity chef (Lagasse) marked their emergence in the national restaurant world. Chefs and food writers on the mainland as well as the James Beard Foundation had now recognized the excellence of the HRC chefs and were presenting them to a national audience.

The Second Stage, January 1995 to December 1999

During the second stage of its development, the HRC movement gained momentum. Its chefs opened more restaurants, and most of those still working at hotel restaurants left to strike out on their own. As Yamaguchi was being recognized and celebrated, he opened three more Roy's restaurants, in Tokyo, Guam, and the Philippines. In May 1994, Josselin opened a second restaurant, also A Pacific Café, on Maui, and Yamaguchi opened two more restaurants that year, his sixth, Roy's Poipu Bar & Grill in a resort town on the south coast of Kaua'i, and his seventh, Roy's Pebble Beach, in Pebble Beach, California, his first on the mainland.[55] Celebrity chefs typically open more restaurants after they are recognized by the national media, which usually means that they are no longer simply the chef-owners of a single, well-regarded restaurant but now are the owners of an emerging corporate entity. In the 1990s, Yamaguchi was well on his way to establishing a corporate empire and what food writer Michael Ruhlman called a "media presence."[56]

The following year, after two years of careful planning and preparation, Alan Wong opened his eponymous restaurant in Honolulu.[57] While he was at the CanoeHouse on the Big Island, Wong had caught the eye of Francis Higa, the co-owner of the highly successful Zippy's fast-food chain in Hawai'i. They talked, and Higa agreed to back Wong's new restaurant and to house it in an office building he owned in the McCully district of

Honolulu, a working-class area about a mile from both downtown Honolulu and Waikīkī. That year, too, Yamaguchi opened his eighth restaurant, Roy's New China Max, in Hong Kong.

The HRC chefs opened still more new restaurants in 1996: Josselin's third, A Pacific Café, in the Ward Center in Honolulu; Choy's fourth, Diamond Head Restaurant, near Waikīkī on the second floor of a building on Kapāhulu Avenue that housed a popular Chinese restaurant; and Yamaguchi's ninth, Roy's Waikoloa Bar & Grill, this time on the Big Island. Given the national media attention the HRC chefs were receiving, it is not surprising that these three restaurants were less than a mile from tourist hotels. In 1997, Josselin opened two more restaurants, A Pacific Bakery & Grill near Līhue on the island of Kauaʻi and A Pacific Café in Honolulu, and Ferguson opened Oodles of Noodles in a strip mall in Kona on the Big Island.[58] In 1998, two of the last four HRC chefs still working at hotels opened their own restaurants: Mavrothalassitis, who had left La Mer for the Four Seasons on Maui, opened Chef Mavro, a block from Alan Wong's in the McCully district in Honolulu; and Padovani opened Padovani's Bistro & Wine Bar in the DoubleTree Alana—Waikiki Beach.[59] In September 1999, Wong opened the more casual Pineapple Room in the flagship store of Liberty House, the venerated department store located in the Ala Moana Shopping Center, not far from Waikīkī. The new restaurants immediately caught the attention of locals as well as tourists, thereby increasing the HRC chefs' local and national visibility. No doubt encouraged by all of the attention, Wong opened Alan Wong's Hawaiʻi in Tokyo Disneyland in July 2000.[60]

As all of this was happening, Dikon and Strehl, who were among the founding HRC chefs and ran well-regarded hotel restaurants, left the islands for jobs elsewhere. In 1996, Dikon opened a restaurant in Quito, Ecuador, his wife's hometown, and in 1999 Strehl became a chef-partner at the Park Café in Telluride, Colorado.[61] Both Dikon and Strehl stayed on good terms with the other HRC chefs, returning often for anniversary and benefit dinners.

In April 1995, Choy hosted the Big Brothers / Big Sisters of Honolulu benefit dinner at one of his restaurants and continued to do so every year after that. Later that year, Yamaguchi hosted a Farm Bureau Benefit Dinner at his Hawaiʻi Kai restaurant and also continued to do so for the next three years. In May 1997, Josselin and visiting chefs celebrated the first anniversary of the opening of A Pacific Café, raising $10,000 for the Easter Seal

Society of Hawai'i. The "A Taste of Oregon" benefit dinner for the Multiple Sclerosis Society of Hawai'i was held on February 24, 1999, featuring guest chefs Ferguson, Josselin, Mavrothalassitis, Padovani, and Wong and raising $18,000. Although the HRC chefs would be the first to say that they did not do benefit dinners to gain visibility, their willingness to appear and cook at these events surely enhanced their presence in the islands' increasingly competitive food scene, especially since celebrity chefs' offering their services to benefit dinners had become an established feature of the larger restaurant world on the mainland.

More cookbooks further enhanced the HRC chefs' visibility in the islands and on the mainland. In 1995, Choy's *With Sam Choy* and Yamaguchi's *Roy's Feasts from Hawaii* were published.[62] Choy then published two more cookbooks in quick succession: *The Choy of Cooking* in 1996 and *Sam Choy's Island Flavors* in 1999.[63] In September 1996, Maui food writer Kaui Philpotts published *Great Chefs of Hawaii* as a companion to a television series that aired that year.[64] Seven HRC chefs were among the twenty-eight featured on *Great Chefs*. In addition, Gannon was featured in Beverly Russell's *Women of Taste*, published in 1997, and Wong released his first cookbook, *Alan Wong's New Wave Luau*, in 1999.[65]

HRC chefs also gained visibility in a fourth way, by sweeping the food awards in the islands year after year in the second half of the 1990s. They won many of *Honolulu Magazine*'s Hale 'Aina awards, published annually in August. Roy's won the Hale 'Aina award for the best restaurant in 1995, and Alan Wong's won that award in 1996, 1997, and 1999. Merriman's won the Hale 'Aina award for Best Restaurant on the Big Island in 1995, 1996, 1997, 1998, and 1999; and A Pacific Café usually won the Hale 'Aina award for Best Restaurant on Kaua'i.[66] The HRC chefs also consistently won the *Honolulu Advertiser*'s 'Ilima awards, although many other chefs won these awards from time to time as well.

As this was happening in the islands, the HRC chefs attracted more national media attention. The year before he left the islands, Dikon was invited to be a guest chef at the James Beard House in New York in 1995. In 1996, Strehl participated in a James Beard program, Best Hotel Chefs of America. That year, too, the *Great Chefs of Hawaii* television series premiered, and the accompanying cookbook, written by food writer Philpotts, highlighted thirty local chefs, including seven HRC members. Gannon appeared on *Good Morning, Hawai'i* on December 10, 1997, to show how to "wrap 'n' roll." In 1999, *Travel & Leisure* placed Yamaguchi's original

Hawai'i Kai restaurant and Ferguson's two-year-old Kona restaurant, Oodles of Noodles, on its list of the fifty best restaurants in the United States.[67] Finally, some of the HRC chefs were invited to design meals for the airlines that flew to the islands: Yamaguchi for Continental Airlines, Choy for United Airlines, and Wong and Barbara Stange for Aloha Airlines.[68] Apparently this meant not only that passengers en route to the islands would have better and more interesting meals but also that visitors would encounter HRC cuisine while traveling to and from the islands.

Nothing, however, attested to the HRC chefs' new national reputation and their place in the US restaurant world as well as the visits of celebrity chefs to the islands. The significance of these visits, food scholar Krishnendu Ray observed, is that "the contemporary chef that counts is the one in the network of chefs who references others," and these chefs now were coming to the islands.[69] In January 1995, Nobuyuki Matsuhisa from Matsuhisa in Los Angeles, George Morrone from Aqua in San Francisco, and Makoto Tanaka from Mako's in Beverly Hills cooked at Roy's sixth anniversary fest in Honolulu.[70] The Lodge at Koele, the luxury resort on Lāna'i, brought as guest chefs, first, Lagasse, whose television program *Essence of Emeril* was a great hit, and then Thomas Keller, the chef-owner of the French Laundry in Yountville, California. The visits of celebrity chefs beginning in the late 1990s underscored the fact that Hawai'i now had more food and wine events than any other state in the country.

The Kapalua Wine & Food Symposium was one of these events. Conceived by pioneering Napa winemaker Robert Mondavi in 1981 to introduce California wines to food and beverage directors at island hotels, this festival was one of the oldest wine gatherings in the country. Three other food and wine events were held annually: Cuisines of the Sun, held at the Mauna Lani Bay Hotel & Bungalows on the Big Island in early summer; Big Island Bounty, held at the Ritz-Carlton Mauna Lani in midsummer; and Winter Wine Escape, usually held in November at the Hapuna Beach Prince and Mauna Kea Beach Hotels on the Big Island.

The visiting celebrity chefs always were paired with local chefs, including many HRC chefs. Consider, for instance, some of the pairings from May 1996 to April 1998: In May 1996, Jean-Louis Palladin, one of the country's top French chefs and the owner of Jean Louis in Washington, DC, participated in the Big Island Bounty event and was paired with Gary Strehl.[71] Two months later, Larry Forgione, winner of the 1993 James Beard Outstanding Chef Award and the chef-owner of An American Place in New York City, participated in Cuisines of the Sun and was paired with Alan Wong.[72] Two months after that, Hans Röckenwagner and Ferguson teamed up at the Grand Chefs on Tour event at the Kea Lani Hotel on Maui.[73] In February 1997, Grand Chefs on Tour brought Dean Fearing, winner of the Beard Award for Best Chef: Southwest in 1993 and a founder of Southwestern Cuisine, pairing him with Gannon. A month later, Grand Chefs on Tour paired Michael Foley, a well-known Chicago chef, with Ellman; in May, Grand Chefs on Tour paired Matsuhisa and Strehl; and in July, Lagasse was paired with Choy; in October, Douglas Rodrigues was paired with

Alan Wong. Courtesy of Alan Wong's.

Yamaguchi; and in December, Bradley Ogden was paired with Honolulu chef Russell Siu. In February 1998, the same program paired Keller and Wong and Mario Batali and Ellman. These pairings gave the HRC chefs visibility on the mainland and brought them into a new network of celebrity chefs, thereby affirming their place in the larger US restaurant world.[74]

With their new national visibility, it is no surprise that the HRC chefs were nominated for James Beard Foundation awards year after year. In 1995, Choy, Ferguson, and Josselin were nominees for Best Chef: Pacific Northwest.[75] The following year, Choy and Josselin were again nominated for the same award, as was Wong, whose new restaurant, Alan Wong's, had been open for only ten months. Remarkably, Wong won the award that year, becoming only the second HRC chef to win that coveted prize. For many years, Choy and Josselin continued to be nominated for the Beard Award for Best Chef: Pacific Northwest, a real tribute to the excellence of their restaurants. In 1999, Alan Wong's also received DiRoNa's Award of Excellence.[76] By the end of the 1990s, Hawai'i Regional Cuisine was firmly established in the US restaurant world, thanks to the recognition of the James Beard Foundation and also the new restaurants, new cookbooks, and the visits of leading celebrity chefs from the mainland.

The Third Stage, January 2000 to December 2011

In 2001, the local food writer John Heckathorn summed up the story of Hawai'i Regional Cuisine on the tenth anniversary of its founding. In "How We Got Our Own Cuisine," he offered four astute observations about the HRC movement. First, "[it] changed the way we ate, taking its vitality from local food, playing on the multiculturalism of a population that was more than willing to eat Chinese noodles and prime rib in the same meal, or shrimp tempura and kal-bi, or lumpia and lomi lomi salmon—or maybe all of these from the buffet table." Second, the movement "caused local food to evolve." "HRC started in high-end restaurants," Heckathorn reminded his readers, "but it revolutionized the menus at plate lunch parlors and lunch wagons. Since the advent of HRC, you can, for instance, get seared 'ahi on Waimānalo greens at a bar like Side Street Inn, or spicy 'ahi poke katsu with miso wasabi cream from an everyday café like Jurison's Inn in Waikele. HRC was a kind of realization that we have great food and ought to demand it in all circumstances."[77] Here, Heckathorn was sounding like sociologist Howard Becker, who would have described HRC cuisine as an "esoteric world" that became an "exoteric" one.[78] Third, the movement also "changed the perception of Hawai'i as a visitor destination," so, as food writer Henderson once observed, "You used to go to Hawai'i to surf, snorkel and have fun in the sun. Now you go to dine." Finally, the HRC movement "changed the lives of farmers." As Big Island farmer Tane Datta revealed, "I gave a speech ten years ago, and I said that things would really have gone full circle when the farmers could afford to eat in some of those restaurants and could drive there in a new truck."[79] Heckathorn's article was published just as the HRC movement reached its peak.

Nothing symbolizes the new heights to which a chef, restaurant, or food movement has risen quite as well as an invitation to cook at the James Beard House in New York City. Gannon and Ellman were invited to prepare such a dinner there on October 17, 2001. Their menu included "kalua pig and taro spring rolls, duck mochi, crab potstickers, chawan mushi with moi and truffle, 'ahi carpaccio, glazed lobster with musubi, shiitake-crusted Parker Ranch tenderloin with Moloka'i sweet potato and coconut flan with caramelized pineapple."[80] This dinner, the "third in a series of Hawai'i Regional Cuisine dinners," confirmed the movement's prominent place in the national restaurant world.

The twenty-first century, however, brought several unexpected developments. As happens when a regional cuisine movement matures and its chefs gain more and more recognition, the HRC chefs opened new restaurants and closed some old ones, but they also began to experience disappointments and setbacks. Confirming his emergence as a celebrity chef, Yamaguchi opened four more Roy's restaurants in Hawai'i in 2000 and sold his mainland restaurants to Bloomin' Brands.[81] Josselin closed A Pacific Café at the Ward Center and opened 808 in Caesar's Palace in Las Vegas, which was fast emerging as what chef Tom Colicchio called "the number one dining spot in the country" outside New York City.[82] The next year brought more bad news: Josselin filed for Chapter 11 bankruptcy, closing his A Pacific Café restaurants on both Maui and Kaua'i.[83] Two years later, HRC chefs opened four new restaurants, two in the islands and two on the mainland: Padovani opened a second Padovani's Restaurant & Wine Bar in San Francisco in March; Josselin opened 808 La Jolla in San Diego in April; and Merriman and Wong opened restaurants on the Big Island in

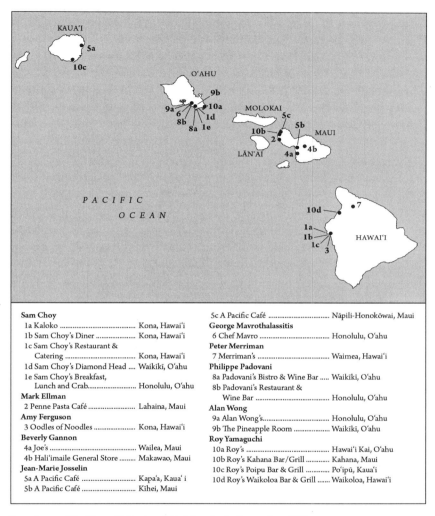

Locations of the Hawai'i Regional Cuisine chefs, December 2001.

December, Merriman's Market Café at the Waikoloa Beach Resort and Alan Wong's Hualalai Grille at the Hualalai Resort.[84]

The opening and closing of restaurants continued during 2006 and 2007. Padovani closed Padovani's Restaurant & Wine Bar restaurants in San Francisco and Honolulu before opening Chocolates by Padovani in February 2006.[85] Mavrothalassitis opened Cassis in Honolulu in April 2007.

That summer, Padovani and Donato Loperfido opened Elua Restaurant & Wine Bar in Honolulu; Ferguson decided to sell Oodles of Noodles; and both Merriman and Josselin finalized plans to open restaurants in a new development on the south shore of Kaua'i.[86]

More restaurant closings followed in 2008. Mavrothalassitis closed Cassis in February, Choy closed his Diamond Head Restaurant in June, and Wong left the Hualalai Grille in December.[87] Only Yamaguchi, the "rock star" of the HRC group, managed to keep his head completely above water. As he approached the twentieth anniversary of Roy's restaurants in 2008, he was operating five restaurants in Hawai'i and five overseas.[88] Yamaguchi celebrated this anniversary with two dinners in the islands and a nine-city culinary tour on the mainland that took him to Roy's restaurants in Orlando, Los Angeles, Las Vegas, San Francisco, Chicago, Philadelphia, New York, Atlanta, and Baltimore.[89]

What were the causes of these openings and closings? The first was the failing Japanese economy, whose effects had begun to be felt in the 1990s, but then the attacks of September 11, 2001, and the Iraq War cast even longer shadows on tourism in the islands. The number of Japanese tourists coming to the islands plummeted. On September 10, 2001, Mavrothalassitis was on his way to France for a vacation, "but when September 11 happened," he thought, "Oh, my god, I'm dead."[90] The reported decline in visitors to the islands tells the story. Mavrothalassitis was right: 3 percent fewer Japanese came to the islands in 2002 and 10 percent fewer in 2003. This was only the beginning. The recession in Japan continued through the first decade of the twenty-first century, and this may have had an even greater impact on fine dining in the islands than the September 11 attacks did. After dropping by 3 percent in 2002 and 10 percent in 2003, tourism from Japan then rose by 11 percent in 2004 and 2 percent in 2005 before dropping again by 10 percent in 2006, 5 percent in 2007, and 9 percent in 2008.[91] What helped was that tourism from the West Coast picked up some of the slack, rising 5 percent in 2002, 4 percent in 2003, 7 percent in 2004, 10 percent in 2005, and 6 percent in 2006. But when the Great Recession set in on the mainland, the flow of tourists from the West Coast declined precipitously, by 15 percent in 2008 and 2 percent in 2009.[92] Mavrothalassitis closed Cassis, and Choy closed Diamond Head Restaurant in 2008. No one, certainly not restaurateurs, could have predicted the impact of external events on their businesses.

In March 2000, Josselin was nominated for the Beard Award for Best Chef: Pacific Northwest for a sixth time. In 2002 and 2003, Mavrothalassitis was nominated for the same award and finally won it in 2003, the third HRC chef to do so.[93] The following year Sam Choy's Kaloko in Kailua-Kona won a James Beard Foundation America's Classics Award, and both Merriman and Gannon were nominated for a Beard Award. It was the same year that Charles Phan, chef-owner of the Slanted Door, an upscale Vietnamese restaurant in San Francisco, won the Beard Award for Best Chef: California, and Mavrothalassitis was invited to cook a dinner at the James Beard House in New York City. Beginning in 2006 and for three years afterward, Wong was a semifinalist for a Beard Award for Best Chef.[94] That year, Gannon and Merriman were semifinalists for Best Chef: Pacific Northwest, as was Enrique Tariga, the chef at the Seascape Maʻalaea Restaurant at the Maui Ocean Center. In 2000, the James Beard Foundation recognized as an

George Mavrothalassitis. Courtesy of George Mavrothalassitis.

American Classic Helen Chock's Helena's Hawaiian Foods, an iconic west Honolulu institution that had the distinction of being the oldest restaurant in the islands serving Hawaiian food.[95]

The HRC chefs brought home other national awards. In 2001, Wong won a string of awards: a Médaille de Mérite for Outstanding Service to the Chaîne des Rôtisseurs and DiRoNa's Award of Excellence, and he also was named one of the top ten chefs in the United States.[96] The awards continued in 2002: Alan Wong's was inducted into *Restaurant News'* Hall of Fame, and Wong himself was named one of the top ten culinary innovators in the United States. Wong's *sous chefs* Lance Kosaka and Steve Ariel received Bertolli Sous Chef Awards and put in cooking stints at Daniel and Daniel Boulud in New York City.[97] In 2003, Alan Wong's again received DiRoNa's Award of Excellence, and Mavrothalassitis' Chef Mavro received the coveted Five Diamond Award in 2008.[98]

National food writers continued to give the HRC chefs good press. Several of their restaurants were on the leading food magazines' lists of the country's best restaurants. In 2000, *Bon Appétit* included Alan Wong's in its "Our Favorite Restaurants" list.[99] Later that year, *Gourmet* named Padovani's Bar & Grill the best French restaurant in Honolulu; and Alan Wong's, the best regional cuisine restaurant in Honolulu, calling Wong "the Tennyson of teriyaki, the Proust of poi, and the Lorca of lomi lomi."[100] *Gourmet* also included Alan Wong's in its list of Best Restaurants.[101] The following year, it named Alan Wong's the sixth-best restaurant in the nation and, in 2002, named Chef Mavro one of "America's Best Restaurants."

Occasionally, the leading food and wine magazines even featured HRC chefs. In 2000, Mavrothalassitis and his restaurant Chef Mavro were featured in *Wine Spectator*'s cover story, and Alan Wong's was included in *Food & Wine*'s "Best Reflects the City."[102] In September 2003, *Bon Appétit* recognized Wong as "Master of HRC."[103] In August 2006, *Restaurant Business* listed Wong's Chinatown Roast Duck Nachos one of the nation's best dishes.[104] Later that year, *Gourmet* magazine named Merriman, Wong, and Neil Murphy "local pioneers."[105] Murphy was the chef at Merriman's in Waimea. (*Gourmet* also named Waters a "local pioneer."[106]) The HRC chefs continued to be featured on national television, and no one more than Yamaguchi, the islands' leading celebrity chef. In 2001, Yamaguchi debuted as an iron chef on *Iron Chef USA* and was featured in a PBS series, *Hawaii Cooks with Roy Yamaguchi*. The following year, he was featured in the Food Network's *My Country, My Kitchen*, and in 2003, he cooked for the

Grammy Awards in New York City and filmed the sixth season of *Hawaii Cooks with Roy Yamaguchi*.[107] In 2004, he appeared on the Home Shopping Network, where his signature line of cookware and culinary products was showcased, and he and Wong cooked at a benefit dinner in Los Angeles for the Go for Broke Foundation, a Japanese American veterans' organization. In 2005, Yamaguchi was invited to join Chef Michael Lomonaco on the Travel Channel's cooking program *Epicurious* as an in-studio guest and also was seen on *Live with Regis and Kelly*. That same year, he prepared dinner for guests on the Sarasota Film Festival cruise to the Cannes Film Festival and cooked for Thai princess Soamsawali's charity Save a Child's Life from AIDS Project, sponsored by the Thai Red Cross. In 2006, Yamaguchi made other television appearances: first, on *Emeril Live*, then on the *Today* show, and finally on *CBS Morning*. He also was invited to join the board of trustees of the Culinary Institute of America, his alma mater. He was the featured celebrity chef on the South Africa Winelands Tour & Safari. Given this visibility in the national media, Yamaguchi's restaurants made more than $100 million in 2006. More television appearances followed in 2007: the *CBS Early Show*, the *Today Show* with Al Roper, Bravo's *Top Chef* program, and iVillage. Clearly, Yamaguchi was a celebrity chef.

Besides hosting celebrity chefs from the mainland and Asia, the HRC chefs brought in young star chefs. In April 2000, Grant MacPherson, executive chef at the Bellagio Hotel in Las Vegas, returned to Hawai'i to cook for the first anniversary of Padovani's Bistro & Wine Bar. In early October of that year, Wong and Ming Tsai, chef-owner of Blue Ginger restaurant in Wellesley, Massachusetts, were featured at the Kea Lani Food & Wine Festival.[108] The following year, 2001, found Choy appearing with Lagasse at a luau at the Hilton Hawaiian Village Beach Resort & Spa. The event was filmed for the May 18 *Good Morning America* show. That summer, Cuisines of the Sun brought more than a half dozen celebrity chefs: Ben and Karen Barker of Magnolia Grill in Durham, North Carolina; Hiroki Sone and Lissa Doumani from Terra in St. Helena, California; Johanne Killeen and George Germon of Al Forno in Providence, Rhode Island; Lee Hefter of Spago in Beverly Hills; and George Morrone of the Fifth Floor in San Francisco. Wong and Yamaguchi were there as well.[109]

The HRC chefs also continued to maintain their media presence at home, hosting benefit dinners for a variety of causes and often along with celebrity chefs. Choy continued to host the Big Brothers/Big Sisters of Honolulu benefit dinner year after year and even invited a series of well-known guest chefs, including Ming Tsai; Andrew DiCataldo, the chef at Patria in New York City; and Charles Phan, chef-owner of the Slanted Door in San Francisco. Roy's Hawaii Kai continued to host the Farm Bureau Benefit Dinner, as it did in June 2000. In 2001, Josselin's new television show *A Taste of Hawaii with Jean-Marie Josselin* aired on local television. In August, the HRC founding chefs gathered for a tenth anniversary dinner, which was held at the Sheraton Waikiki, and all twelve of the founding HRC chefs were there, even those who had left the islands. On May 4, 2002, Taste of the Stars, a benefit dinner for Leeward Community College, brought together as guest chefs Mavrothalassitis, Padovani, Russell Siu, Yamaguchi, and Wong. Four months later, Yamaguchi teamed up with Matsuhisa and Yūji Wakiya at Roy's Hawaii Kai to cook a benefit dinner for college culinary programs in the islands.[110] Matsuhisa had become a celebrity chef with restaurants all over the United States and the world, and Wakiya was the well-known Japanese chef-owner of Turandot in Yokohama, which served some of the best Chinese food in Japan.[111]

Although many fewer celebrity chefs visited in 2003, this changed in succeeding years. In April 2004, Wong, Yamaguchi, and others again cooked at Leeward Community College's Taste of the Stars benefit dinner.[112] In August 2005, benefit dinners for the Oʻahu Art Center were held at Sam Choy's and Roy's Ko Olina, and in April 2006, Choy and Paul Prudhomme cooked at a benefit dinner for victims of Hurricane Katrina and Kauaʻi's months of torrential rains at Sam Choy's Diamond Head Restaurant. In February 2007, Wong hosted a $1,000-a-head benefit dinner at his restaurant for Hale ʻAina Ohana's culinary education efforts. The guest chef was Jonathan Benno, from New York City's Per Se, the winner of the Beard Award for Best New Restaurant in 2005 and the recipient of three Michelin stars in 2006. In April 2007, Choy, Yamaguchi, and Göran Streng (who opened Tango, near Waikīkī, the following year) cooked for the school fair at the ʻIolani School, a local prep school, and half a year later, Mavrothalassitis and Choy cooked for the Chopsticks and Wine benefit Twilight in Tuscany dinner held at the Sheraton Waikiki. Finally, in September 2008, Ellman was one of several chefs who cooked at the Chefs of Aloha dinner that the Hawaiʻi Restaurant Association sponsored to raise funds for local culinary students.

The HRC chefs managed to remain visible in other ways. In 2005 Wong and Yamaguchi designed kitchens for luxury residences,[113] and Yamaguchi

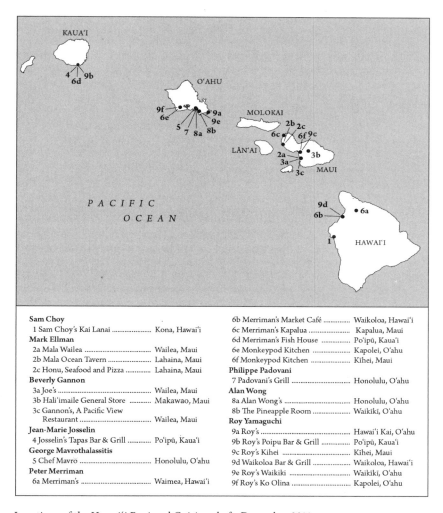

Sam Choy
1 Sam Choy's Kai Lanai .... Kona, Hawai'i
Mark Ellman
2a Mala Wailea .... Wailea, Maui
2b Mala Ocean Tavern .... Lahaina, Maui
2c Honu, Seafood and Pizza .... Lahaina, Maui
Beverly Gannon
3a Joe's .... Wailea, Maui
3b Hali'imaile General Store .... Makawao, Maui
3c Gannon's, A Pacific View
     Restaurant .... Wailea, Maui
Jean-Marie Josselin
4 Josselin's Tapas Bar & Grill .... Po'ipū, Kaua'i
George Mavrothalassitis
5 Chef Mavro .... Honolulu, O'ahu
Peter Merriman
6a Merriman's .... Waimea, Hawai'i

6b Merriman's Market Café .... Waikoloa, Hawai'i
6c Merriman's Kapalua .... Kapalua, Maui
6d Merriman's Fish House .... Po'ipū, Kaua'i
6e Monkeypod Kitchen .... Kapolei, O'ahu
6f Monkeypod Kitchen .... Kīhei, Maui
Philippe Padovani
7 Padovani's Grill .... Honolulu, O'ahu
Alan Wong
8a Alan Wong's .... Honolulu, O'ahu
8b The Pineapple Room .... Waikīkī, O'ahu
Roy Yamaguchi
9a Roy's .... Hawai'i Kai, O'ahu
9b Roy's Poipu Bar & Grill .... Po'ipū, Kaua'i
9c Roy's Kihei .... Kīhei, Maui
9d Waikoloa Bar & Grill .... Waikoloa, Hawai'i
9e Roy's Waikiki .... Waikīkī, O'ahu
9f Roy's Ko Olina .... Kapolei, O'ahu

Locations of the Hawai'i Regional Cuisine chefs, December 2011.

was named to the "Honolulu 100" and recognized at the Centennial Gala Celebration in Honolulu. In April 2006, Wong cooked plantation-era dishes at Plantation Village, and on January 21, 2008, he featured Hamakua Mushroom Farms at his Farmer Series Dinner, and then on July 23, 2008, he highlighted butterfish and halibut from Troutlodge Marine Farms at his Farmer Series Dinner. On May 10, 2008, Yamaguchi was honored at the

Lʻulu, Leeward Community College Culinary Arts Gala, the third annual benefit dinner for the college's culinary arts program.

The HRC chefs also continued to write cookbooks. Three appeared in 2000: Gannon's *Haliʻimaile General Store Cookbook* and Choy's *Sam Choy's Cooking* and *Sam Choy's Sampler*.[114] Over the next two years, Choy released three more cookbooks: *Sam Choy's Cooking with Kids, Sam Choy Woks the Wok,* and *Sam Choy's Polynesian Kitchen.* The year 2003 brought a bumper crop of cookbooks by HRC chefs, beginning with Yamaguchi's *Hawaii Cooks with Roy Yamaguchi* and followed by Choy's *Sam Choy's Little Hawaiian Cookbook for Big Appetites* and Ellman and Barbara Santos' *Maui Tacos Cookbook.* In 2004, Choy published *A Hawaiian Luau* with the Makaha Sons, a well-known local vocal group, and *Sam Choy's A Little Hawaiian Poke Cookbook. A Hawaiian Luau* won an award of excellence at the annual Ka Palapala Poʻokela Book Awards. Over the next three years, Yamaguchi published *Roy's Fish & Seafood* and *Roy's Feasts from Hawaii,* and Choy published *Aloha Cuisine,* which won a Ka Palapala Poʻokela honorable mention award in the cookbook category.[115]

The HRC chefs' restaurants continued to sweep the islands' culinary awards. Alan Wong's won *Honolulu Magazine*'s Hale ʻAina award for the Best Restaurant in 2000, 2001, 2005, 2006, 2007, and 2008. Roy's won the same award in 2002 and 2004. As it had from the inception of the Hale ʻAina awards, Merriman's continued to win the Best Restaurant on the Big Island award. The HRC chefs also dominated the *Honolulu Advertiser*'s ʻIlima Awards, winning the Best Restaurant award year after year. Alan Wong's won ʻIlima's Best Restaurant Award, readers' choice.[116] Chef Mavro won ʻIlima's Best Restaurant Award, critics' choice; and Roy's won ʻIlima's Best Restaurant Award, people's choice.[117] In November 2008, Gannon was named the state's Small Business Person of the Year.[118]

The awards, the new cookbooks, the steady stream of articles in local as well as national newspapers and food magazines, and the television appearances enhanced the place of the HRC chefs and their restaurants in the island and the national restaurant scene. Once again, there was no better affirmation of Hawaiʻi Regional Cuisine than the first of many visits by President and Mrs. Barack Obama to Alan Wong's on January 20, 2008. The Obamas became regulars, visiting at least once every time they came to the islands during the eight years of the Obama presidency, and on several occasions, Wong and his staff staged luaus at the White House.

Conclusions

On March 9, 2011, Wong and Mavrothalassitis were invited to cook a special dinner at the James Beard House in New York City.[119] The two chefs and their assistants offered what might be called vintage HRC cuisine. Their menu consisted of the following dishes:

Hors-d'oeuvres

Chilled Tomato Soup and Grilled Mozzarella Sandwiches with Foie Gras and Kalua Pig

Garam Masala–Dusted Shrimp with Hearts of Palm, Green-Apple Rémoulade, and Oʻahu Sea Asparagus Tempura

Maui Cattle Company Roast Beef Rolls with Pho Flavors

Winter Vegetable Meli-Melo with Sumida Watercress, Chickpea Fritters, and Eggplant Tahini

Dinner

Poached Truffle–Infused Petersons' Upland Farm Egg with Potato Mousseline and Jinhua Ham Ribbons

Chopped Ahi Sashimi and Avocado Salsa Stack on Crispy Wonton with Spicy Aïoli and Wasabi Soy

Crisped Onaga with Poha Rice, Braised Green Papaya, and House-made Tamarind Curry

Butter-Poached Kona Lobster with Eryngii Mushrooms, Green Onion Oil, and Katsuo Soy

Lamb Pissaladière

Big Island "Wow" Farm Tomato Tart with Lamb Bacon, Maui Onions, Black Olive Powder, and Lamb Jus

Dessert

Kula Strawberries Romanoff

Goat Cheese Panna Cotta with Kula Strawberry-Hibiscus Soup, Yogurt Sorbet, and Hawaiian Vanilla Sabayon

Many of these dishes, and their flavor profiles, would be familiar to those who dined often at Chef Mavro or Alan Wong's, as would the names of the producers—Maui Cattle Company, Peterson's Upland Egg Farm, and Sumida Watercress Farm—and their locations. It was a brilliant selection of dishes that exhibited the chefs' culinary skills, the range of their repertoires, the quality and variety of their ingredients, and their shared vision of Hawai'i Regional Cuisine.

In many ways, this dinner, the fifth at the James Beard House to feature HRC chefs between 1991 and 2011, symbolized the extraordinary success of the movement. Consider what the HRC chefs had done over the course of nearly twenty years: they had opened and closed sixty-five restaurants and were operating thirty-eight restaurants in 2011; published twenty-seven cookbooks; raised several hundred thousand dollars for both national and local causes; appeared regularly on television programs; and become part of a global network of celebrity chefs, with several becoming celebrity chefs themselves, with corporate empires consisting of restaurants, television exposure, and even their own cookware. The HRC chefs continued to be finalists for the Beard Award for Best Chef: Pacific Northwest as late as 2010.[120]

The HRC chefs' achievements are important, too, for giving them a voice in what Krishnendu Ray terms the national discussion of "taste." Using Ray's language, one might describe the HRC chefs as bridging the existing "hierarchies of taste and ethnic difference" with their "Euro-Asian" cuisine. What helped make this possible was the emergence of several regional cuisines in the United States and the transformation of Japanese cuisine from an "ethnic cuisine" to a "foreign cuisine," comparable to French and Continental cuisine. Without these other changes in the national restaurant world, what the HRC chefs were making at their restaurants between 1991 and 2011 would not have made complete sense to the national tastemakers and thus would not have been recognized. This twenty-year trajectory is revealed as well in the dishes that HRC chefs made over the life of the movement, the subject of chapter 3.

3 | Cuisine

> Cooking is evolution, cooking is life. . . . The restaurant is
> not stagnant, it grows, it evolves. It started twenty years ago.
> We are still working on it. Dishes will be different tomor-
> row because of sheer evolution, because of the life of food.
>
> Thomas Keller, 1998

We have seen how the Hawai'i Regional Cuisine chefs revolutionized the food scene in the islands, shattering the racial hierarchies governing haute cuisine and inspiring a new locavorism.
They also created a new regional cuisine that gave them a place in a larger
national restaurant world, as was clear from their coverage in the national
print and television media, their relationships with leading chefs on the
mainland and around the world, and their many impressive awards. How
was their brand manifested in what they served at their restaurants? Was
there a distinctive HRC culinary style, something akin to a Hawaiian version of the nouvelle cuisine that emerged in France in the 1960s?

The second question is an obvious but not the right one, because Hawai'i
Regional Cuisine cannot be defined in these terms. Unlike the French chefs
who created a nouvelle cuisine in the 1960s, the HRC chefs did not have a
manifesto. They had nothing like the ten-point "formula" that Henri Gault
and Christian Millau described in their *Gault et Millau se mettent à table*
to sum up their new approach.[1] There was no definitive HRC culinary style.

Roy Yamaguchi agreed when I asked him this question.[2] Instead, the
HRC chefs created dishes that reflected their biographies (where they were

born and raised, what they ate at home, and where they learned to cook) and their careers (where they had worked) and how long they had been in the islands. After all, the HRC chefs hailed from many different places: the Hawaiian islands, the mainland United States, Europe, and Australia. Their culinary education and training also were quite varied. Only three of them were products of the same institution—Roger Dikon, Gary Strehl, and Yamaguchi had graduated from the Culinary Institute of America— and Jean-Marie Josselin, Peter Merriman, George Mavrothalassitis, and Philippe Padovani had worked at restaurants in Europe before they came to the United States. Two even had their own, well-regarded, restaurants before they came to the islands. Amy Ferguson had Baby Routh's in Houston, and Yamaguchi had 385 North in Los Angeles. Accordingly, rather than ask about an "HRC style," we should ask what was distinctive about HRC cuisine and what identified an "HRC dish."

Sam Choy was the first chef to have a clear sense of what would become Hawai'i Regional Cuisine. Several years before the August 1991 meeting, he talked about what he called "Cuisine Hawai'i," defining it as "home-grown ingredients dressed in gourmet fashion."[3] Yamaguchi and Alan Wong always pointed to the ethnic diversity of the islands. In his first cookbook, *Pacific Bounty* (1994), Yamaguchi described "Hawaii's new cuisine" as a "cuisine of many cultures, for Hawaii itself is defined by a population of immigrants."[4] Indeed,

> [i]t only makes sense that we should have a cuisine of many cultures, for Hawaii itself is defined by a population of immigrants. More than 1,000 years ago, the earliest Hawaiians grew fish in man-made shoreline ponds, planted taro (a nutritious tuber) and cooked pigs in imu (underground ovens). In the mid to late 19th century, Chinese and Japanese sugar plantation workers brought, respectively, wok cooking and exquisite preparations of raw fish. Over the decades they were followed by Portuguese, Koreans, Filipinos, Mexicans, Vietnamese and other ethnic groups, each of whom contributed unique culinary styles to their new home.[5]

Echoing Yamaguchi, Wong insisted that his dishes always harked back to the "cross-cultural cooking" of the plantations.

> If you can imagine, back in the day on the pineapple field, the workers take their lunch break. It would be very common that they form a little circle, they all squat and put their food in the middle. They each get their own pail

rice, but otherwise they're all sharing their food. . . . So we get the Japanese guy with his *musubi* sitting next to the Filipino guy with his *pinakbet*, next to the Korean, next to the Chinese, next to the Portuguese. . . . That's how cross-cultural cooking started.[6]

Later, in an interview in 2009, Wong elaborated on the "cross-cultural cooking" of the islands:

I say to the cooks [at my restaurant] that HRC started a long time ago. I talk about the three great migrations that came to Hawaii. The Polynesians from the South Pacific. The second, the big boats . . . the missionaries and the whalers. They brought things with them. I like this kind of stuff. Because there's a story here. So, the second migrations, whalers, the Portuguese whalers brought chili pepper water. That's why there's chili pepper water on the table, you know, and soy sauce. On the ship, scurvy. Vitamin C. That's how we got lomilomi salmon, *bacalhau* from those boats. The chili peppers are high in vitamin C. OK?

Then during that time, somebody brought sugarcane. The plantations were born. Then the disease set in, and over 50 percent of the Hawaiian population died. So they were working in the fields. The Hawaii Plantation Village can document that. Then they went to China first. They brought these men over for three-year contracts. They made $9 a month or something like that. They stayed. They became the first business merchants and the store owners. They still kept their wife. Imagine that: the Chinese man marrying the Hawaiian girl. Imagine the Chinese man hungry for Chinese food, trying to teach the Hawaiian girl how to cook Chinese food. She no can. The Hawaiian girl trying for get him to eat Hawaiian food. But he no like. So what you get is cross-cultural clash.

Then the Japanese came. I love the scene in *The Hawaiians*. Charlton Heston. You remember the *ofuro*. Remember they're freaking out because they're taking off their clothes and going into the bathtub. Charlton Heston comes in. That's one of my favorite movies.

Anyway, so the Hawaiian Plantation Village is all about that: sugarcane, the Chinese, the Japanese, the Portuguese, the Puerto Ricans, the Koreans, Okinawans, and last, the Filipinos. And what they brought with them. So this exchanging of cultures and food. So the Japanese guy is making tofu, the Portuguese guy's making bread out in their *fornos* . . . and so on and so on. They're planting all their vegetables in their backyards. They exchange, they barter. They're only making $69 a month. They're poor. That's how it is. I have a friend who grew up on a farm that fed thirty people every night. He talks of stories of one stick kamaboko, five pounds green beans. Stir-fried.

And if you're last, you only get beans, you no more kamaboko. Or one can Spam and five pounds green beans.

So let me finish, so let me finish—can I finish? . . . Then the immigrants were the third immigration, and so that's how I explain to the young cooks today. This Chinese man marrying the Hawaiian girl. The Japanese girl marrying the Pordagee guy or whatever. HRC actually started that long ago. This cross-cultural thing. My mom is from Japan. So even today, her beef stew, her Western-style beef stew has a lot of ginger in it. 'Cause she no like the smell.[7]

Although highly romanticized, Wong's narrative offers a picture of HRC cuisine that shares much with Yamaguchi's vision, and their culinary creations reference these views.

The HRC chefs with island roots admitted, too, that memories of what they ate as children inspired many of their dishes. Choy, who was raised in Lāʻie on the windward side of Oʻahu, remembered what he called "my Hawaiʻi." "I grew up with a fishing spear in one hand and chopsticks in the other," he wrote in the introduction to his first cookbook.

It always seemed more natural to go out and catch food for a meal than to stop by the corner market and buy it. It was also a lot more fun!

For centuries, the people of Hawaii have done the same thing. They've drawn their food primarily from the environment, harvesting fish, shellfish and seaweed from the sea and working the land to grow vegetables and fruit.

Today I still follow that tradition, one which I learned from my parents and their parents before them.[8]

Wong, who grew up in Waipahu, a plantation town in central Oʻahu, has powerful memories of the Chinese, Filipino, and Japanese ingredients, dishes, and flavors that graced his family's table. "I'm used to all of those ingredients and flavors," he would say.[9]

Wong's memories of eating Hawaiian food as a boy were formative as well. He once described a dish that he served at CanoeHouse in 1992, called "Grilled Chicken Marinated in Macadamia Nut Oil with Taro Sauce," as "a delicate breast of chicken marinated in herbed oil, grilled and served in a pool of taro and leek puree and topped with a slightly fiery tomato relish." It was inspired by "the way I eat Hawaiian food": first, mounding some poi in a bowl, adding a layer of laulau or kālua pig, and topping with lomilomi salmon.[10] Especially powerful was Wong's memory of eating kālua pig, the pièce de résistance at celebratory Hawaiian feasts: "I grew up eating kalua pig. . . . It was the easiest way to eat poi: Kalua pig and lomi went into the poi. It's very regional, very Hawai'i." These memories, he adds, inspired what he called "Da Bag," a signature dish at Alan Wong's, and the caesar salad, pizzas, and kālua pig BLT served at the Pineapple Room.[11]

Many of Yamaguchi's dishes were inspired by his binational family's cooking and meals: "My mom used to make pork with miso, green onions, and scrambled eggs—it's one of my all-time favorites. . . . They wanted that meal to be on the table and for the kids to enjoy the meal they served. No matter what the flavors were, you never forget the flavors you have as a kid."[12] Obviously, the HRC chefs who did not grow up in the islands do not share these views, so their dishes have other sources.

The HRC chefs' various visions of their cuisine nonetheless converge at two points. First, they all share a commitment to locavorism: they always highlight the locally sourced vegetables, meat, fruit, shellfish, and fish used at their restaurants. Since the late 1980s, local sourcing was the idée fixe of Merriman, Dikon, Ferguson, Padovani, and Strehl and the main reason that the HRC chefs met in August 1991. In fact, Merriman once described his technique as one that "favors use of local—rather than imported—food products, a practice that caught both restaurant patrons and fellow chefs by surprise. 'They didn't think that you could do this,'" Merriman explained. "'They didn't think that you could go out and talk to farmers and encourage them to grow or raise what you wanted.'"[13]

Yamaguchi agreed and acknowledged the importance of his food purveyors. "We all want to work with the farmer, the people out there fishing, so we can bring out an awareness of all the products."[14] Continuing in the same vein, Yamaguchi wrote in 1994: "We are a growing legion of chefs who go out of our way to get the plumpest ahi (yellowfin tuna) at the Honolulu fish auction. We get dirt under our fingernails in order to taste sweet upcountry Maui strawberries. We milk floppy-eared Nubian goats on the Big Island to learn how rich Puna goat cheese is made. We monitor the availability of crops from one end of the archipelago to the other, and we urge growers to cultivate products with us in mind."[15] Having come from California, where Alice Waters initiated her own farm-to-table movement to supply Chez Panisse in the 1970s and where Wolfgang Puck served the "freshest vegetables" he could find at Spago in the 1980s, Yamaguchi knew this locavoric vision was feasible, as did the HRC chefs who had trained or worked in Europe, where local sourcing was a given.[16]

For Mavrothalassitis, one of those French-trained chefs, fresh ingredients are one of the things that distinguish "good cooking" from "great cooking." "The difference between good cooking and great cooking," he explained, "the difference between a one-star Michelin restaurant in France and a three-star one, is in the details. Everything is fresh and cooked to perfection."[17] The other thing is culinary skill.

The HRC chefs also agreed that theirs was a "regional cuisine," a second point of agreement. As noted in chapter 1, they even decided early on to label their food "Hawai'i Regional Cuisine." Merriman may have been the first to use the term "regional cuisine" and one of the first to cook a Hawai'i-centric cuisine.[18] Ferguson brought firsthand knowledge of the concept and practice of a "regional cuisine," since before she moved to the islands in 1985, she had been part of what came to be known as Southwestern Cuisine.[19]

The term "Hawai'i Regional Cuisine" clearly resonated with a broader public, both in the islands and nationally. In fact, when looking back many years later, Yamaguchi could say categorically that Hawai'i Regional Cuisine was a form of "regional cooking." In a 2009 interview, he carefully explained that

> HRC isn't really about a style of cooking. It's about a bunch of chefs who got together who wanted to make a regional cooking entity but not through the cooking style. Because if you take a look at everybody today [2009], no one really does the same thing. The ones who are left over in Hawai'i, Alan Wong, myself, Sam Choy, Mavro, Philippe Padovani, who comes in and out. For instance, I make a lot of sauces, a tremendous amount of sauces, whether it be Asian, Chinese or whatever different flavors come into mind. You get somebody like Peter Merriman that does pretty much . . . no sauces; it's more salsas and stuff like that. And take Alan Wong, who is a combination of using more . . . poi or li hing mui and stuff like that. And everybody has resources of what Hawai'i has to offer. That was the most important part of HRC: *It was regional cooking. It's not the style of cooking . . . but the products you get to make that regional cooking.*[20]

When asked whether that was true from the beginning, he replied:

> Yeah, yeah. Always. Back then we all cooked differently, even back then when Roger Dikon was still here, when Gary Strehl was here . . . Amy Ferguson, everybody had different styles of cooking. But *what brought everybody together was to get better products to make our food better. That was the most important. We didn't say that we were going to cook alike, because*

that would defeat the purpose. Everybody has their own style of cooking. But what's important [is,] let's utilize what Hawaii has to offer, whether it be agriculture or aquaculture, whether it be the fish from the ocean, whether it be the taro from the land.[21]

All twelve HRC chefs would have agreed, first, that they were practitioners of a new "regional cuisine" and, second, that what they served at their restaurants was made with locally sourced, incomparably fresh, high-quality ingredients supplied by a small army of farmers, fishermen, ranchers, and others in the islands.

The same quest for fresh ingredients also inspired chefs involved in other regional cuisine movements, notably California Cuisine and New American Cuisine. As they were beginning their careers, they, too, like the HRC chefs, discovered that many of the top restaurants in San Francisco and New York City were not using what was available locally. In the 1970s, David Kamp reports, "Even the white-tablecloth French restaurants across the bay in San Francisco were using frozen steaks and pre-butchered poultry," and Jeremiah Tower, who may have cooked one of the first California Cuisine dinners at Chez Panisse in Berkeley, remembered that "you couldn't buy fresh herbs."[22] In the 1980s, when Charlie Palmer was beginning his career at the top French restaurants in Manhattan—La Côte Basque, La Petite Marmite, and Le Chantilly—he was shocked to find that their chefs were using frozen Dover sole. Why were they doing this, he asked, "When we can get the best fish in the world right in New York City?" Like Dikon, Palmer even had groundskeepers at the Waccabuc Country Club, where he worked for a time, create an herb garden for him when he worked there.[23]

Ingredients

Ingredients, then, were what made the new HRC cuisine. All the HRC chefs followed Ferguson's advice to "use the best ingredients."[24] Mavrothalassitis certainly did, declaring that he always started with the ingredient. "Regional cuisine is not a style of cooking, it is more a philosophy," he observed. "It's cooking with what we find wherever we are. . . . We do not say, 'I have a recipe and I'm going to find the ingredient.' We say, 'I have an ingredient and I'm going to find a recipe.'"[25] Yamaguchi, as well, stressed the importance of *fresh* ingredients. "I want to only buy food for that day," he stated; that way, "we can provide the freshest food possible."[26] As expected, local fish, meat, seaweed, fruits, and vegetables were highlighted on the menus at HRC restaurants.

Yamaguchi's television program *Hawaii Cooks* featured these locally sourced ingredients, introducing them first to an island audience and later to a mainland one. He and his producer agreed "to show all the ingredients that make a dish before it is cooked. . . . That includes the land it came from, the people that grow it, the cultures that created it: Cooking is only a part of it. There are a lot of regional products grown in Hawaii that will be featured . . . everything from macadamia nuts to papayas to our wonderful fish to prawns. And we'll be visiting specialist chefs to get their flair."[27] The local ingredients used in the cookbook that resulted from this program include coconuts, eggplants, guavas, Hawaiian chilis, Hawaiian chocolate, Hawaiian salt, Kahuku shrimp, Ka'ū oranges, Keāhole shrimp, Kona coffee, Kona crabs, Kona oysters, Lāna'i venison, liliko'i, local fish, macadamia nuts, mangoes, Maui onions, papayas, Puna goat cheese, and Waimea tomatoes, as well as veal, Wagyu beef, elk, and lamb from the Kahua Ranch on the Big Island.[28]

Yamaguchi's locavorism was shared by the other HRC chefs. Given the abundance of fresh fish in the islands, they always made a point of serving locally caught fish, such as ahi (yellowfin tuna), onaga (long-tail red snapper), mahimahi, ono (wahoo), moano (goatfish), 'ōpakapaka (short-tail pink snapper), moi (Pacific threadfin), shutome (swordfish), and nohu (scorpion fish). The chefs also featured locally grown coconuts, mangoes, and pineapple, 'ulu (breadfruit), beautiful microgreens, tomatoes, pohole (fiddlehead ferns), and Molokai sweet potatoes, as well as an array of indigenous seaweeds such as limu. Even the somewhat expensive shellfish 'opihi (limpet) found its way onto HRC restaurant menus.[29]

Crucial here were the HRC chefs' relationships with local food producers, which ensured a steady supply of fresh and high-quality ingredients. Merriman cultivated farmers and ranchers on the Big Island, beginning with Tane Datta, Erin Lee, Richard Ha, and Monty Edwards. Yamaguchi turned to Dean Okimoto, who had a small farm in Waimānalo, on the southeastern side of O'ahu, and who supplied the microgreens and herbs used by chefs in Honolulu and Waikīkī for several years. Padovani liked the chervil grown by Big Island farmers Pam and Kurt Hirabara and became a regular customer for that and much else that they grew.[30] Many of these relationships have survived to the present, but now, of course, there are many other producers, even a new generation of farmers, ranchers, fishermen, and food producers.

In gratitude, the HRC chefs always have gone out of their way to recognize their producers.[31] Merriman was one of the first to do this, crediting Lee for her tomatoes, the Hirabaras for their greens, and Richards for his lamb. From the beginning, photographs of them, and of other farmers and ranchers, graced the walls of Merriman's first restaurant. Wong, too, has always identified those who supplied his kitchens. Early on, he let his customers know that his tomatoes were from Ha's Hamakua Springs Country Farms, his smoked meat from the Alex Jardine / Kimo Ha operation, his mushrooms from Bob Stanga's Hamakua Mushroom Farm, and his goat cheese from Heather Threlfall's Hawaii Island Goat Dairy.[32] Wong even made a point of serving locally produced coffees from the Big Island and Kauaʻi, beginning with Eddie Sakamoto's vintage Kona coffees from Hōnaunau on the Big Island.[33] Beverly Gannon went to great lengths to substitute local ingredients for what was used on the mainland: pohā berries for gooseberries and Maui onions for leeks.[34] Josselin even hoped to rely solely on local sources for his vegetables, fruits, and herbs as well as his meat.[35] The HRC chefs' locavoric approaches brought them to the attention of the national restaurant world.[36]

In Janice Wald Henderson's *The New Cuisine of Hawaii* and Yamaguchi's *Pacific Bounty*, both published in 1994, many of the HRC chefs' favorite ingredients were staples of Asian and Pacific cuisines, from what Gannon called "a big table" of ingredients—Japanese, Filipino, and Hawaiian, as well as French.[37] Josselin pointed to three ingredients in particular—"soy sauce, Chinese mustard, and Chinese duck"—explaining that "there are certain things that they [his customers] just love."[38] In the early 1990s, the Asian Pacific ingredients most widely used by at least ten HRC chefs were coconut milk, lemongrass, shoyu, ginger, sesame oil, Kaffir lime leaves, and shiitake mushrooms.

At least five HRC chefs also regularly used hoisin sauce, nam pla (a fish sauce), Szechuan chili sauce, macadamia nuts, rice wine vinegar, mangoes, and snow peas. Two chefs even used bok choy, five-spice powder, Hawaiian salt, Japanese chilis, lilikoʻi, mirin, miso, mung bean sprouts, nori, orange peel, star anise, tamarind, taro, and wasabi. The HRC chefs' recipes in cookbooks published between 1994 and 2001 confirm that these Asian Pacific ingredients continued to be widely used in the first decade of the movement.

THE NEW CUISINE OF HAWAII
Recipes from the Twelve Celebrated Chefs
of Hawaii Regional Cuisine

JANICE WALD HENDERSON

Cover of Janice Wald Henderson's *New Cuisine of Hawaii*. Courtesy of Mark Ellman.

In their second decade (2001–2011), the HRC chefs greatly expanded this palette of ingredients. They continued to use coconut milk, curry powder, fish sauce, ginger, hoisin sauce, lemongrass, liliko'i, miso, peanut oil, rice vinegar, sesame oil, and soy sauce, as before. But after 1999 they began to use even more Asian Pacific ingredients. The list of new ingredients is an impressively lengthy one: arare, arrowroot, bitter melon, Chinese cabbage, choy sum, coriander seeds, daikon, dashi, edamame, enoki mushrooms, fermented bean curd, *fukujinzuke*, furikake, galangal, *gochujang*, green tea, *ikura*, 'inamona, Japanese eggplant, kabocha, *kai choy, kaiware, katsuobushi, kecap manis, kinome*, kombu, kudzu starch, li hing mui, linguica, lotus root, *masago*, matsutake mushrooms, *mentaiko, mitsuba*, mizuna, *mochigome, nagaimo*, nam pla, natto, nuoc mam, pipi kaula, pohā berries, poi, *rayu*, rice paper, saffron, *sansho*, sea asparagus, *shichimi*, shiso, somen, *tatsoi, umeboshi, uni, wonbok, shaoxing, yuba*, and yuzu. It is significant that most of these ingredients are commonly used in Asian Pacific cuisines.

No one used as many different "Asian" ingredients as Yamaguchi, the HRC chef who grew up in Asia. When he did, as one food writer put it, it was to "draw . . . on Hawaii's already multifaceted cuisine—a lattice of Japanese, Chinese, Philippine, and Southeast Asian flavors—and deftly combine . . . them with his technical skills to create an entirely new food culture," skills that were French in origin.[39]

We should not overlook the non–Asian Pacific ingredients that the HRC chefs used. Food writer Henderson was the first to point this out. In 1991, in an article on Yamaguchi's new restaurant Roy's, she observed that he "throws a curveball at conventional cooking wisdom by boldly blending Pacific Rim ingredients and techniques with Western ones."[40] Indeed, a close analysis of the HRC chefs' first cookbooks, those published in the movement's first decade (1991–2001), confirms Henderson's observation. Many chefs made ample use of heavy cream, sour cream, and both red and white wine.[41] Wong, in *Alan Wong's New Wave Luau* (1999), and Gannon, in *The Haili'imaile General Store Cookbook* (2000), used olive oil more than any other ingredient, Asian or Western. This reliance on non–Asian Pacific ingredients persisted into the second decade of the HRC movement (2001–2011). In fact, olive oil, heavy cream, and shallots were the most widely used ingredients in two HRC chefs' cookbooks published in the second decade, Yamaguchi's *Hawaii Cooks* (2003) and Gannon's *Family-Style Meals at the Haili'imaile General Store* (2009). Interestingly, the outlier is Wong, who, in his most recent cookbook, *Blue Tomato* (2010), relied much less on heavy cream, olive oil, sour cream, and red and white wine than he did earlier. To understand why, we should look at the dishes that the HRC chefs prepared over the course of two decades.

Dishes

Hawaiʻi Regional Cuisine's distinctive "new food culture," to use Lisa Peterson's term, offers answers to these questions. First, the HRC chefs were doing more than simply mixing various ingredients to make new dishes. Chefs do not cook in a vacuum. As noted earlier, the dishes served at HRC restaurants reflected many things: the chefs' culinary training and professional experience but also their personal experience, or what food scholar Krishnendu Ray calls their "embodied experience."[42] Second was the way that the chefs used their fresh and locally sourced ingredients, and the resulting dishes offer their interpretation of Hawaiʻi Regional Cuisine. Each chef had, of course, what Yamaguchi termed his or her own "style of cooking," and each called on a different array of culinary techniques.[43]

At the outset, Yamaguchi was the most explicit about what he and his fellow HRC chefs were doing. "We are not slaves to European or Asian techniques," he wrote rather pointedly in the introduction to his first cookbook, *Pacific Bounty*.[44] Beginning in the 1990s, he repeatedly stated that he was combining both European and Asian techniques and making what he called "Euro-Asian" dishes. In fact, he even claimed to have invented "Euro-Asian cuisine" in 1980.[45] He once remarked that the term "'Euro-Asian' has a nice looseness about it" and is "applicable to anything from Fresh Opakapaka in Uni Chardonnay Sauce to mixed-plates of Baby Back Ribs, Duck Dim Sum, Shrimp Stick & Rice."[46] The term "Euro-Asian" describes many of the dishes that he and the other HRC chefs were making in the 1990s. For example, Mark Ellman offered Chinese chicken salad, crab with black bean sauce, and wok-fried fish; on Merriman's menu was a caesar salad with sashimi and a spinach salad with pipi kaula; and Padovani had wok-fried moano with tabbouleh salad, tomato and nicoise olives vinaigrette.[47] The HRC chefs also openly borrowed from one another and adapted Euro-Asian dishes they had tried at one another's restaurants, less as a form of competition than as a way of affirming their shared vision of their new cuisine and their "new food culture."[48] Fern Tomisato Yoshida, a former chef and culinary arts instructor, explained: "They shared everything. Their knowledge palette was open for all who were interested, so there's so much opportunity just in that. . . . It's not about my job, and I cannot share it— you know, if I share it with you, then I'm going to lose my job."[49] In its early stages, the new HRC cuisine could therefore be described as Euro-Asian.

The ubiquity of Euro-Asian dishes on HRC menus in the 1990s was important also because they were the rage on the West Coast from the early 1980s, when Puck opened Spago (1982) and Chinois on Main (1983), Yamaguchi opened 385 North (1984), and the Tsunoda family opened La Petite Chaya and Chaya Brasserie (1984), all in Los Angeles. This may explain Yamaguchi's assertion that he invented Euro-Asian cuisine in 1980 and was making Euro-Asian dishes. Moreover, in 1996, when he hosted mainland chefs at the sixth-anniversary celebration of Roy's, the menu for this commemorative dinner was filled with quintessentially Euro-Asian dishes: George Morrone of Aqua in San Francisco made oven-roasted oysters flavored with saffron, caviar, and leeks; Nobuyuki Matsuhisa of Matsuhisa in Los Angeles offered Hawaiian shutome with asparagus, shiitake mushrooms, and wasabi pepper sauce; and Makoto Tanaka of Chinois on Main contributed grilled squab with sautéed goose liver in cherry ginger port sauce.[50] Thus, a full appreciation of the HRC chefs' Euro-Asian dishes must include their debt to what was going on in Southern California from the 1980s through the 1990s.

By the HRC movement's second decade (2001–2011), certain Euro-Asian dishes even achieved classic status, notably wok-blackened ahi and grilled salmon drizzled with ponzu sauce and sprinkled with furikake.[51] Today, the menus at Yamaguchi's restaurants are full of what one food writer called "novel classics, such as butter-basil Hawaiian mahi mahi with Maine lobster sauce; Mongolian pork tenderloin roasted with sake, soy and pineapple sauce; and a delicate Napoleon showcasing haupia, a traditional Hawaiian coconut custard."[52]

These Euro-Asian dishes are important because they reveal a culinary paradigm. A close reading of the HRC chefs' recipes confirms that through the 1990s, they worked comfortably within the Euro-Asian framework and innovated in two rather different ways. Many followed a more classical (that is, French) approach, using their wonderfully fresh and locally sourced ingredients to create dishes that reprised what they had learned as apprentices at French restaurants or in cooking school. The vinaigrettes and sauces that several chefs used, for instance, were clearly French in origin, echoing recipes in Auguste Escoffier's classic *Le Guide Culinaire*, the "bible of chefs trained in the classical French tradition."[53] Merriman's Coconut Crème Brûlée, for example, comes very close to reproducing Escoffier's *Crème à l'Anglaise*.[54] The crepes in Gannon's Duck Salad with Warm Goat Cheese and Chive Crêpes and Wong's Shredded Coconut-Chili Beef with Taro Crêpes are made with exactly the same ingredients as the crepes in *Le Guide Culinaire*, but with the addition of chives and taro.[55] In fact, many recipes in Yamaguchi's *Pacific Bounty* and Henderson's *New Cuisine of Hawaii* are the result of their creators' "French" training: Gannon's recipes for Grilled Ahi in Tomato Beurre Blanc and Big Island Goat Cheese and Maui Onion Tart with Red Pepper Coulis; Ferguson's Warm Mango Custard; Mavrothalassitis' Bouillabaisse of Hawaiian Fish; Padovani's Coconut-Tapioca Pudding with Mango and Papaya; Strehl's Asian Duckling Confit with Wild Mushrooms; Wong's Lychee-Ginger Sorbet; and Yamaguchi's Coconut-Crusted Big Isle Goat Cheese Tartlets with Macadamia Nut Praline.[56] In addition, the chefs' Francophilia shows the dominance of French cuisine in contemporary haute cuisine after World War II.[57]

In an interview, Ferguson described how she once made a dish in a culinary competition that used both French technique and local ingredients. She recalled that she made a Laulau Tureen with a Surinam Cherry Compote. "Common sense told me . . . [to] treat taro leaf the way I'm supposed to, like a laulau, and cook it. And . . . [to] pull together a pork aspic, and make a traditional aspic, using salted pork, or was it smoked?" When I mentioned that this seemed very French, she agreed, "It was very French, because that was my background, my training."[58] Ferguson's dish followed a more conservative, French approach, but one that fit comfortably within the Euro-Asian paradigm.

The HRC chefs also took liberties with the French dishes they knew so well. Their recipes use the Euro-Asian framework more playfully, riffing on old, known, dishes in *Le Guide Culinaire* and inventing bold new ones. Already in the early 1990s, for example, they were making sauces that only faintly recalled Escoffier's *sauce vin blanc* (white wine sauce) and *sauce batârde* (butter sauce). Ferguson's Nori Fettucine with 'Opihi and Garlic-Chili Butter Sauce is a good example. With a nod to her French training, she calls for a sauce made with white wine, shallots, garlic cloves, whipping cream, and butter. But she adds *sambal olek*, a spicy Indonesian paste, to the sauce and then pairs it with nori fettucine. Moreover, her garlic-chili butter sauce is far from even Escoffier's Orientalist tribute to the East, his *Sauce currie à l'indienne*.[59] Similarly, Padovani's Fresh Kona Oysters with Hawaiian Mignonette uses local oysters in an unmistakably French preparation, but with the addition of ginger, mirin, and ogo, a local seaweed.[60]

Amy Ferguson. Courtesy
of Tony Novak-Clifford.

What Ferguson did with her sauce and Padovani with his mignonette are
more liberal renditions of iconic French preparations.

At the same time, some HRC chefs made unmistakably "Asian" dishes.
Yamaguchi's miso-glazed butterfish is one of the best examples; it is a standard in the Japanese *kappō* repertoire.[61] "Marinating fish in miso is a traditional Japanese preparation," he wrote, adding, "I owe the idea for this
recipe to Nobu Matsuhisa."[62] For his version, Yamaguchi often used locally
sourced sablefish and Asian ingredients—miso, sake, and mirin—and anyone who has had this dish at his restaurants knows that it is *always* cooked
perfectly.[63] Gannon once observed that "as Hawai'i Regional Cuisine got
going, more and more Asian-influenced dishes showed up on the menu,"
including her Szechuan Barbecued Salmon, which became a Hali'imaile

General Store classic.[64] Merriman's restaurants offer a cucumber namasu, a vinegary Japanese dish that dates from the seventh century and is a distant ancestor of sashimi.[65]

The HRC chefs' cookbooks written in the second decade of the movement show that they also stretched the Euro-Asian paradigm, adding a third element, dishes from the local culinary vernacular. Gannon's Portuguese Bean Soup is a good example. It is based, she tells us, on a recipe that her bookkeeper, Patrice Tuzon, gave her. Similarly, Merriman's Chinese-Style Braised Beef Short Ribs was inspired, he admits, by local Chinese barbecue.[66] Merriman even made a Hawai'i-Style Jerk Chicken, his nod to the Puerto Rican laborers brought to the islands around 1900 to work on the sugar plantations. He explained: "While driving around the main Hawaiian islands, you might notice roadside vendors offering pateles, which are Puerto Rican tamales made with grated green banana. Too much work to include in this cookbook [*Merriman's Hawaii*], but I mention them because they are a part of another legacy that has contributed to Hawaiian cuisine."[67] In *Merriman's Hawaii*, Merriman even includes a recipe for saimin, the local version of Chinese *lamian* and Japanese ramen, which is not a dish usually served at haute cuisine restaurants in the islands.[68]

The move toward the local also informed the dinner that Mavrothalassitis cooked at the James Beard House in May 2004. He served his versions of several local dishes, such as Duck Foie Gras "Manapua Style" and Confit Hamachi, Lomi Lomi.[69] Manapua is a local version of what is known globally as dim sum, and lomilomi salmon is a fixture at luaus. The addition of local dishes like these expanded the Euro-Asian paradigm to what might be called a "Euro-Asian / Pacific-Local" paradigm.

In addition, since many of the HRC chefs were from the mainland, classics from the American culinary vernacular began to appear as well on the menus of their restaurants and in their cookbooks. A native Texan, Gannon unapologetically offers renditions of several favorite American classics at her restaurants. In fact, she devotes a whole section to casseroles in her cookbook *Family-Style Meals at the Hali'imaile General Store*, writing, "Casseroles in our house were an afterthought, a mishmash of leftovers with a white sauce or canned cream of mushroom soup. . . . When she [Gannon's mother] did a tuna-noodle casserole, she used canned Chicken of the Sea albacore tuna, canned Le Sueur peas, sliced mushrooms out of a jar, canned cream of celery or cream of mushroom soup, and kosher squiggly noodles with crushed potato chips on top."[70]

Beverly Gannon. Courtesy
of Beverely Gannon.

But make no mistake. Gannon knows she is in the islands and tweaks
these classics accordingly. Consider her New Wave Tuna-Noodle Casserole.
She begins by asking, "How do you take a classic dish and make it part of
the contemporary food scene in Hawai'i?" Her answer: "[F]irst you start
with fresh tuna instead of canned; it would be sacrilegious to do otherwise.
Then you add the flavors from our mostly Asian community and you come
up with a dish that says, 'This is Hawai'i Regional Cuisine today, a dish that
goes to a whole new level of delicious flavor.'"[71] Gannon uses fresh tuna
steaks, seared on the outside but rare on the inside. She substitutes sautéed
shiitake mushrooms for cream of mushroom soup and adds sliced onions,

baby corn, water chestnuts, minced garlic and ginger, and edamame. She then finishes the dish with a sauce made with chicken stock, oyster sauce, fish sauce, sriracha, fresh lime juice, and chopped cilantro; and a wasabi pea–panko (Japanese bread crumbs) mixture is substituted for crushed potato chips. In the 1990s, Gannon even started making her versions of dishes from what she calls her "Tex-Mex youth," dishes such as enchiladas. But her version uses kālua pig, the savory pork dish cooked in an underground oven called an "imu" favored by Hawaiians, and she declared that "[i]f Pancho Villa knew about kālua pork, I guarantee you that Mexicans would use it in all their pork dishes."[72]

In *Merriman's Hawaii*, Merriman even reprised several American culinary standards. His recipe for Pineapple Upside-Down Cake in a Skillet is typical, as it follows very closely Irma Rombauer's Skillet Cake or Upside Down Cake in the canonical *The Joy of Cooking* but uses fresh instead of canned pineapple, because, as Merriman put it, "Hawaiian pineapples are famously sweet."[73] Similarly, Merriman's tongue-in-cheek Not-the-Usual Cashew Chicken is his whimsical take on an American chop suey classic, one, no doubt, that he or his chefs from the mainland remember from their childhoods. After all, even Irma Rombauer has a version of cashew chicken in *The Joy of Cooking*.[74]

Invention

The Euro-Asian / Pacific-Local-American paradigm is significant because it gave the HRC chefs room to be creative, daring, and even outrageous. No one has done more with this framework and been more inventive than Wong. Consider a dish he calls "rice creams." At first glance, rice creams sounds like a cross between a French cream sauce and a Chinese congee, but this is not the case at all. Wong explained how he invented it. "One day I came to work and wasn't feeling very well, so I took some cooked rice and boiled it with some water, just like my mother would do when I was a kid and wasn't feeling very well. I ate it with some ume (Japanese pickled plum), shiso (beefsteak leaf) and nori (dried seaweed). I felt better."[75] Wong found that these rice creams were a good substitute for "compound butters—butters flavored with herbs, spirits, or whatever"—and could be used as "a thickening agent, binder and flavor enhancer."[76] Wong's rice creams are an example of an HRC chef using the Euro-Asian

/ Pacific-Local-American paradigm to invent a new dish inspired by a childhood memory. Wong also devised something else, a concoction he calls "tomato water," which food writer Joan Clarke described as "water flavored with tomato scraps, dripped and filtered—to enhance the flavor of vegetable dishes."[77]

Wong also reimagined local dishes. Recognizing Spam's popularity in the islands, food writer Joan Clarke once asked Wong what he thought about it. He responded by making "the equivalent of Spam." She described his version as "[a] pork terrine that looked like Spam w/ its characteristic pink color. It smelled like Spam as it fried to a crisp. And by golly, it tasted like Spam w/ the texture of Spam, all without as much fat and salt as the real thing."[78] Wong also riffed on another local favorite, seafood tempura, producing "nori-wrapped tempura salmon," which food writer Matthew Gray described as "salmon wrapped in nori, flash-tempur'd, then thinly sliced and fanned around the plate. The salmon is sushi-raw, and melts in your mouth."[79] By the late 1990s, Wong and his staff had reimagined a number of local dishes: they made kālua pig quesadillas, 'opihi shooters, and luau on a plate.[80] At the Pineapple Room, his second Honolulu restaurant, his chefs, with culinary tongues in cheek, offered pizzas with a local twist: huli-huli chicken pizza with mozzarella and mac-nut pesto; kālua pig, onion, and Boursin cheese with shiitake mushrooms, sausage, olives, and Puna goat cheese.[81]

Wong took his culinary playfulness a step further, deconstructing and then reconstructing local dishes. He did this most famously with the loco moco, a dish said to have been devised in Hilo on the Big Island in 1949 for working-class boys who needed something substantial enough to sustain them through football games.[82] The loco moco usually consists of a plate of cooked short-grain rice with a fried hamburger patty, brown gravy, and a fried egg on top. Wong's 1998 version of the loco moco, true to the locus classicus, consisted of a miniature hamburger patty topped with brown gravy and a fried quail egg.[83] A year later, Wong developed another version of the loco moco that food writer Joan Clarke described as "tender braised organic Big Island beef in a mushroom gravy . . . over rice, topped with a poached egg."[84] Several months after that, the Pineapple Room started serving a breakfast loco moco, "a Thai-inspired loco moco" that consisted of "a poached egg with a shrimp/pork hash patty (juicy good) in lemongrass chili garlic black bean sauce over rice."[85] In the first decade of the 2000s, Wong's version of the loco moco morphed once again into an elegant and refined dish that substituted deep-fried mochi rice for steamed rice and topped it with a Wagyu beef and unagi [eel] patty and a fried quail egg, with kabayaki sauce poured over it. Wong was obviously having fun as he concocted these versions of this local icon. Any analysis of HRC cuisine must begin with fresh and locally sourced *ingredients*, followed by *dishes* that both copied and diverged from classics in *Le Guide Culinaire*, and then reimagined local and American standards.

Culinary Technique

HRC cuisine has a third constituent element, culinary technique. The HRC chefs' recipes confirm their mastery of French and Asian Pacific culinary techniques, so when they combined Asian Pacific and Western ingredients, they often used either French or Asian Pacific culinary techniques or a combination of the two. Food writer Henderson recognized this in 1991. Fully aware of what had been going on in Los Angeles since the 1980s, she pointed out this blending of what she termed "Pacific Rim [that is, Asian Pacific] . . . techniques with Western ones."[86] In *The New Cuisine of Hawaii*, this was obvious in Ellman's Chinese chicken salad, crab with black bean sauce, and wok-fried fish, and in Merriman's caesar salad with sashimi and spinach salad with pipi kaula.[87] It was apparent as well in many of the recipes in Yamaguchi's *Pacific Bounty*, including Gannon's fusion of Cajun-style grilled ahi and a simple shoyu and wasabi sauce in her Sashimi Sampler.[88]

No one better understood the benefits and hazards of this two-pronged approach than Yamaguchi, whose decade of training and experimentation in Los Angeles had taught him the importance of striking a balance between French and Asian techniques. "A lot of chefs, when they don't know what they're doing, may put too much Asian influence into a sauce, and it really doesn't go with what we're trying to do as a whole. . . . It's not an Asian restaurant. We want that balance of French, the balance of Asia, the balance of contemporary, the balance of tradition."[89] Yamaguchi's call for balance points to the dualism informing HRC cuisine, a dualism with both spatial and temporal dimensions. After he opened the first Roy's in 1988, he admitted many years later, his culinary horizons expanded. "I got more involved in adding Korean, or Thai, or Vietnamese. More Asian cultures came into the picture." When asked whether this involved culinary technique or an ingredient like hoisin sauce, he replied, "Hoisin sauce, or say, for instance, fish sauce, lemongrass, Thai curries, coconut milk. Stuff like that came into the picture. Whereas at 385 North, I didn't really have that. Not much of that."[90] In fact, Yamaguchi even used the word "fusion" instead of "balance" when he spoke of "my Asian kind of fusion cooking" at La Serene (1981–1982) in Los Angeles.[91] At that time, he created dishes such as napa cabbage stuffed with *uni* and bathed in a seaweed cream sauce of white wine, onions, cream, and dashi made with wakame; and a pounded duck leg marinated in teriyaki sauce, grilled and plated on salad greens with a dressing made with hazelnut oil, chopped shallots, and sherry vinegar. He later described these over-the-top dishes as the "East meet[s] West type of deal."[92] As a pioneer, Yamaguchi had experimented with both good and not-so-good results.

Yamaguchi's evolving dishes summed up his personal biography. Promotional literature for Roy's dating from 1992 recounts his arduous and demanding culinary journey: "[F]rom the beginning Roy has always preferred 'Euro-Asian.' Probably because it best describes his own personal journey: being born and raised in Japan (as the son of a Maui-born career military man); his study at the Culinary Institute of America in New York; further development under the influence of such *nouvelle cuisine* masters as Jean Bertranou in West Hollywood's L'Ermitage; and finally, a spiritual homecoming to the Islands in '88."[93] The reference to the nouvelle cuisine reminds us that Yamaguchi was lucky enough to learn this new approach from one of its American masters, Jean Bertranou.

When asked about the nouvelle cuisine, Mavrothalassitis admitted his own complicity and that of others, too. "'Nouvelle cuisine' was a 'revolution'; we burned *Escoffier,* but we forgot 'flavors'; 'what about the flavors?' 'emotion,' 'emotion in the mouth'; [unclear] advised him 'if it tastes good' is all that matters." Mavrothalassitis noted that he was not the only one to backtrack from the nouvelle cuisine. "[Alain] Ducasse did too, as did [Pierre] Gagnaire's pastry chef, who also was Mavrothalassitis's pastry chef."[94] Mavrothalassitis described his approach as one that "emphasizes traditional cooking of the Mediterranean."[95] When asked what he would call the cuisine that his restaurant offers, he said: "It's contemporary original cuisine. 'Original' because this is only what I believe. 'Contemporary' because, OK, I don't cook in the classic way, but I have a classical foundation.

Very strong. Even if in the beginning I burn the book, I took the book back from the ashes. I know the . . . book, you can open, ask me a question, you're gonna be surprised."[96] Mavrothalassitis and Yamaguchi had traveled a similar route—from the classic *Le Guide Culinaire* to the nouvelle cuisine and then back to classic French cuisine.

Wong's approach to blending Asian and Western (that is, French) culinary techniques also is instructive, but in a different way. Food writer Wanda Adams recounted how Wong came up with his version of the Filipino dish *pinakbet*, which consists of vegetables stir-fried in bagoong, a fermented shrimp or fish sauce. "Last week . . . a village volunteer [from Plantation Village in Waipahu] spent a day in Wong's kitchen, sharing her recipe for the Filipino vegetable dish pinakbet. Wong can't serve anything that plain at a \$125-a-ticket event, but [he] watched closely as she stir-fried the eggplant, long beans, bitter melon and tomatoes with bagoong, the potent fermented fish paste. His interpretation: a French-style confit of akule filets, slow-cooked in oil with garlic, bay leaf, thyme and black pepper, topping a stir-fry of pinakbet vegetables, but with a patis, shoyu and sesame sauce." Notice Adams' description of Wong's *pinakbet* as "a French-style confit of akule filets, slow-cooked in oil with garlic, bay leaf, thyme and black pepper, topping a stir-fry of pinakbet vegetables, but with a patis, shoyu and sesame seeds." Wong himself described what he was doing: "[Mine is] a sort of deconstructed pinakbet. . . . But before you can do something like that, you have to really understand the roots of the dish. You have to go back to Mama's cuisine or Grandma's cuisine and really understand the ingredients." His method had the following steps: first, watching closely the cooking of the original dish; second, retaining the original combination of ingredients, vegetables and bagoong; third, adding elements prepared with French technique—adding the confit of akule (big-eyed scad) fillets and slow-cooking them in oil with garlic, bay leaf, thyme, and black pepper; and fourth, serving the confit of akule fillets on the vegetables with a sauce of bagoong-derived *patis*, shoyu, and sesame oil.[97] Thus, while the original dish and ingredients were unmistakably Filipino, Wong's technique was quintessentially French.

On occasion, however, Wong leaned in the other direction—toward Asian culinary technique. We see this in his account of how he created ginger-crusted onaga, the most popular dish at his flagship restaurant.[98] When asked how he came up with that dish, Wong explained:

My Chinese grandfather was the cook in the house. When we went to Dad's house, I was exposed to good cooking. My mom was from Japan, [and] they seasoned their food just right, what constitutes perfect seasoning. So I kinda grew up with Chinese and Japanese food. I like cold ginger chicken, but I would never say I am a Chinese chef or Japanese chef. What I rely on is a memory of taste or flavor, palate memory, . . . so I set out to make the recipe, following the technique; tried it on hot chicken, tried it on a steak, tried it on every fish imaginable. Finally, I did onaga [long-tail red snapper], and we sold twenty or something that night. We were doing miso dressing with boiled octopus, the way locals did; we had a spinach dressing with orange and pipi kaula, [and] I combined the two dressings [and] partnered that with the onaga. We were big on corn—the corn from Pahoa was really sweet—with mushrooms.[99]

Here, Wong first settled on the Chinese culinary technique of simmering to make cold ginger chicken and then searched, through trial and error, for a suitable dressing before settling on the miso-based dressing that the Japanese in the islands serve with boiled octopus. The technique was Chinese and the dressing Japanese. Yet even though Wong was inspired by a Chinese dish and a Japanese sauce, he still invoked French cuisine, calling the dressing "Miso-Sesame Vinaigrette," although the dressing was not French at all, a revealing culinary slip of the tongue.[100]

Semiotics

Wong's slip of the tongue points to another, a semiotic, dimension of Hawai'i Regional Cuisine. In fact, semiotics offers a way of understanding what the HRC chefs were doing. Although French culinary technique informs so much of what they do, the obvious allusions to French cuisine in the names of HRC dishes—such as crepe, nage, vinaigrette—sometimes say very little about many dishes. Consider the Miso-Sesame Vinaigrette that accompanies Wong's Ginger-Crusted Onaga. His calling that sauce a "vinaigrette" is a case in point: it is simply a label, a hollow marker. There is nothing French about that sauce. When the ginger-crusted onaga is analyzed more closely, many other things matter more than does the verbal nod to French cuisine: notably, its local ingredients, its Chinese and Japanese culinary techniques, and its obvious reference to local cuisine.

Perhaps Wong was simply being playful, but I argue that even more is going on than meets the eye.

Given the history of haute cuisine in the islands, the diminution of French cuisine, represented by the hollow signifier, is important. Wong is turning Continental cuisine on its head. To demonstrate this, we first must recognize that the name of an HRC dish and its many other references often mean more than anything else, more even than the technique used to make it. Think of what Wong was doing with the highly refined loco moco he made in the first decade of the twenty-first century: first, he valorized a local dish, the loco moco; second, he used a Chinese culinary technique, deep-frying; third, he highlighted a well-known Japanese dish, unagi kabayaki (grilled eel); and fourth, he featured a supremely expensive Japanese ingredient, Wagyu beef. Obviously, Wong's loco moco is more complex than the average loco moco served at a local drive-in.

In fact, Wong's loco moco is polysemous, conveying multiple, coexisting meanings. But these multiple meanings also do more than just coexist; they contradict one another and, together, comprise the dish semiotically; that is, when the various elements of Wong's loco moco—the local culinary vernacular, the Japanese and Chinese elements—are taken together, they form a new construction and generate new meanings. In fact, Wong's loco moco may be an example of what contemporary philosophers call a "mediated reference," alluding, first, to a dish from the local culinary vernacular, the loco moco; second, to a Japanese dish, unagi kabayaki; and third, to a Chinese culinary technique, deep-frying. Informing Wong's loco moco is his highly refined culinary sensibility, one that reflects his extensive French training, first at Kapiʻolani Community College (KCC) in Honolulu, then at the Greenbrier in West Virginia, and finally at Lutèce in New York City. At first glance, these references might seem to contradict one another, but when taken together, they represent something with semiotic complexity and depth.

Other Wong classics evince the same qualities. Consider his Pan-Steamed Opakapaka (Short-Tail Pink Snapper) [with] Shrimp Pork Hash, Truffle Nage, Gingered Vegetables, and Tapioca Pearls, another Wong classic. A glance at the ingredients in the dish as it appears on the menu at Alan Wong's reveals *six* different references: the first is to a local ingredient (ʻōpakapaka); the second to the *Le Guide Culinaire* (the butter nage); the third to Honolulu Chinatown (pork hash); the fourth to a Chinese culinary technique (steaming); the fifth to an important ingredient in southern Chinese cuisine (cilantro); and the sixth to the now popular tapioca pearls.[101]

What is important is that these two dishes—the loco moco and the 'ōpakapaka combined with shrimp pork hash in a truffle nage—may resemble the highway strip featured in architectural historian Robert Venturi's classic *Learning from Las Vegas*. As the architectural historian Ritu Bhatt described it in her commentary on Venturi's analysis: "[I]n the architecture of the highway strip, buildings do not inherently mean something. Instead the fronts of the buildings disengage themselves from the building mass and recombine themselves as a complex formation of false fronts standing perpendicular to the highway as big signs, competing and competing with each other."[102] Or as the philosopher Nelson Goodman himself observed about Venturi's interpretation of Las Vegas architecture: "[W]hen Robert Venturi writes of 'contradiction' in architecture, he is not supposing that a building can actually assert a self-contradictory sentence but is speaking of exemplification by a building of forms that give rise when juxtaposed, because they are also severally exemplified in architecture of contrasting kinds (for example, classical and baroque), to expectations that contravene each other. The 'contradiction thus arises from indirect reference.'"[103] That "contradiction thus arises from indirect reference" is key.

When read in this way, a dish like Wong's pan-steamed 'ōpakapaka with shrimp pork hash in a truffle nage disengages itself from the plate and its explicit or implicit names (dish, ingredients, techniques, producers, and other references) and recombines them in a complex formation made of what once were simply one-dimensional words. Echoing Bhatt, a dish like the 'ōpakapaka with shrimp pork hash in a truffle nage embodies an "undefined number of symbols," and "the symbol system . . . has an indefinite number of symbols, so that between any two there is a third. There is no claim that all of these symbols occur within a single work. Rather the point is that if there are infinitely fine differences between symbols of the system, it is not clear exactly which symbol belongs to the work."[104] Thus, we might see Wong's 'ōpakapaka with shrimp pork hash in a truffle nage in the following way: First is the name of the dish; second is the names of key ingredients ('ōpakapaka, shrimp, pork, truffles, and cilantro); third is the implied culinary techniques, Chinese and French; and fourth is the culinary references, the pork hash pointing to Honolulu Chinatown. The following figure presents the relationship of these four sets of elements schematically.

name

1

ingredient   2   3   technique

4

other references

Bhatt would remind us that although the dish consists of four "symbols"—name, ingredient, technique, and other references—each of which can stand alone, two symbols together can point to a third symbol, three to a fourth, and four to a fifth. Thus, the semantic plenitude of Wong's 'ōpakapaka with shrimp pork hash in a truffle nage is inexhaustible.

The semiotic richness of a single Wong dish is expanded even further when we add the names of his producers: farmers, ranchers, fishermen, cheese makers, and so forth. I feel sure that Wong would insist that his producers not be left out of the analysis. After all, he posts their photographs in the elevator that carries diners from street level to his restaurant and also adds their names to the menu, thus reaffirming the HRC commitment to using the best, locally sourced ingredients available. When added to an analysis of Wong's dishes, the names of his producers become, in Bhatt's terms, another set of symbols.

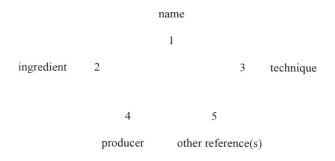

name

1

ingredient   2   3   technique

4   5

producer   other reference(s)

When we read a menu at Alan Wong's in this way, we account for each of the many constituent elements in each dish and in the entire dinner, as shown in table 3.1. This table offers the name of each dish, its ingredients, the producers of its ingredients, the techniques used to make the dish, and its other references, to other dishes, chefs, cuisines, restaurants, and

April 30, 2007

CURRY BEEF VEGETABLE SOUP
Chili Pepper Aioli Crostini
$6.50

LUAU STEW "EN CROUTE"
Short Rib and Pork Belly
$7.50

GARLIC BLACK BEAN BBQ DUCK "TACOS"
Lomi Tomato, Asian Guacamole, Big Island Smoked Goat Cheese
$10.50

YUKARI CRUSTED SEARED AHI
Myoga, Ma'o Farms Ruby Streak Greens, Creamy Soy Tofu Dressing
$15.00

PANKO CRUSTED AHI POKE
Tomato Ginger Relish, Yuzu Soy Butter Sauce
$15.00

PAN SEARED YELLOWFIN AHI
Kahuku Sea Asparagus, Hamakua Eryngi Mushroom, Pickled Onion and Nori Tsukudani
$29.00

PAN ROASTED KONA KAMPACHI
Tomato Curry Powder, Hawaiian Hearts of Palm Puree, Waialua Asparagus
$36.00

5–COURSE MENU SAMPLING

Prix Fixe Dinner: $75.00 per person • With Wine Pairings: $105.00 per person

APPETIZER DUO

GINGER CRUSTED ONAGA
Organically Grown Hamakua Mushrooms and Corn, Miso Sesame Vinaigrette

BUTTER POACHED KONA COLD LOBSTER
Shrimp, Honda Tofu Cake, Jalapeño Tokyo Negi Sauce

TWICE COOKED SHORTRIB, SOY BRAISED AND GRILLED "KALBI" STYLE
Gingered Shrimp, Ko Choo Jang Sauce

DESSERT DUET
Chocolate "Crunch Bars" and Coconut Tapioca

CHEF'S TASTING • 7 COURSES
Prix Fixe Dinner: $95.00 per person • With Wines: $135.00 per person • available only for entire table

Courtesy of Alan Wong's.

locations. All these elements together compose a rich and complex system of symbols. Each word on the menu matters, reminding us that HRC dishes are often more than the sum of their parts.

We should notice, too, that no single element—whether the name of the dish, ingredient, producer, culinary technique, or other

TABLE 3.1. A Semiotic Reading of a Dinner at Alan Wong's

Dish	Dish	Dish	Dish
Name 1	Name 2	Name 3	Name 4
Ingredient(s) 1	Ingredient(s) 2	Ingredient(s) 3	Ingredient(s) 4
Producer 1	Producer 2	Producer 3	Producer 4
Technique 1	Technique 2	Technique 3	Technique 4
Other dish 1	Other dish 2	Other dish 3	Other dish 4

references—dominates the HRC dish. All its constituent elements coexist in the dish. We cannot miss the obvious diminution of French cuisine, which once dominated menus at fine-dining establishments in the islands. To be sure, some French elements persist, for instance in the many vinaigrettes, nages, crepes, and fine sauces in the HRC chefs' cookbooks and menus. But they now *coexist* with many other elements—local, Asian Pacific or even American ingredients, dishes, culinary techniques, producers, and restaurants.

Conclusions

Hawai'i Regional Cuisine gave the islands a "new food culture" that was, by definition, locavoric, using what local growers, ranchers, fishermen, and others offered. Second, it created a cuisine that evolved over the life of the movement, appearing first in one form and then in others. Third, in the movement's first decade (1991–2000), the HRC chefs initially used many of the ingredients found in Continental, Asian Pacific, and American cuisines as they worked to create a "Hawai'i regional cuisine." In the second decade (2001–2011), they became more creative and even playful, diverging from the original palette of flavors. Fourth, each chef used different culinary techniques, with some leaning toward French cuisine and others toward Asian Pacific and even American cuisines. Fifth, the dishes the HRC chefs created had many obvious sources, such as their childhood memories, their culinary education, and their professional experience.

The "new food culture" represented by Hawai'i Regional Cuisine was significant in another way. In *The Ethnic Restaurateur*, Krishnendu

Ray writes of the "clear tension between the embodied experience of the ethnic chef and the professional proficiency of the expert chef with his designer restaurant, which encapsulates the incongruence between the two kinds of identities."[105] Ray's comment immediately brings to mind Choy, Yamaguchi, and Wong, all of whom had to achieve the "professional proficiency of the expert chef" before they could express their "embodied experience" as "ethnic" chefs. Choy's Cuisine Hawaiʻi echoed his Lāʻie childhood, and Yamaguchi's Euro-Asian paradigm allowed him to give a culinary voice to his memories of trips to his paternal grandparents' home on Maui. Wong demonstrated his mastery of French culinary technique even as he played with his memories of an Asian Pacific culinary vernacular, recasting the local ethnic cuisine. Choy, Yamaguchi, and Wong also broke the racialized barriers of colonial Hawaiʻi with their professional achievements, awards, and recognition, but their contributions to the new Hawaiʻi Regional Cuisine did even more. It became the foundation for what would evolve into a "Euro-Asian-local-American" paradigm that was capacious enough to accommodate not only the HRC chefs with ties to the islands but also those who came from other places, each with his or her own "embodied" experiences.

Finally, the HRC movement destabilized and reconfigured the relationship of French and Asian Pacific cuisines, as well as the formerly denigrated "local foods," so that French cuisine no longer dominated the others as it had for so long. It is hardly an accident that this diminution of Continental and French cuisine took place as regional cuisines appeared on the West Coast and in the Southwest, Chicago, and New York and as Japanese cuisine moved from being an "ethnic" to being a "foreign" and "high-status" cuisine.

4 | Successors

> The apples of its second Eden have the tartness of
> experience.
>
> Derek Walcott, "The Muse of History"

The Hawai'i Regional Cuisine movement has had a huge impact in the islands. Fresh, locally sourced ingredients are now widely available and universally valued. Farmers' markets have appeared in many cities and towns and have become a fixture in the lives of those lucky enough to live near them. The HRC chefs' locavoric philosophy also has set new standards for locally grown produce, locally caught or gathered seafood, and locally raised beef, pork, and lamb, as well as local cheeses, coffee, and eggs. Restaurants of every type continue to be sites of culinary innovation, offering dishes informed by the humor and playfulness that the HRC chefs displayed in their second decade. The leading chefs of the next generation, whom I call the "post-HRC chefs," continually express their undying respect for their HRC mentors and their achievements. Nonetheless, they have eschewed the HRC chefs' idealized vision of colonial Hawai'i and plantation life and have struck out in bold, new directions, creating their own distinctive cuisine.

The Post-HRC Chefs

The HRC movement's demographic impact is unmistakable. The top chefs who emerged in the islands between 2005 and 2015—those who attracted national attention and were nominated for the top national awards—are an impressively diverse group. Although they all are homegrown, they represent different ethnicities and cultural backgrounds as well as different geographic and social origins. Their culinary training and their careers are quite varied: all of them studied at the top national and local culinary schools, but upon graduation, some chose to begin their careers in the kitchens of the finest restaurants on the mainland, others worked in famous restaurants in the islands, and a daring few followed their own visions from the outset, despite the formidable challenges and risks this posed. What is noteworthy about these chefs is that they are comfortable with themselves as local, homegrown chefs whose identities were not defined by national tastemakers, long apprenticeships at haute-cuisine restaurants on the mainland, or French cuisine.

Ed Kenney is the acknowledged leader of the post-HRC group, as he has, by far, the most extensive restaurant experience. He also may be the first graduate of the Punahou School, a leading college preparatory school in Honolulu, to make a name for himself as a chef. After graduating from Punahou in 1986, he went to the University of Colorado, graduating in 1990 with a degree in business. He then returned to the islands and worked in real estate for four years before spending a year traveling around the world with his girlfriend (now his wife).[1]

When Kenney returned to the islands in 1995, he decided to try the restaurant business. High school friends had opened an Italian restaurant in Kailua, a suburban beach town on the east coast of Oʻahu, and Kenney helped out there for a time. He then worked at a succession of Honolulu restaurants—Indigo, Shipley's, and Roy's—and these experiences led to his decision to enroll in the culinary arts program at Kapiʻolani Community College in Honolulu, the same program that produced Sam Choy and Alan Wong. In his last semester there, Kenney drew up a business plan for a restaurant, which suggested what was on his mind. After graduating in 1998, he was hired as the executive chef at the Café Monsarrat in Kaimukī. When that restaurant closed, Kenney became the executive chef and general manager of the café at the Lanikea YWCA on Richards Street in downtown Honolulu. All of this gave him valuable experience.[2]

In 2005, Kenney opened his first restaurant, Town, located by choice in Kaimukī. If Café Monsarrat was located in what might be called Upper Kaimukī, Town was down the hill in Lower Kaimukī. Kenney knew this area well, as he had visited coin and stamp shops there as a boy, taking the

Ed Kenney. Courtesy of Ed Kenney.

bus from Kāhala, where his family lived. To help him at Town, he hired chef Dave Caldiero from Donato's, a well-regarded Italian restaurant in Mānoa, and together they offered what they described as an Italian-influenced "California Cuisine" or "California Mediterranean."[3]

Michelle Karr-Ueoka is the other Punahou graduate in the group of post-HRC chefs. Like Kenney, she started out on a completely different track. She attended Lewis & Clark College, a well-known liberal arts college in Portland, Oregon, but left after a year. She returned to the islands and enrolled at the University of Hawai'i at Mānoa, graduating in 1998 with a degree in business and travel industry management. To satisfy a requirement for her major, she served an externship at Alan Wong's, despite never having done any serious cooking. After graduating from the University of

Hawai'i, she was hired at Alan Wong's. She worked on the savory side for a number of years but then decided to focus on desserts. In 1998, she enrolled in the three-year course at the Culinary Institute of America in Hyde Park, New York, and in 2000 she returned to work full time at Alan Wong's, but now as a pastry chef. Along the way, she staged at Thomas Keller's fabled French Laundry restaurant in Yountville, California.[4]

Wade Ueoka is a graduate of another Honolulu prep school, Mid-Pacific Institute. His culinary career began the summer after his junior year in high school, when he got a job at a branch of Zippy's, a popular local fast-food chain, in his hometown of Kailua. In 1993, when he graduated from high school, he was hired by Zippy's as a line cook, and in 1996, he enrolled in the culinary arts program at Kapi'olani Community College. When a

Michelle Karr-Ueoka. Courtesy of Michelle Karr-Ueoka.

classmate there mentioned that her husband had a job at a new restaurant called "Alan Wong's," Ueoka contacted the restaurant and was hired as a dishwasher. He quickly moved up to line cook and worked there for seventeen years, becoming the chef de cuisine in 2002. Ueoka is unusual in that his culinary education took place almost completely at Alan Wong's, with stages at the French Laundry in Yountville and at Alex in Las Vegas.[5]

Both Michelle Karr-Ueoka and Wade Ueoka were working at Alan Wong's when in April 1996 Wong won the James Beard Foundation Award for Best Chef: Pacific Northwest. They both developed as chefs at Alan Wong's, and given their tenure there—a combined thirty-one years—they were practically family. It is hardly surprising, therefore, that they use

Wade Ueoka. Courtesy of Wade Ueoka.

familial metaphors when talking about their former mentor and their time at his restaurant. They also got married in December 2011.

In February 2013, Ueoka left Alan Wong's to cook at Tsunami, a Honolulu bar run by a friend. He and his wife, Michelle, also opened food booths at local farmers' markets and did a weekly pop-up at Taste, a favorite venue among new and rising chefs. Clearly, they were testing the waters. Then in August 2013, they announced that they would be opening a restaurant called "MW," in the old KGMB Building on Kapiʻolani Boulevard, across the street from the Ala Moana Shopping Center. MW opened on October 24, 2013.[6]

The most likely successor to the HRC chefs, the one with the best and most rigorous French training, was Kevin Chong, another local culinary talent. Chong was born in Seoul in the Republic of Korea but came to the islands with his family when he was one. He grew up in the Mōʻiliʻili area of Honolulu and attended local public schools. After graduating in 1994 from McKinley High School, Chong left the islands to attend the Culinary Institute of America in Hyde Park. During the summer after his first year there, he worked briefly at L'Uraku, a well-known French restaurant in Honolulu. While a CIA student, Chong also had a four-month externship at Joachim Splichal's Pinot Bistro in Los Angeles. It was a good choice, as Splichal had impeccable credentials as a chef, having worked at hotel restaurants in Canada, Israel, Morocco, Norway, Sweden, and Switzerland before beginning his serious culinary training in France. He was hired as a *saucier* at La Bonne Auberge in southwest France and then as a *sous chef* at Jacques Maxim's Chanticleer Restaurant in Nice. In 1981, Splichal moved to California to become the executive chef at the Regency Club, an exclusive private club in Los Angeles founded by billionaire David Murdock and patronized by the city's leading businessmen.[7] Splichal then was hired to open the Seventh Street Bistro, in Los Angeles' financial district, before opening Max au Triangle, the first of his many acclaimed restaurants. It was Chong's good fortune to work at Splichal's restaurants shortly after Splichal won the Beard Award for Best Chef: West in 1991.[8]

Chong's externship at Splichal's Pinot Bistro may explain the course of his culinary career. Upon graduating from the Culinary Institute of America in October 1998, he landed a job at Le Cirque, one of New York City's best French restaurants. His first job there, he recalled, was to cook dinner for the chef's dog. It got worse. For several months, the more senior chefs never called him by his name; he was simply "piece of shit" and was

Kevin Chong. Courtesy of Kevin Chong.

allowed to speak only when spoken to. To his credit, Chong stuck it out and eventually earned the respect of the Le Cirque staff. After four years, they paid him the highest compliment: they sent him to Mexico City to open a branch of Le Cirque in April 2002. It was a huge and onerous responsibility for the twenty-five-year-old Chong, as it entailed overseeing the entire operation and managing a staff of nearly sixty people. After two frenetically busy years in Mexico City, Chong got married and returned to the islands in November 2004. George Mavrothalassitis, one of the founding HRC chefs, immediately hired Chong as chef de cuisine at Chef Mavro, and he worked there for seven years. Given his CIA training and his stints at Pinot Bistro, Le Cirque, and Chef Mavro, Chong became a chef's chef and was, by his own admission, "old school."⁹ One of the young chefs he mentored at Chef Mavro was Andrew Le, a young Vietnamese American whose biography resembled in many ways his own.

Like Chong, Le was the son of immigrants. His family had fled Vietnam in the closing days of the Vietnam War and was on a flight to a new home in Arkansas when his pregnant mother began to go into labor. They got off the plane in Honolulu and never left. Le's parents opened a video game shop in Kaimukī, and he grew up in Hawai'i Kai, a suburb east of Honolulu. He attended a local elementary school and then the intermediate and high school levels of Saint Louis School, a well-known Catholic boys school.[10] After graduating in 2001, Le enrolled at the University of Hawai'i at Mānoa, where he dabbled in the fine arts. He dropped out in 2003 and began exploring a culinary career, working first at the Garden House and then at Duc's Bistro: Traditional Vietnamese and French Cuisine, both in Honolulu's Chinatown.[11]

Andrew Le. Courtesy of Andrew Le.

In the fall of 2004, Le enrolled in the three-year bachelor's degree program at the Culinary Institute of America in Hyde Park. In the summer of 2005, he staged at Kenney's new restaurant, Town, and the following summer he staged at Alan Wong's. After graduating in 2007, Le came home to the islands for the summer, intending to return to the mainland to look for a job. An offer from Chef Mavro proved irresistible, however, and he worked there for nearly four years, mentored by the restaurant's new chef de cuisine Kevin Chong. By all accounts, Chong was a tough and demanding mentor, but Le learned much from him.

In the summer of 2011, Le began to think about opening his own restaurant, so he did what chefs in this situation now do: he opened a pop-up. He chose Hank's Haute Dogs, a Honolulu hot dog joint that serves high-end wieners, and called his pop-up The Pig and the Lady.[12] That fall, Le left Honolulu to spend six months staging at Rich Table, a newly opened restaurant in San Francisco's Hayes Valley district. His experience there taught him much about opening and running a new restaurant of the "smart casual" style.[13] After he returned to the islands in 2012, he put what he had learned to good use and began planning a brick-and-mortar restaurant. He and his crew also tested their dishes at local farmers' markets. In November 2013, he opened The Pig and the Lady in Honolulu's Chinatown, and almost overnight, Le attracted the attention of local and national food writers and other chefs.[14]

Sheldon Simeon is the last of the post-HRC chefs that I will discuss. He is the only neighbor-island chef in this group, and his path to culinary prominence is quite different. Like Chong and Le, Simeon has immigrant roots. His father's parents immigrated to Hawai'i from the Philippines, and his mother came directly from the Philippines. His family settled on the northeast side of the Big Island, first in Pāhoa and then in Hakalau, where his grandfather and father worked on the sugar plantations.

Simeon attended public schools in Hilo, fifteen miles away, graduating from Hilo High School in 2000. He then enrolled in the culinary arts program at Leeward Community College on O'ahu, and after just a semester there, he secured an internship in the kitchens at Disney World in Orlando, Florida. These two big moves in one year introduced Simeon to the new worlds and new challenges he apparently craved. In 2001, he returned to the islands and enrolled at the Maui Culinary Academy in Kahului. Simeon completed the program in 2002 and was immediately hired to work at Aloha Mixed Plate, a local eatery with a prime location on Front Street in

Sheldon Simeon. Courtesy of Sheldon Simeon.

picturesque and touristy Lahaina. His first job was, in effect, his apprenticeship. In 2010, the owners of Aloha Mixed Plate opened two new restaurants, Star Noodle and Leoda's Kitchen and Pie Shop, with Simeon at the helm. Star Noodle made him famous.[15]

National Attention

The restaurant world on the mainland quickly noticed the post-HRC chefs, with Kenney the first to gain national recognition. One month after Town opened, *Gourmet* magazine gave it a short, favorable review. The magazine's food writer Peter Lindberg wrote, "In a city where less invariably means too much Town sends out simply plated, perfectly executed gnocchi with peas and sage brown butter, and a lovely fritto misto of scallops, lemon slices, celery hearts, and fat white beans."[16] A year later, Town was included on Condé Nast's "hot list."[17] Kenney had done his homework: Town was the sort of "casual dining" restaurant that had begun to win awards on the mainland. It had many of the features of what has been called a new "smart casual" or "haute food" dining style: first, it was in a "found" space (a former fast-food restaurant); second, its wait staff affected an informal style; and third, its eclectic menu included both high and low cuisine and artisanal beers as well as wines.[18] This was a very promising beginning for the senior member of the post-HRC group.

In February 2009, Chong, then chef de cuisine at Chef Mavro, was named a semifinalist for the Beard Award for Best Chef: Pacific Northwest, the same award that Mavrothalassitis, his mentor and employer, had won in April 2003. Although Chong did not win, he was a semifinalist for the same award a year later as well.[19]

Beginning in 2011, nearly all the post-HRC chefs were semifinalists for Beard Awards. In fact, two were in the running for the Beard Award for Rising Star Chef of the Year several times: Simeon in 2011 and Le in 2013, 2014, and 2015. Another island chef, Christopher Kajioka, who had trained at the Culinary Institute of America and worked at Per Se in New York City for several years before returning to the islands in 2012, was also a semifinalist for this award. But no one in the post-HRC group was a semifinalist for the Beard Award for Best Chef: West more often than Kenney, who received that honor in 2013, 2014, 2015, and 2016. Karr-Ueoka was a semifinalist for the Beard Award for Outstanding Pastry Chef three times—in 2014, 2015, and 2016—and MW, the restaurant that she and her husband opened in 2013, was a semifinalist for the Beard Award for Best New Restaurant in 2014 and 2015. In the national restaurant world, simply being named a semifinalist for a Beard Award is a high honor, even if one never actually wins it. The attention these young chefs were getting from the James Beard Foundation boded well for their futures.

They collected other awards too. In December 2012, Le and Simeon were named 2012 Hawai'i Rising Star chefs.[20] Then in 2012–2013, Simeon was invited to compete on the television show *Top Chef*, the first island chef invited to do so. He acquitted himself well, reaching the finals in Los Angeles. As I will discuss later, what made Simeon's success so extraordinary was that he did this by making typical Filipino dishes, which earned him global attention and acclaim. In 2014, *Food & Wine* included him on its "Best New Chef, People's Choice" list.[21]

Restaurants

These chefs' growing national recognition encouraged them to open new restaurants. In 2007, Kenney opened Downtown at the new Hawai'i State Art Museum in downtown Honolulu. More changes came in 2013: in October, Karr-Ueoka and Ueoka opened MW, and in November Le opened The Pig and the Lady. In January 2014, Simeon, with the backing of HRC chef Mark Ellman, one of the original HRC chefs, and impresario Shep Gordon, opened the Migrant Maui Restaurant at the Wailea Beach Marriott Resort on Maui's south coast. In August of the same year, Kenney opened Kaimuki Superette, across the street from Town, and, eight months later, Mud Hen Water next door. In 2016, Kenney opened Mahina & Sun's in the Surfjack Hotel, a boutique hotel in the center of Waikīkī.

The locations of the post-HRC chefs are important. Following the lead of their mentors, several accepted positions at oceanside resorts or major hotels. In 2011, Chong became the executive chef at the 'Ama'Ama restaurant at the new Disney Aulani resort just north of Pearl Harbor. The appeal of 'Ama'Ama for Chong is not hard to fathom: he had been trained and worked in famous French restaurants for eleven years and had opened and run a branch of one of them for two years, doing everything an executive chef is required to do. As the flagship restaurant at a new and well-known resort, 'Ama'Ama spared Chong the intensity and demands of the first-rank French eateries where he had worked.[22] Remarkably, Simeon had never had his own restaurant before he opened Migrant Maui Restaurant in 2014 at the posh Wailea Marriott Resort. The restaurant was a kind of gift, as it was co-owned by Ellman and Gordon, who, among other things, had managed the career of French chef Roger Vergé, a leading chef of nouvelle cuisine. Simeon and Kenney had clearly learned from their HRC mentors, most of whom had worked at the beginning of their careers at large resort hotels and whose success there had encouraged them to open their own restaurants.

The post-HRC chefs who opened brick-and-mortar restaurants chose the kinds of repurposed spaces and locations favored by restaurateurs committed to the "new casual" dining style. Kenney decided to open not one but three "neighborhood restaurants" in repurposed spaces in Lower Kaimukī: Town, Kaimuki Superette, and Mud Hen Water. As he once explained, the area appealed to him for sentimental reasons:

There used to be a stamp-and-coin shop up here. My older brother was
really into collecting coins. Basically a Thrifty Drug, a Kress, and [a] Kwang
Ung Chinese and crack-seed store, which is still here. The transfer spot for
the Number 14 [bus] was right here on Koko Head Avenue. So I grew up
in the sort of business district as a kid, and I just loved it. And it's a sleepy
town and never really went anywhere, and after going to college and expe-
riencing these hip, trendy, bohemian suburban towns, or even urban streets
in San Francisco—they've got Chestnut Street, Union Street. Basically
every city has these streets that had thrift shops, cafés, and bookshops.[23]

The Ueokas, Michelle and Wade, opened MW, their ninety-seat restaurant, in the old KGMB building on Kapiʻolani Boulevard, very close to
good shopping. Michelle's older brother, a local businessman, found the
space. Le's restaurant The Pig and the Lady was located in Chinatown only
because the space and funding were available. The space had been occu-
pied by another Vietnamese restaurant, Lemongrass, and was owned by
the Pacific Gateway Foundation, a nonprofit serving individuals from
immigrant, refugee, and low-income communities in the islands. Le
agreed to embrace the foundation's mission and in return got an eighty-
six-seat eatery in a historic building with appealing industrial features in a
thriving multiethnic community.

MW, The Pig and the Lady, Town, Downtown (now closed), Kaimuki
Superette, and Mud Hen Water are also some distance from the tourist
hotels and resorts. All are located in or near urban residential areas: Town,
Kaimuki Superette, and Mud Hen Water are in Kaimukī; Downtown was
close to downtown Honolulu; MW is in Ala Moana; and The Pig and the
Lady is in Honolulu's Chinatown. All are near major retail shopping areas
as well. Downtown was on the edge of Honolulu's business district, and The
Pig and the Lady is at the center of a vibrant immigrant community and
just blocks from the famed Chinatown produce, seafood, and meat markets,
where local residents shop daily. Town, Kaimuki Superette, and Mud Hen
Water are in a thriving working-class community close to the University
of Hawaiʻi campus and suburban Mānoa. MW is across the street from the
Ala Moana Shopping Center, the world's largest open-air shopping center
and, in 2009, the United States' second-most-profitable mall.[24]

All six restaurants also are located on or near major traffic arteries.
Downtown and The Pig and the Lady are on or near King Street, the west-
east artery that runs from Chinatown through downtown Honolulu to
Kapahulu and Lower Kaimukī. Town, Kaimuki Superette, and Mud Hen

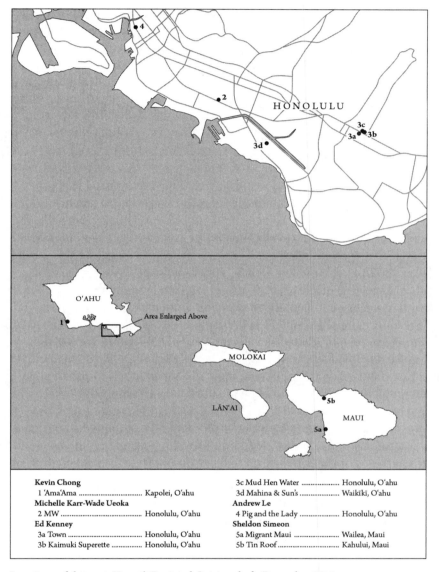

Kevin Chong
1 'Ama'Ama .... Kapolei, O'ahu
Michelle Karr-Wade Ueoka
2 MW .... Honolulu, O'ahu
Ed Kenney
3a Town .... Honolulu, O'ahu
3b Kaimuki Superette .... Honolulu, O'ahu

3c Mud Hen Water .... Honolulu, O'ahu
3d Mahina & Sun's .... Waikīkī, O'ahu
Andrew Le
4 Pig and the Lady .... Honolulu, O'ahu
Sheldon Simeon
5a Migrant Maui .... Wailea, Maui
5b Tin Roof .... Kahului, Maui

Locations of the post–Hawai'i Regional Cuisine chefs, December 2016.

Water are on Wai'alae Avenue, which starts where King Street ends and runs three miles through Upper Kaimuki into the tony suburb of Kāhala. MW is on another major, west-east artery, Kapi'olani Boulevard, which runs parallel to King Street but is several blocks closer to the ocean. All of these restaurants are within a mile of the H-1 freeway, the state's most heavily used highway, which brings commuters to Honolulu from the west, north, and east.

These restaurants' locations reveal their targeted clientele as well. Those at hotels or resorts are obviously targeting tourists: this is the case with Simeon's Migrant Maui Restaurant and Kenney's Mahina & Sun's. Migrant (now closed) was in the Wailea Marriott Resort on southwestern Maui, and Mahina & Sun's is in the Surfjack Hotel, a boutique hotel in the heart of Waikīkī. When Chong was there, 'Ama'Ama attracted both tourists and locals from the nearby Mililani and Kapolei communities. In contrast, the restaurants located some distance from the tourist hotels and resorts are targeting mainly locals. As pointed out earlier, Kenney had sentimental reasons for choosing working-class Kaimuki for three of his restaurants. The Ueokas chose to locate MW in an old working-class district close to the best shopping on the island. MW and the Kenney restaurants are not far from Waikīkī, but the food they offer is intended mainly for a local clientele, although tourists do find their way there. The locations of these restaurants confirm the importance of "place" for some of these chefs and signal their turn away from the HRC chefs.

Careers

This move away from the HRC chefs is easy to miss. On the one hand, all the post-HRC chefs openly acknowledge their debt to the HRC chefs and the movement they started. Chong remembers idolizing them as a high school student. "Everybody had that book [*The New Cuisine of Hawai'i*]," he said. "We saved up our money just to go to their restaurants."[25] Chong even took his girlfriend to dinner at La Mer, the renowned French restaurant at the Halekulani Hotel in Waikīkī, where Mavrothalassitis was then the chef.[26] Simeon recalled visiting the Maui Culinary Academy's library and discovering the HRC chefs' cookbooks. After that, he says, *Alan Wong's New Wave Luau* was always "by my side."[27] Kenney still remembers as clear as day his first encounter with Roy Yamaguchi's new

"Euro-Asian cuisine." It was 1989. He had come home from college in the summer after his sophomore year, and his mother told him about a new restaurant in Hawai'i Kai that they had to try. "We walked into this place," Kenney remembered. "And it was loud; it smelled like smoke. It was crazy pizzas on the menu. I remember, I had the blackened seared ahi with a hot-mustard shoyu beurre blanc [sauce]. We had their crab cakes with another, some sort of cream fusion, French butter sauce. And it was really invigorating and fresh, and new at that time. [But] it was not only the food, but also the smells and the noises and sounds."[28] Nearly thirty years later, Kenney can still see Yamaguchi standing in the kitchen and approving every dish before it was served.[29]

Most of the post-HRC chefs also had contact with the HRC chefs at one time or another, with many being mentored, or advised, by them. Kenney worked briefly at Roy's and Alan Wong's. Chong worked at Chef Mavro for seven years and, while there, mentored a younger chef, Le. Ueoka began working at Alan Wong's not long after it opened in 1995 and stayed there for seventeen years, and Karr-Ueoka was at Alan Wong's for nearly as long.

Simeon remembers seeing the HRC chefs on television. As a boy, he often watched several food-related local programs, such as Hari Kojima's program *Let's Go Fishing* and Mike Sakamoto's *Fishing Tales*. Both featured the hosts cooking what they had just pulled from the ocean. The third and most memorable program was, of course, *Sam Choy's Kitchen*, which premiered in 2002 and featured one of the founding chefs of Hawai'i Regional Cuisine. Simeon claimed not to have missed a single episode of the Choy program and remembered proudly that he even had helped Choy prepare a meal when the chef visited the Maui Culinary Academy.[30]

The HRC chefs thus provided more than just inspiration or advice to these up-and-coming chefs: they offered models of success. No longer was a culinary career the path of the "dummies," and no longer was enrolling in the culinary arts programs at local community colleges shameful, as it once was. Prep school graduates Kenney and Ueoka enrolled in the culinary arts program at Kapi'olani Community College, and Simeon studied culinary arts at both Leeward Community College and the Maui Culinary Academy. All three not only managed to find jobs but also achieved success as chefs and recognition in the larger national restaurant world.

The HRC chefs' careers offered three other possible paths as well. The first path led to the Culinary Institute of America and was pioneered by Yamaguchi and several other HRC chefs. This was the path followed by

Chong, Karr-Ueoka, and Le. Wong blazed a second path: he first earned a community college culinary arts degree and then served an apprenticeship at the Greenbrier in West Virginia, and several young chefs from the islands followed this path. The third path was earning a community college culinary arts degree followed by the short course at the Culinary Institute of America, a more recent path. Today, many fledgling chefs simply complete the culinary arts degree at a local community college in the islands and immediately look for jobs at local restaurants or hotels. Increasingly, with the growing international reputation of the culinary arts program at Kapiʻolani Community College, the opening of the new Culinary Institute of the Pacific on the northern slope of Diamond Head, and the success of would-be chefs with just an associate's degree in finding jobs, this will be the path chosen by more and more of the islands' aspiring local chefs.[31]

The appeal of being a chef is now well established, thanks to the HRC chefs' successes and celebrity. Television food programs had an impact, a point that John Morton made when I interviewed him. He should know, as he is the administrator at the University of Hawaiʻi at Mānoa who oversees the islands' community college system, including the very successful culinary arts programs.[32] Gone are the long shadows of colonial service, embedded for so long in the curricula of the islands' public schools and even at the Kamehameha Schools. The subalterns have emerged and have full agency.

Cuisine

Not surprisingly, what the post-HRC chefs serve at their restaurants reveals their debt to Hawaiʻi Regional Cuisine. These chefs, too, use and highlight fresh, locally sourced ingredients, naming their producers and singing their praises, and their menus even echo those of their HRC mentors. Yet there is much more going on than is apparent at first. What the post-HRC chefs are doing in their restaurants is novel in several ways. Looking back to the foodways of their families and immigrant ancestors, they valorize the cuisine of their local communities, giving their dishes the marked specificity of particular individuals, places, and cultures. They thus are doing more than simply rehearsing the HRC chefs' myths about the islands and their creation of a regional cuisine and reprising their dishes; they are creating new dishes.

What Chong did at 'Ama'Ama at the Disney Resort was closest to the HRC chefs.[33] In fact, he happily worked within the Euro-Asian-local paradigm, using the French techniques he perfected during his six years at Le Cirque and seven at Chef Mavro. Chong admitted as much when he labeled himself "old school." When asked in 2015 which elements of the original HRC vision had survived, he replied, "It's using [the] techniques, ingredients, and philosophy of HRC and just moving on with it. I mean, I can't see anyone passing HRC."[34] This is surprising because he also remembered that when he and other chefs left the islands to study at the Culinary Institute of America, "we were all saying we don't want to do this Pacific Rim stuff. . . . That's why we went abroad, to learn other things."[35] Chong's menu at 'Ama'Ama amply showed his debt to Mavrothalassitis; in fact, he even reprised dishes from Chef Mavro. His mango croquettes are a good example, as is the seafood stew with *vadouvan*, the French version of garam masala, a staple on the Chef Mavro menu.[36]

Chong also departs from the Chef Mavro paradigm, however. He is, for example, more eclectic in his choice of ingredients and dishes. Consider his Kahuku Corn Chowder, which references an American classic and uses locally sourced corn from Kahuku, on the northern tip of O'ahu. Chong adds a tomato-and-salmon combination and taro, calling them by the Hawaiian names of the dish and ingredient that inspired them, lomilomi salmon and kalo. These culinary and rhetorical moves put Chong closer to Wong and to the dialogue between *la grande cuisine* and local food that marks Wong's cuisine.

Michelle Karr-Ueoka and Wade Ueoka also embraced the HRC vision. In fact, they always mention their commitment to carrying on what they call the "tradition" and never miss a chance to express their respect for Wong, their longtime mentor. "We need to make sure the legacy of the Hawai'i Regional Cuisine chefs lives on," is how Karr-Ueoka phrases it.[37] She even quotes Keller, the chef-owner of the French Laundry in Yountville and Per Se in New York City, who once advised her "to be a part of a movement, not a trend."[38]

At the same time, however, the Ueokas have a clear sense of what distinguishes what they are doing at MW from what was done at Alan Wong's. "He did his thing; we do our thing," Karr-Ueoka explained. When asked to clarify, her husband described "their thing" in this way: "We take a lot of the iconic local dishes and try to make them into something contemporary," like the dishes "he had when he was growing up" and the "things that locals are used to."[39] A good example is Ueoka's rendition of oxtail soup, an island favorite. He first creates a rich beef broth by simmering beef short ribs and then makes an oxtail roulade stuffed with ground pork, corned beef, peanuts, and shiitake mushrooms, which he simmers for two and a half hours; and he also makes a risotto. He next warms up slices of the oxtail roulade and serves them on a small mound of risotto, finishing the dish with a ginger-scallion oil.[40] Ueoka's reconfiguration of oxtail soup as a roulade served on risotto immediately calls to mind Wong's Unagi Roulade with Shiitake-Edamame Rice, Kinome, and Kabayaki Sauce and his Velvet Chicken Roulade, which typify his debt to his mentor.[41]

Another good example of the MW approach is Karr-Ueoka's rainbow of colors and flavors in her rococo variations of shaved ice desserts—served with haupia tapioca, strawberry kanten, mochi ice cream, yuzu sorbet, coconut sorbet, panna cotta, and coconut–kaffir lime "air." Most important, the Ueokas are not wedded to the French culinary tradition. Unlike their mentor, they never add French signifiers with no substance to the descriptions of their dishes. Instead, they carefully negotiate the relationship between haute and local cuisine, producing the culinary equivalent of what the architectural historian Kenneth Frampton once called an *arrière-garde* position.[42] Like Walcott's "great poetry of the New World," the fruit of their culinary efforts "is a mixture of the acid and the sweet, the apples of its second Eden have the tartness of experience. . . . [T]here is a bitter memory and it is the bitterness that dries last on the tongue."[43]

The Ueokas thus are unmistakably offering a new version of local food at MW. According to food writer Martha Cheng, "This is local food interpreted by two former Alan Wong chefs, with a little French Laundry and a lot of Zippy's thrown in."[44] When Cheng characterized MW's menu as offering "a lot of Zippy's," she might have been thinking of their rendition of the iconic Zippy's bento, which *Honolulu Magazine*'s readers named Best Bento in 2015.[45]

Interestingly, the pronounced turn toward the "local" seen at MW was anticipated by a number of well-known local chefs. In 1999, when asked to predict the direction of food in the new millennium, Wayne Hirabayashi, the executive chef at the Kahala Mandarin Oriental and a CIA graduate, replied, "We're going back to basics—comfort food with a modern flair." Wong responded to the same query by predicting that "we'll continue to go backward as we move forward. People are looking for honest-to-goodness comfort food, quality stuff. We'll be cooking with honest ingredients—no mystery stuff. In Hawai'i Regional Cuisine, we're going back to basics. A new set of chefs will have to do different things."[46] The Ueokas are those "new" chefs, and they are very definitely doing "different things."

There is more. Consider Ueoka's recipe for mochi-crusted fish with somen. In this recipe, Ueoka, like Wong, uses a locally sourced fish such as 'ōpakapaka, ono, onaga, or kampachi. He adds Japanese ingredients, mochi and somen. He even grates the mochi he uses to encrust the fish, much as Wong grated the ginger in his iconic Ginger-Crusted Onaga with Corn, Mushrooms, and Miso-Sesame Vinaigrette. This is precisely what his mentor might have done. But Ueoka claims that the locus classicus for the mochi in his dish was not his knowledge of Chinese or Japanese cuisine, as it was for Wong's dish.[47] Rather, it was inspired, he tells us, by what his mother did with leftover mochi after New Year's. The power of a personal memory—the familiar soft crunch of mochi-encrusted fish—is crucial here, and this "mode of inflection" is something that Ueoka shares with other post-HRC chefs.[48]

Kenney, Le, and Simeon openly acknowledge their debt to the HRC movement and express their respect for its founders. Yet a close analysis of what they serve at their restaurants confirms that they actually have moved away from their HRC mentors and reveals where and how they have done this.

Kenney is a good example. At first glance, he, too, seems to offer several different variations of the Euro-Asian-local paradigm developed by the HRC chefs. His first restaurant, Town, is well known for a menu that has been called "vaguely Italian" and described as offering "Italian-inflected" dishes; Kenney himself stated that "our spirit is Italian." But he also admitted to being tired of the HRC chefs' Francophilia.[49] "When I started getting involved in the industry," he said, referring to the late 1990s, "I felt like Hawai'i Regional Cuisine hadn't evolved much. It was still doing the French food, French mother sauces with infused flavors. And it was becoming pretty ubiquitous, you know. You could go almost everywhere, and there would be that signature trio of daikon, carrot, and beet curls as a garnish on top of everything, and so that's when I decided to come back in and do what we did." In 2015, Kenney described his philosophy as offering a "Hawaiian sense of plate" and defined it as "cooking Hawaiian food from a more rooted and connected place."[50]

To Kenney, what showed just how far he was from the HRC chefs were the trips to the mainland sponsored by the Hawai'i Visitors Bureau that had him and other chefs doing the "Aloha thing." He remembers the moment of revelation:

> The first time I did it, I showed up with a little rolling cooler. It was this big. I could have put a case of beer in it, max. And I was supposed to be going to these places and cooking for two hundred people. I see these HVB [Hawai'i Visitors Bureau] people just looking at me wide-eyed, freaking out, like "Where is your food? What are you gonna feed these people?" Because they were used to Alan, Roy, and Sam with . . . giant coolers, they would take on their trips everything from Hawai'i to show these flavors of Hawai'i. What I explained to them was that our ancestors, the original voyagers, they traveled . . . with pa'i 'ai, 'ulu, limu, salt, and toasted 'inamona. Wherever they ended up, they would use what was there. That was the true farm-to-table ethic. I think it's not like farm-to-table for us, when we take things with us.
>
> So we would go on these things. We showed up with these five things. We showed up two days early and would go to the Santa Cruz farmers' market or the farmers' market in Seattle or Chicago, and get to know the farmers. While we were going around, we would purchase all this stuff for the dinner, actually go into the parking lot, bust open a pot, cook a bunch, and feed the farmers that we got the food from. Then we would go back and prep for a day, cooking for two hundred people using Hawai'i ingredients. Introduce to them the idea of cooking from a Hawaiian point of view. We called it a "Hawaiian sense of plate" rather than a "Hawaiian sense of place."[51]

This anecdote suggests where Kenney parted company with the HRC chefs.

Kenney's culinary approach is distinguished by his concerted effort to use not only locally produced ingredients but also Hawaiian ingredients and "to showcase [them] in their purest, simplest form."[52] His inspiration was a conversation with a visiting New York food critic, Alan Richman, who, twenty years earlier, had heralded the new Hawai'i Regional Cuisine and predicted that it would take America by storm. On this trip, Kenney recalled, Richman observed that Hawai'i had "fallen off the . . . culinary map."[53] That conversation, which took place in 2008, led Kenney to start "looking more into indigenous cuisine, indigenous cooking techniques" and to respect "man-pounded poi, pa'i 'ai, kalo, 'ulu, and limu and all these things that the ancestors who grew up in this land ate and integrate them into what we do here."[54] Besides a rich array of local fish and shellfish, Kenney uses 'inamona (candlenut relish), limu, kalo, 'uala (sweet potatoes), and ʻulu (breadfruit). At all of his restaurants, he also serves a paʻi ʻai (a kind of pounded taro sometimes called "hard poi") that had never been featured at restaurants in the islands but that he had eaten at home, often for breakfast. Kenney does several things with paʻi ʻai: he sautés, grills, and deep-fries it; he even makes it into a batter.[55] The paiʻi ʻai and akule combination he serves at Mahina & Sun's, for example, even reprises the tested pairing of poi and akule much loved by Hawaiians.[56]

Kenney's effort to use paʻi ʻai required determination, because for some time it was not easily sourced. In 2009, the state department of health prohibited the sourcing of paʻi ʻai made in the traditional way, by stretching and pounding cooked taro with a special stone on wooden boards, because the boards were, by tradition, not sanitized in the way that the department of health required. Kenney recounted how the department's inspectors visited Town and made him "trash all of the paʻi ʻai we had in inventory." It was only when paʻi ʻai makers found a way to sun-bleach their boards that the department of health relented in 2011 and allowed paʻi ʻai made in the

David Kaapu pounding poi. Courtesy of Pan Pacific Press.

traditional way to be sold.[57] One local paʻi ʻai maker, David Anthony, even devised "a non-chemical ozone system" for cleaning his boards, with the result that his paʻi ʻai now is not only widely sourced by restaurants but is even sold at Whole Foods stores in the islands.

Kenney serves other indigenous ingredients and dishes. One of these is ʻulu, which he prepares in several different ways. Another is his version of squid lūʻau, an exquisite dish made with fresh squid and coconut milk that is an icon in the Hawaiian culinary repertoire.[58] Not surprisingly, Kenney also uses ingredients and dishes drawn from other local culinary traditions, such as fermented black beans, pig's feet, and lup cheong (a type of sausage) from Chinese cuisine; miso and shishito peppers from Japanese cuisine; and bean soup and *pao doce* (sweet bread) from Portuguese cuisine. Kenney's restaurant in Waikīkī, Mahina & Sun's, bravely serves these dishes made with indigenous ingredients to a mainly tourist clientele. In this way, Kenney has taken HRC cuisine in a completely new direction, toward not only recovering lost local ingredients and dishes but also "cooking Hawaiian food from a more rooted and connected place."[59] Like the Ueokas, Kenney is negotiating the relationship between haute and local cuisine in a way that the HRC chefs never did.

Le also inherited Hawaiʻi Regional Cuisine's commitment to locavorism. He, too, uses locally sourced ingredients, many of them from the farm run by the Pacific Gateway Foundation in Kunia or the MAʻO Farms in Waiʻanae. Like many of the HRC chefs, Le received a rock-solid education in French culinary technique, first at the Culinary Institute of America in Hyde Park and then at Chef Mavro in Honolulu. "I had just graduated from culinary school, moved back home, and I was going to go back to New York," he remembers. "So I staged at Chef Mavro. At the time, Kevin Chong was chef de cuisine. . . . I got there, and I thought I knew something, but it turned out I knew nothing. They put me in my place right away. They had very high standards."[60] His eight years of French culinary training—three at the Culinary Institute of America and five at Chef Mavro—left its mark. When asked, "What meal changed how you feel about food?" Le recalled a dish he helped prepare at Chef Mavro: "During my stage with Chef Kevin Chong at . . . Chef Mavro, the tako [octopus] carpaccio dish blew my mind. It was sliced paper-thin and arranged on the plate like a beautiful mosaic of tangled tentacles. It was served with pickled green papaya, brushed with a shoyu and sherry gastrique and garnished with ikura, or red salmon roe. To be involved with the preparation, cooking process and plating, and then having the opportunity to eat it was such a special experience." He called it "the first chapter of my career path as a chef."[61]

Le acknowledges another powerful influence, the cuisine of his immigrant Vietnamese family, especially the dishes that his mother, Loan, made. "For our family, food has always been a big part of who we are. It's helped to define our identity. My mom is an amazing cook, and she's one of the primary reasons I was so attracted to food and why I became a chef." He continued: "She's a driving force behind The Pig and the Lady and brings a really authentic style of Vietnamese cuisine to the table. There's so much more to Vietnamese food than spring rolls and pho, and she's able to widen people's understanding of the food."[62] But Le is not simply making authentic Vietnamese dishes; he is doing much, much more.

He is making a *kind* of Vietnamese cuisine. Here a comparison with Wong and Yamaguchi is instructive. In the 1990s, they developed the Asian end of the "Euro-Asian paradigm" using what they knew about Asian and French culinary techniques and Asian ingredients to make their own versions of Asian standards. Yamaguchi's version of miso-glazed cod and Wong's 'ōpakapaka and shrimp pork hash in a truffle nage are good examples: both dishes come out of the Japanese and Chinese culinary repertoire. In contrast, Le starts with his mother's culinary knowledge, "her expertise," in his words. Then, and only then, does he add what he learned at the Culinary Institute of America and at Chef Mavro to create something new, and "the results," he says, "have been really amazing."[63]

Le's collaboration with his mother, however, has not always been easy, because she apparently did not always agree with his ideas. When she disapproved of how he was preparing a Vietnamese dish, she always responded ominously with "You're going to embarrass the Vietnamese community" or resorted to the device that Asian immigrant parents often use with their American-born children: "You're going to shame the family!"[64] Le remembered one particular incident when he was still doing pop-ups:

> We did a variation of . . . rice soup . . . and then they [his parents] were like, "Wait, why are you doing that? Why are you pressing the rice and making it all so fancy? And why are you using sherry vinegar instead of this or that?" It's like, "Don't do that. You're going to embarrass me. You're gonna ruin the family name."
>
> I was like, "Uhhhh. Nah." Like I'm very stubborn. I'm gonna make it. And then I sneak [it in], and they tried it. They were like, "Oh, it's good." I was like, "I told you what I was gonna make." Yeah![65]

In time, Le's recognition as a Rising Star chef and the praise showered on his new brick-and-mortar restaurant improved his culinary relationship with his mother. His restaurant's Facebook site states that Le is "currently the only chef among Hawaii's culinary cognoscenti cooking contemporary food built on Vietnamese flavors—a foundation built on delicious memories first introduced by his mother."[66]

When I interviewed him in the summer of 2015, Le said that what he does in the kitchen is "a swerve away from his French training." When asked to talk about a dish that he learned to make using a French culinary technique, he mentioned a particular beef dish: "You cut it [the beef] about this big, and then you roast it. And then three ways, and three times, and develop it for, like, six hours. And then you reduce it and make a nice sauce. Very intense flavor. And then [you] flavor it any way you want to make a unique sauce. . . . It was like a very rigid way of thinking. It's, like, OK, when I think of making a sauce, I'm gonna use this technique." When asked to point to a dish that he makes not in the French way, he chose Three Pot Chicken:

> You get some fowl, right, and you dry it, and then [store] it in the fridge . . . until the skin dries, and then you fry it. Cut it up, and it's usually, like, a tougher, older bird. And then you gotta braise it. And then you put in all these aromatics—like Thai ginger, lemongrass, kaffir lime, chili, shallots, fish sauce, some sugar. And then you put it all in a big pot and then . . . just let it cook. And it takes, like, an hour, an hour and a half. Once it's done, you open it up, and it's like this incredible aroma. And then you get this jus from the herbs and slow cooking and the aromatics that make this incredible sauce. It's, like, it's delicious. And you eat it with rice. . . . So that's like an example of the type of technique that I use.

Asked whether he was still thinking in "French culinary terms" when he made that chicken dish, Le replied, "Yes, yes, absolutely," but "you try to deviate as far away from what you are familiar with . . . because you need to learn about it." When pressed, he said, "My cooking style is one part Continental . . . and one part Vietnamese. So it's a combination of both."[67] Clearly, Le is inflecting in new ways the French dishes he learned to make at the Culinary Institute of America.

Personal memory obviously informs what he does. When pressed, Le admitted as much: "When you first cook for yourself, there is a distinction between cooking professionally and cooking things you love. . . . My professional cooking was French, but the food that I loved was Asian food.

I grew up eating pho, and I have all these great food memories from my childhood, a lot of aunties and uncles getting dirty with roasted pig face—stuff like that." Particular dishes on the menu of The Pig and the Lady, he added, even evoke certain memories:

> When I look at it, it's like I think about maybe this one time in my life that I had this or this memory of us cooking this together, you know. It means something to be on the menu. And then, but at the same time, we are in the modern age, you know, and I'm a young chef, and there is a lot of interests that we have. So we can't help but be creative here and there. And so I say our cooking style is an appreciation for [the] traditional, but being in the present and always keeping an eye on the future. We create, like, a new cuisine. We offer just a different direction.[68]

Like Kenny and Ueoka, Le offers dishes inspired by memories of what he ate as a boy. By late summer 2015, Le was able to say of this collaboration: "Our food is a reflection of our team's ethnic heritage, with a nod to the past and an eye on the future. . . . We strive to present our dishes with an air of familiarity coupled with flavors and techniques that are new and exciting."[69] The key words are "ethnic heritage." They bring to mind a point that HRC chef Amy Ferguson made in an interview in 2011, when she praised chefs who "create a regional cuisine . . . from the roots up."[70] Here Le is negotiating the relationship of haute and local cuisine, his French training, and what his Vietnamese American family ate to produce dishes that are neither simply French nor Vietnamese but something more, dishes that resolve the clear tension between what Krishnendu Ray termed the "embodied experience" of the ethnic chef and his training as an "expert" chef.[71]

Simeon also admired the HRC chefs, but he had virtually no kitchen time with any of them. His only contact came when he helped Choy prep for a cooking demonstration at Leeward Community College.[72] At first glance, Simeon's cooking might be seen as playing the "Asian" end of the Euro-Asian paradigm. After all, it was his noodles at Aloha Mixed Plate and Star Noodle in Lahaina that brought him to the attention of the restaurant world, first in the islands and then nationally. In fact, in eight years, from 2002 to 2010, his noodles carried him from the position of prep cook to that of a chef and then of executive chef at Aloha Mixed Plate.

In 2009, when Simeon's bosses decided to open Star Noodle, a new restaurant featuring Asian noodles, they took him on a short trip to the mainland, with stops in San Francisco and New York City. No doubt New York chef David Chang's meteoric rise as the chef-owner of Asian noodle restaurants caught their eye: Chang opened Momofuku Noodle Bar in 2004 and then three more restaurants in the New York area, winning the Beard Award for Best Chef: New York City in 2008 and the Beard Award for Best New Restaurant in 2009, and these were just the first of seven Beard Awards that he, his chef Christina Tosi, and his restaurants won between 2008 and 2014. Indeed, when Star Noodle opened in February 2010, food writer Martha Cheng called it a Momofuku look-alike.[73]

Despite the superficial similarities, Simeon was doing more than just reprising Momofuku dishes at Star Noodle. His dishes were clearly meant to appeal to locals, as they included ramen, udon, yakitori, and pork buns, as well as one standout dish, pohole (fiddlehead fern) salad with shredded squid, kombu, and tomatoes.[74] Within just ten months of its opening, Star Noodle was a semifinalist for the Beard Award for Best New Restaurant; Simeon was a semifinalist for the Beard Award for Rising Star Chef of the Year;[75] and a year later, he was added to *Food & Wine*'s list of nine regional winners in its annual Best New Chefs, People's Choice poll.[76]

It was Simeon's appearance on *Top Chef* that brought him national and international visibility. Two things stand out about his appearance on this widely watched national food show in its thirteenth season. The first was that he was the first island chef to appear on the program. The second was his decision to make well-known Filipino dishes, ranging from old standbys such as pork adobo, *halo halo, miki, kilawin,* and *sinigang* and *balut* (duck embryo).[77] Even though Simeon was making upscale versions of these dishes, no one had ever made them on national television. He called the concept informing his renditions of these dishes "URBANo." The judges responded with obvious enthusiasm. Danny Meyer took a sip of Simeon's sour tamarind soup with pork belly, shrimp, and snapper and declared, "It makes you sit up straight." Tom Colicchio called his pork adobo "the best tasting dish of the night" and announced, "You don't get many Filipino restaurant concepts like that. Maybe we are waiting for a chef like you to do that."[78] Simeon's appearances on *Top Chef* attracted a lot of attention, and viewers in both the United States and the Philippines went wild.[79] It was, Simeon says, the "proudest moment of my whole career. I put Filipino food out there, and everyone received it well."[80] This is an understatement: the truth is that they went nuts.

Simeon's decision to make Filipino dishes on *Top Chef* says much about his sense of himself. He grew up in a plantation community northwest of Hilo, most of whose inhabitants were Filipino and where families like his "grew and harvested their food [and] raised animals in their backyard."[81] Simeon's immigrant grandparents had a deep appreciation of the land and the food they grew, and they passed this on to his father and then to him. Simeon remembered that they all were wonderful cooks and that he "grew up cooking." "I've been surrounded by good cooks my entire life—my dad, my mom, and my grandparents all were amazing cooks." Because his father worked two jobs and his mother had health problems, Simeon and his older brother "started cooking . . . when we were kids."[82] They learned to cook by imitating their father, he remembered, cutting in the way he cut, adding what he added, and so forth. Often he and his brother had dinner ready when their father returned from work. Not surprisingly, they also made what they liked, and Simeon's breakfast was often a bowl of Maruchan ramen.[83] Today one of his favorite dishes is *miki*, a Filipino noodle soup made with chicken broth, which his mother used to make for him, and "to this day, I remember that about my mom."[84]

When Migrant Maui Restaurant opened in January 2014, Simeon offered a kind of Filipino home cooking "rooted in his family's recipes."[85] On his menu were *kinilaw*, a kind of ceviche; pancit, Chinese-style fried noodles; adobo, a vinegary dish made with pork or chicken; *tocino*, often called "Filipino sweet pork"; and *kare kare*, a rich savory stew made with pig's feet, ham hocks, and offal. In these dishes, he also used such Filipino ingredients as kalamansi and made sauces inspired by Filipino cuisine, like his adobo glazes. He also "Filipinized" dishes, as he did, for example, with his popular hand-cut chow fun noodles. Simeon explains his Hand-Cut Chow Fun Noodles with Lechon and Parmigiano-Reggiano in this way: "*chow fun* noodles remind me of gnocchi, so that's why there's Parmesan . . . [, and] I looked for Filipino flavors to go with it. So we used Italian techniques, but this dish is straight-up Filipino."[86] This is Italian and Filipino cuisines having a conversation.

The menu at Migrant was, not surprisingly, highly eclectic. The names of his dishes tell the story: Ahi Kinilaw, Pancit Noodles, French Onion Mazemen, "Dry Mein" Tsukemen, and "Tone" Katsu. Simeon's descriptions of each of these dishes show the variety of Asian and non-Asian ingredients and the culinary techniques used to make them.

Ahi Kinilaw: Sashimi-Grade Big-Eye Tuna, Young Coconut Gelee, Leche de Tigre, Sweet Onion, Argumato Lemon Olive Oil, Red Shiso, Molokai Sweet Potato Chips

Pancit Noodles: Oahu Noodle Factory Canton Noodles, Roasted Pork Belly, Black Tiger Shrimp, Market Vegetables, Garlic Chives, Fried Garlic

Hand-Cut Fat Chow Fun: Steamed Tapioca Fat Chow Fun Noodles, Chopped Lechon Pork, Pipinola Shoot Salad, Brown Butter Achuete Jus, Grated Parmigiano-Reggiano

French Onion Mazemen: Iwamoto Ramen Noodles, Kula French Onion Soup, Comte Cheese, 12-Hour Braised Boneless Short Ribs, Fried Leek "Hay" Cilantro

"Dry Mein" Tsukemen: Paia Saimin Noodles, Garlic Schmaltz, Char Siu Pork, Fried Egg Ribbons, Kamaboko Fish Cake, Sunflower Sprouts, Served with Shiro Tare Dashi

"Tone" Katsu: Twice-Cooked 14-oz. Duroc Pork Chop, Bacon Shiitake Cream, Roasted Oyster Mushrooms

Absent here is the careful balance of the "Euro" and the "Asian" that Yamaguchi championed in the late 1990s. Also missing are the carefully mediated references that Wong added to the names of his menu items, such as their ingredients, producers, and implied culinary techniques. In contrast, Simeon's menu offers a completely different kind of semiotic complexity, one rooted in his family's story and pointing in the same direction as Kenney's pa'i 'ai dishes, Chong's chowder with kalo and lomilomi salmon, Ueoka's mochi-crusted fish and somen, Karr-Ueoka's shaved ices, and Le's pho. Kenney's description of New York chef Chang's food may sum up what the post-HRC chefs are doing: "It wasn't [like the] Asian fusion that was going on in Hawai'i. It was simpler, but more complex. It was based on who he was."[87] The cuisine of the post-HRC chefs was, in short, who they were and not what they wanted, or hoped, to be. They were cooking their community, as Simeon once put it.

Conclusions

John Heckathorn once described the HRC chefs' achievement as a "revolution."[88] If he was right, and I think he was, then what their successors have done early in the twenty-first century may amount to a second revolution. Of course, they are too respectful of their mentors and too modest to make such grand claims. Yet a close reading of everything they say about their restaurants and what they serve there suggests that they are moving in a dramatically new direction, straight toward the "local."

The younger chefs are not wedded to French culinary technique. Instead, their cuisine is based primarily on a genuine nostalgia for forgotten ingredients, overlooked dishes, and even lost culinary techniques, a nostalgia served by powerful personal memories. Kenney's boyhood memories of a *place*, Lower Kaimukī, where he spent many afternoons after school, led him to open three restaurants there. Karr-Ueoka's memories of a *favorite childhood snack*, shaved ice, led her to create elaborate shaved-ice desserts, and Ueoka's memories of particular *dishes* that his Kailua family ate, such as his mother's mochi-crusted dishes, inspired much of what he serves at MW. At first glance, Ueoka seems to be following in the footsteps of his mentor, but his memories seem more personal and less romantic than Wong's. Ueoka's are more everyday Kailua than fabled plantation meals. Similarly, Le's culinary creations at The Pig and the Lady were prompted by memories of *another country*, Vietnam, but since he was born and raised in the islands, these are not really his memories but those of his mother and her sister. Simeon's dishes originated in his memories of what his *immigrant family* ate when he was growing up outside Hilo: his pohole salad, for example, makes reference to the pohole growing in his grandparents' backyard.

The memories animating the post-HRC chefs' culinary creations are recovered memories of ingredients, dishes, and culinary techniques lost during migrations and with the passage of time or effaced by lapses of memory. These are memories that survived the homogenizing effects of the impulse "to become American" or, perhaps, "to eat American." They also are memories that were distorted by the totalizing narratives of "aloha" and the official multiculturalism produced by government and professional agencies. But make no mistake. These chefs are not simply reproducing the cuisines of their ancestors, families, or home countries or trying to recover a lost vernacular cuisine. They have created a new vernacular that is the product of a dialogue between a once dominant, universal (read French) cuisine and a local cuisine, the result of an ongoing culinary conversation between the tastemakers guarding the fine-dining tradition in the United States and the post-HRC chefs. Perhaps we could call what these chefs offer at their restaurants "Hawai'i Regional Cuisine once removed."

These younger chefs have also bridged the identities of the ethnic cook and chef.[89] Kenney did this by reviving Hawaiian dishes and ingredients, Le by channeling his family's "Vietnamese cuisine," Simeon by making the dishes that his grandparents and parents made for him, and Karr-Ueoka and Ueoka by making their favorite local dishes. Without embarrassment or anxiety, all five chefs allude to their experience of their communities' goût de terroir, or "taste of place."[90] They are cooking from what Walcott called a position of "elation."[91]

Finally, the younger chefs' food work exhibits another inspiration, the new casual style of dining that emerged early in this century. They have been watching what has been happening in the restaurant world on the mainland, in the Bay Area, Los Angeles, Chicago, and New York. Like the young chefs on the mainland, such as Chang, Danny Bowien, Roy Choi, Jeremy Fox, Josef Centeno, and Carlos Salgado, they are driven by new conceptions of ethnic cuisine, the local, and place, conceptions not known in the islands before 2010.

5 | Legacy

It was just a desire to have good fresh foods to work with, but it's helped the state economy. It helped farmers get started.

Peter Merriman

The Hawai'i Regional Cuisine chefs had a very good run. In the decade after their August 1991 meeting, they gained visibility first in the islands and then nationally. By 2000, ten of the twelve founding chefs had their own restaurants, and the other two had left the islands. As befit a celebrity chef, Roy Yamaguchi owned thirty-two restaurants by 2011, whereas the other chefs had many fewer.[1] Although the HRC chefs' locavorism and their new regional cuisine are the main reasons for their success, credit also should be given to the farmers, fishermen, aquaculturists, ranchers, coffee growers, cheese makers, and others who supplied them. The local journalists who wrote about their restaurants and the television producers who introduced their new regional cuisine to the islands played a part, too, as did the chefs, food writers, and tastemakers on the mainland who brought Hawai'i Regional Cuisine into the larger national restaurant world. Clearly, even as the HRC chefs worked hard to succeed as restaurateurs, to promote their brand, and to serve their community, they accomplished much, much more.

Food Scene

The chefs' most enduring impact has been on the food scene in the islands. They created a regional cuisine that featured locally sourced fish, shellfish, vegetables, beef, lamb, pork, eggs, coffee, and cheeses. They elevated humble, everyday fare into haute cuisine, with chefs from the mainland adding American standbys—like casseroles, popular desserts, and Chinese American or Tex-Mex dishes—to their menus, and chefs with island roots transforming "local food" into fine dining. These chefs' "Euro-Asian-Pacific-American" culinary paradigm diminished the dominance of French cuisine, thereby creating room for innovation, experimentation, and even humor.

All this enabled the next generation to bridge the "ethnic" and "expert" chef divide and to create new, *local* cuisines. Their successors now can cook from a position that finds them recovering not only lost ingredients, lost dishes, and lost cuisines but also family, community, and place. What the post-HRC chefs are offering is more than a simple return to vernacular cuisines: they are reimagining what had been forgotten, overlooked, or obscured or even what they never knew.

The HRC chefs also ushered in a new era that opened doors that had long been closed to both chefs of color and women in the islands. Because of Sam Choy, Alan Wong, and Yamaguchi, chefs of color who once "didn't go into that business except as short-order cooks," now cook at the top restaurants in the state.[2] After Amy Ferguson was named executive chef at the Hotel Hana Maui and then at the Ritz-Carlton Mauna Lani, and after Beverly Gannon showed herself capable of running three successful restaurants, similar paths opened for women, who now are in charge of the kitchens at top fine-dining spots in the islands.

This demographic revolution accounts for the huge impact that the HRC chefs have had on culinary education in the islands. Inspired by their example, many more young people found new pride in becoming chefs and cooks, with even graduates of Honolulu's top prep schools entering the restaurant world. In the first decade of this century, enrollments in the islands' culinary arts programs steadily rose.[3]

Agriculture

As happened with other regional cuisines, Hawai'i Regional Cuisine had an extraordinary impact on local agriculture. Initially, a small group of farmers grew the vegetables the HRC chefs needed, planting more varieties than they knew existed and learning where to plant, how to nurture, when to harvest, and, above all, how best to ship their products to preserve their freshness. With the increased demand from other chefs who embraced the new locavorism, the platoon of farmers gradually became a small army, which now includes many younger farmers as well.

Hawai'i Regional Cuisine was significant in another way. When the sugar and pineapple plantations that were the mainstay of the state's economy started to close in the 1980s, the new locavorism pointed to a possible solution: diversified agriculture.[4] State officials saw this, too. In 2003, former governor George Ariyoshi claimed in an editorial that "in fixed dollars, diversified agricultural crops—flowers, ornamentals, herbs, fruit, vegetables and nuts—have made up for the massive losses of sugar." He cataloged the benefits of diversified agriculture: "Crops are pleasing to see, and obviously an asset for the travel industry. We have healthy, fresh food in our markets. An island cuisine derived from fresh fruit, vegetables, herbs and fish is becoming known worldwide."[5] Later that year, Sandra Lee Kunimoto, the newly appointed chair of the state department of agriculture, added that "it does things like give us open, green, working spaces and . . . recharges our aquifers and gives us products for both local consumption and export."[6]

Local agencies throughout the state also did what they could to help farmers. In 2005, the University of Hawai'i's College of Tropical Agriculture and Human Resources, the Hawai'i Farm Bureau Federation, and the Hawai'i Department of Agriculture started the "Buy Local, It Matters" campaign to encourage local consumers to make a "conscious decision . . . to purchase locally grown produce."[7] The following May, Governor Linda Lingle announced the creation of the Hawai'i Seals of Quality program, which, like similar programs on the mainland, promoted local products.[8] In 2009, the North Kohala Eat Locally Grown community initiative on the Big Island was launched to "Keep Kohala, Kohala," and in 2014 a Growing Agricultural Tourism in North Kohala program was started to attract tourists "seeking an authentic, educational, rural experience in Hawai'i and to bring an additional revenue stream to the farmers."[9] Similar Kauai Made and Grown on Maui programs were begun, too.[10]

The HRC chefs' locavorism led to the appearance of farmers' markets in the first decade of the 2000s. One ardent advocate of these markets was Dean Okimoto, the farmer whom Yamaguchi persuaded to grow microgreens for his restaurants in the early 1990s. As the president of the Hawai'i Farm Bureau Federation, Okimoto, together with food writer Joan Namkoong, opened farmers' markets that featured locally grown vegetables, fruits, and flowers. The first market opened in 2003 in the parking lot of Kapi'olani Community College on the northern slope of Diamond Head, and its immediate success led to the creation of more markets. Although this first market was criticized for attracting mainly well-heeled white and Asian consumers and hordes of tourists but excluding low-income residents, the Hawai'i Farm Bureau's three other markets do currently cater to a "more diverse population."[11] Several new types of farmers' markets also emerged that solved the access issue, but they posed another problem: many of their vendors sold imported vegetables and fruits, whose lower prices made them more attractive to many buyers.[12] This problem plagues farmers' markets on the mainland as well, and state and county officials are still trying to resolve it.[13]

In the twenty-first century, the HRC chefs found other ways to promote local produce. For example, Peter Merriman has become the face of the farm-to-table movement in the islands and frequently takes visitors to meet producers on Maui, not only farmers, but also famous artisans like Marie McDonald, a renowned lei maker.[14] Wong holds periodic Farmer Series Dinners at his eponymous restaurant that celebrate those who supply his restaurants with fresh produce, fish, shellfish, meat, butter, cheese, and eggs. One of these dinners, held at Alan Wong's on May 20, 2009, featured no fewer than twelve suppliers and their products.[15]

Fishing

Given the abundance of fresh seafood on restaurant menus in the islands, it is not surprising that the new regional cuisine had an oversized impact on fishing. The demand for local fish, shellfish, and seaweed has increased dramatically, and although much of what is served at local restaurants originates in island waters, the supply is not boundless. In the 1990s and first decade of the 2000s, when the overfishing of deepwater bottomfish

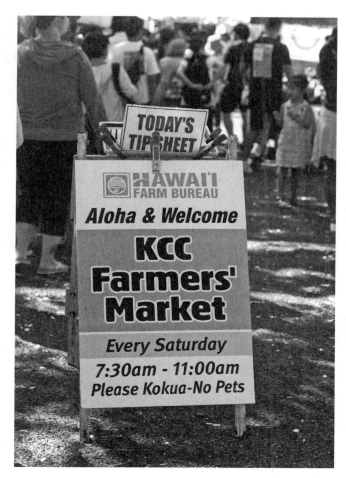

Kapiʻolani Community College Farmers' Market. Author's collection.

species became a serious problem, the HRC chefs, among others, brought this to the attention of the public.

Merriman raised this issue in a long editorial in the *Honolulu Advertiser* in December 2006: "While a healthy competition within Hawaiʻi's thriving culinary scene generates awareness among residents and visitors about the benefits of local farming and the joys of food . . . there is one important arena where the competition fails: off-island, within our Hawaiian waters."[16] As Merriman explained, the overfishing problem had two manifestations: first, the catch rates of 'ōpakapaka (short-tail pink snapper) and onaga (long-tail red snapper) rose and then steadily fell between 1991 and 2006, with 226,000 pounds of 'ōpakapaka caught in 1998, 133,000 pounds in 2003, and 92,965 pounds in 2006.[17] The second problem, according to Merriman, was that growing numbers of "immature onaga" also were caught, and since onaga take four years to mature and spawn, the availability of this fish would soon be greatly diminished.[18]

In 2008, federal and state authorities addressed the problem of bottomfish overfishing. The National Maritime Fisheries Service began monitoring the commercial landing of seven deepwater bottomfish varieties, and when a fixed poundage was reached, it simply closed the fishing of these varieties in Hawaiian waters. In 2010, for example, when the catch of deepwater bottomfish reached 254,000 pounds, fishing in the "Main Hawaiian Islands" was closed from April 20 to August 31, 2010. The same action was taken in 2011 and 2012. The results were gratifying: the deepwater bottomfish catch remained above 300,000 pounds from 2006 through 2014, except for 2010 and 2012, when it dropped below that figure. In addition, the catch of 'ōpakapaka from 2007 through 2014 remained above 100,000 pounds except for 2013, when it dropped to 95,377. After 2008, the catch of the slow-maturing onaga never rose very far above 100,000 pounds, confirming Merriman's warning. Although state records show that the limits have generally been observed, only time will tell whether the vigilance of federal and state authorities, as well as the attention of local chefs, will reverse the steady decline observed between 1990 and 2010.[19]

Aquaculture

The HRC chefs have been enthusiastic promoters of aquaculture, not only because of the overfishing problem, but also because annual seafood consumption in the islands has always been higher than the US average.[20] In 1997, John Corbin, manager of the state's aquaculture development program, reported that Hawai'i residents were consuming an enormous fifty million pounds of seafood a year, 80 percent of which was imported, 18 percent caught locally, and 2 percent produced by aquaculture.[21] His hope was that increasing production through aquaculture, together with careful management of the fishing industry, could reduce this dependence on imported seafood.

Aquaculture took off in the 1990s, helped by two developments. The first was the decline of the sugar and pineapple industries, which freed up both land and water resources.[22] As a result, the number of aquaculture businesses rose from 71 in 1991 to 100 in 1999 and then fell to 70 in 2009. Sales in the nascent aquaculture industry climbed around 10 to 15 percent a year in the 1990s, from $6.9 million in 1991 to $18.1 million in 1999 and to $25.3 million in 2009, an impressive 267 percent increase over the eighteen-year period. In 2012, the number of aquaculture businesses rose to 75, and sales totaled $55.7 million.[23] The second development was the wise decision by island aquaculturists to focus on particular species of fish, shellfish, and seaweed: principally shrimp, moi (Pacific threadfin), microalgae, lobsters, ogo (an edible seaweed), flounder, and ornamental fish.[24]

Another significant development has been the use of traditional Hawaiian fishponds for aquaculture. Ke Kuaʻaina Hanauna Hou, a cooperative on Molokaʻi, began raising limu in fishponds there in 1989. This is important because naturally grown limu had virtually disappeared by the 1980s because of overharvesting. The use of existing fishponds was attractive for three reasons: first, it offered an ecologically sustainable aquacultural medium; second, it affirmed an indigenous form of aquaculture that had a proven record of success;[25] and third, it provided economic opportunities for Molokaʻi, where the unemployment rate was nearly 22 percent in 1998.[26] Today, many fishponds on Molokaʻi continue to be used to raise limu, and others are currently being restored.[27]

The HRC chefs have encouraged the development of the aquaculture industry in another way, by featuring its products on their menus. For example, several chefs serve abalone, kampachi (amberjack), and lobster from the Kona area, in addition to sea asparagus from the north shore of Oʻahu and shrimp from Kauai.

Ranching

The HRC chefs have had much less impact on ranching. As is well known, this industry has virtually insoluble problems. According to state data, the number of beef and pork producers fell precipitously in the 1970s, with the number of ranches producing beef dropping from 1,410 in 1970 to 850 in 1980 but rising slightly to 900 in 1990. The number fell again to 800 in 2000 and then rose to 1,100 in 2007, before falling back to 1,000 in 2008.

The decline in pork-producing operations has been even more dramatic, from 1,820 producers in 1960 to 700 in 1970, to 650 in 1980, to 500 in 1990, and to 230 in 2000, where it remained through 2010. This is an 87 percent drop over thirty years.[28]

Food writer Joan Namkoong discussed this issue in several thoughtful articles that appeared in the Honolulu dailies in the first decade of this century. As she explained, the ranching industry in the islands faces a major structural problem. The methods that island cattle ranchers used for decades became economically unsustainable in the 1970s. Until that time, they raised their calves on grass and then "finished" them on local feedlots, where they were fed grain imported from the mainland. In the 1970s, the rising cost of imported grain forced local ranchers to ship their calves to the mainland for finishing.[29] When the value of calves fell, shipping them to the mainland became less attractive, but the practice nonetheless continued. In 2014, for example, 32,900 cattle were shipped to the mainland.[30]

One solution, according to Namkoong, would be to produce local grass-fed beef. Grass-fed beef, however, is more expensive and tastes different: it is juicier but also chewier. Grass-fed cattle in Hawai'i also consume tropical

Parker Ranch. Hawai'i State Archive.

grasses that are "low in energy" and do not promote their growth as well as cool-season grasses do.[31]

To their credit, the HRC chefs and others have actively promoted grass-fed beef, but they have had to educate their clientele about this product. Wong took the lead here: "One hundred percent grass-fed beef has less fat, less moisture, [and is] more firm. It's old-school beef. You gotta chew it. More flavors. The old-timers will say, ah, this reminds me of the old beef we used to buy in Chinatown. You have to chew it. When you chew it, then you have all the different flavors coming out. Because people today are conditioned to fork-tender filet mignon, which you can cut . . . with your fork. For some old-timers, that's not enough flavor. So you're trading off texture for flavor."[32]

Wong even teamed up with former state veterinarian Calvin Lum, who raised grass-fed beef on a one-thousand-acre ranch on Oʻahu and whose goal was to raise hormone- and antibiotic-free beef.[33] Lum's beef made fabulous hamburgers, and not surprisingly, Wong's Pineapple Room hamburgers were voted "Best Hamburgers in Town." Eager to serve this beef at Alan Wong's, Wong eventually persuaded "Doc" to sell him beef aged for twenty-eight days. "We helped promote his product," Wong recalled. "We publicized it, and it caught on. And people today are now more aware of the benefits of eating 100 percent grass-fed beef."[34] Maui chef Gannon also had to educate her customers about grass-fed beef: "I use Maui Cattle Company beef upcountry, and I've had to educate . . . people about grass-fed beef. Because it's not like grain-fed beef at all. And the minute we started telling them on the menu, 'It's a little chewier, it's a lot more flavorful but it's chewier.' . . . They get it."[35]

Ranchers, chefs, and food writers have promoted grass-fed beef in other ways. First, they tout its health benefits. As Namkoong pointed out, "Research has shown that grass-fed beef is better nutritionally, providing more beta carotene that is converted to vitamin A, more vitamin E, and more omega-3 fatty acids than conventionally raised beef. Conjugated linoleic acids, a group of polyunsaturated fatty acids, are present in higher levels in grass-fed than grain-fed beef."[36] Ranchers and chefs on the Big Island also have promoted grass-fed beef, lamb, and goat as a way of saving "Hawaii's 160-year-old ranching tradition,"[37] and others have described it as a more sustainable product.[38] In 2014, Parker Ranch and the Ulupono Initiative created the Paniolo Cattle Company and promised "to hold back

1,400 animals annually for the local grass-fed market," which would double the quantity of grass-fed beef available for local consumption.[39]

By promoting grass-fed beef, chefs and journalists have drawn attention to the larger and virtually insoluble declining-ranch problem. The truth is that no matter how much grass-fed beef is produced in the islands, it will not meet local demand. In the end, Hawai'i will have to remain dependent on the large mainland operations for its beef and pork even as more grass-fed beef is produced locally.

Sustainability

The ranching industry's predicament points to the larger issue of sustainability. Because the islands are located 2,500 miles from the mainland United States, Hawai'i has long had to rely on food imports, a reality that most island residents have learned to accept. What they may not know is that precontact Hawai'i was actually self-sufficient economically, sustaining nearly a million Hawaiians with the fruits of the land and sea. During the nineteenth century, however, this "indigenous food system" was undermined by American missionaries and businessmen and subjected to the forces of global capitalism.[40] Until World War II, Hawai'i consumed locally produced milk, eggs, and meat, which were supplemented by imported canned, dried, and refrigerated foods.[41] Nonetheless, the state maintained its self-sufficiency in eggs and dairy production through the 1970s.[42]

Recognizing the problem posed by this reliance on imports, state authorities convened a group of planners, politicians, businesspeople, consultants, and scholars who were asked to draw up a long-term plan for what was termed the "sustainable future of Hawai'i." The product of those deliberations, the *Hawai'i 2050 Sustainability Plan*, is a remarkable document. First, it catalogs the problems facing the state and recognizes their severity as "the steady deterioration of public infrastructure, lack of affordable housing, continued reliance on a service-based economy, the vulnerability of Hawai'i in a volatile global energy market, possible interruptions in travel and critical food supplies, threats to our fragile island ecosystems, and the increasing numbers of residents and visitors."[43]

The plan also lays out annual benchmarks and longer-term "intermediate steps" to gauge progress toward the goals to be achieved by 2020 and

2050.[44] These benchmarks and goals, in turn, have inspired several state-wide institutions and agencies to articulate their own goals. For example, the state department of energy proposed the 2008 Clean Energy Initiative to achieve "70 percent clean energy by 2030,"[45] and in 2015, the University of Hawaiʻi adopted policies designed to make its campuses carbon neutral by 2050.[46]

The *Hawaiʻi 2050 Sustainability Plan* is notable for a third reason: it affirms the wisdom of what was described as the "traditional Kanaka Maoli [Hawaiian] concept of the ahupuaʻa [land division] resource and behavioral management system as a philosophical foundation for a sustainable Hawaiʻi."[47] Hawaiʻi is one of a small number of states that have recognized the value of indigenous institutions and their relevance in the twenty-first century. Alaska allows Alaska Natives and long-term residents to enjoy "subsistence fishing and hunting" rights, and US Supreme Court rulings allowed Washington and Minnesota to stop subjecting Native Americans to state game laws.[48]

Despite these efforts, Hawaiʻi is still dependent on imports overall, but it now is less dependent on imported fruits and vegetables.[49] Between 2005 and 2011, approximately 33 to 35 percent of the fruits and vegetables consumed in the islands were grown locally,[50] and in 2011, the College of Tropical Agriculture and Human Resources at the University of Hawaiʻi at Mānoa reported that by 2020, the state may be able to produce 85 percent of its fruits and vegetables.[51] This is the reasoning behind the Buy Local, It Matters, Kauai Made, and Grown on Maui initiatives, and why state and county officials have been searching for ways to help the small and midsize farmers on the neighbor islands with favorable property tax and water programs.[52] Even more important, the broader public recognizes that diversified agriculture, more than many other sectors of the local economy, offers opportunities for greater self-sufficiency.[53] In fact, beginning in 2005, Hawaiʻi residents have shown "a growing interest . . . [in efforts] to increase the State's ability to produce more of its own food. More consumers are seeking access to local fresh produce, and retailers are responding by labeling local products and building new connections to local producers. Some grocers and many restaurants have made it part of their brand to promote fresh and flavorful local products and preparations."[54] Local fruit and vegetables offer the greatest potential for sustainability.

The HRC chefs have long championed sustainability. Jean-Marie Josselin may have been the first to declare, in the 1990s, that his goal was to rely entirely on local produce. Ferguson and Gannon showed how self-sufficiency might work by using local ingredients in recipes.[55] Merriman has been the most active advocate of sustainability. He made the case in two powerful editorials arguing for locally produced food that is grown in a sustainable way. In the first, he explained that "locally grown food has the advantage of freshness and flavor, supports Hawai'i's economy," and perpetuates "Hawai'i's agricultural economy." In the second editorial, Merriman announced that "the time has come for Hawaii to support its farmers, growers, and ranchers as never before," pointing out that "one acre of agricultural land that's approximately the size of a football field can produce 42,800 pounds of strawberries, 35,000 pounds of lettuce, or 11,600 pounds of sweet corn."[56] Merriman also has championed the "nose-to-tail" approach to butchering, in which chefs use the entire animal and even those cuts of beef that are hard to sell.[57] By 2011, Merriman could claim that 90 percent of what his restaurants served was locally produced.[58]

Among the younger chefs, the most vocal advocate of sustainability is Ed Kenney, with his "local first, organic when possible, with aloha always" mantra. He not only has embraced the "nose-to-tail" approach; he has made it part of the business plan for his restaurants, which has allowed him to use all the parts of the pigs he buys from Shinsato Farm in Kahalu'u on O'ahu.[59] As he explained, "A slow-roasted shoulder will last for four nights, braised pork belly two nights, cured ham two nights," and the liver, kidneys, and head can be made into sausage, pâté, and terrines. He also has been a Cooking for Solutions Chef Ambassador, with a commitment to serving and promoting ocean-fresh seafood.[60] Other chefs with island roots stress as well the importance of what Kenney calls the "aloha 'āina, love of the land, love of that which provides us with food" and realize that this vision will be one of the many challenges facing the next generation in the islands.[61]

Final Thoughts

What the HRC chefs achieved over the nearly three decades since their meeting in August 1991 is, by any measure, impressive. They helped undo the racialized and gendered regimes still operating in the kitchens of the best restaurants in the islands in the 1980s. They created a distinctive regional cuisine based on a new locavorism and brought the fine-dining scene in the islands in line with the "food revolution" taking place on the mainland in the 1980s and 1990s. By attracting the attention of national tastemakers, Hawai'i Regional Cuisine brought its creators and their restaurants unexpected celebrity and a place in a larger national, and even global, restaurant world. They celebrated "local foods" and favorites from a broader American culinary vernacular, eroding the dominance of French/Continental cuisine and paving the way for their successors and the smart-casual dining style of the early twenty-first century. In short, they reimagined the local culinary idiom. Now, however, the HRC chefs and their successors face a final and most difficult challenge: the creation of a food scene in the islands informed by a plausible sustainability, with chefs and consumers buying more and more locally produced vegetables and fruits, accepting the limits on the catch of deepwater bottomfish, recognizing the structural problems plaguing ranchers in the state, and supporting local aquaculture operations.

Glossary

adobo: Filipino stew made by cooking pork or chicken in vinegar, garlic, and soy sauce

ahi: Yellowfin tuna (*Thunnus albacares*)

ahupua‘a: Hawaiian term for parcel of land extending from the uplands to the sea

akule: Big-eyed scad (*Selar crumenophthalmus*)

ali‘i: Hawaiian chief

arare: Japanese rice crackers

arrowroot: Starch made from roots of a plant (*Maranta arundinacea*) found in Asia and the Pacific

bacalhau: Portuguese dried and salted cod; also spelled "bacalao"

bagoong: Filipino version of fermented fish or shrimp sauce

balut: Filipino dish made with a hard-boiled chicken or duck embryo served in its eggshell

bento: Portable Japanese lunch consisting of rice, protein, vegetables, and pickles

beurre blanc: French sauce made by blending cold butter with a reduction of vinegar or white wine and shallots

bitter melon: Melon (*Momordica charantia*) common in Chinese and South Asian cuisine

black beans: Fermented and salted soybeans used in Chinese cooking

bok choy: (*Brassica rapa* subsp. *chinensis*), a type of cabbage common in China and Southeast Asia

bouillabaisse: Type of fish soup or stew common in Mediterranean countries

Boursin: Type of cheese that originated in Normandy, France

ceviche: Mexican dish made by marinating filets of fish in lime or lemon juice and olive oil

char siu: Cantonese-style barbecued pork

Chinese cabbage: Type of cabbage (*Brassica pekinensis*) cultivated chiefly in north China

chow fun: Cantonese-style fried rice noodle dish made with beef or pork

choy sum: Chinese flowering cabbage (*Brassica chinensis* var. *parachinensis*) native to south China

confit: French dish made by preserving meat or fowl in its own fat

congee: Type of rice porridge popular in south China

coriander seeds: *Coriandrum sativum*; used as a spice in Europe, South Asia, and South America

coulis: French puree or sieved sauce made from vegetables or fruit

daikon: Giant white radish (*Raphanus sativus*)

dashi: Japanese stock made from dried anchovies, dried kelp, or smoked bonito

dim sum: Southern Chinese dumpling of chopped meat, seafood, fowl, or vegetables wrapped in paper-thin dough and steamed or fried

edamame: Pod soybean (*Glycine max*), typically boiled and eaten

enchilada: Mexican dish consisting of a tortilla rolled around a filling and sauced

enoki: Winter mushroom (*Flammulina velutipes*) used in one-pot dishes in Japan

fish sauce: Sauce made by fermenting fish in brine and drawing off the supernatant liquid; used widely in Southeast Asia

five-spice powder: Chinese spice mixture made of star anise, fennel, cloves, cassia, and Sichuan peppers

fukujinzuke: Japanese pickle made of seven thinly sliced, salted, and pickled vegetables

furikake: Japanese rice topping made of toasted seaweed, sesame seeds, and dried fish

galangal: Aromatic ginger-like rhizome in the *Zingiberaceae* family used in Southeast Asian cuisine

garam masala: Mixture of spices such as cardamom, black cumin seeds, whole cloves, and peppercorns that is sprinkled on Indian dishes as they are being finished

ginger: Root of a plant (*Zingiber officinale*) consumed fresh or dried

gochujang sauce: Korean chili paste made from glutinous rice, fermented soybean powder, chili powder, and salt

guava: Fruit of a plant (*Psidium guajava*) grown in Central America, Asia, and Hawai'i *halo halo:* Filipino dessert made with shaved ice, fruit, sweet beans, and condensed milk

haupia: Hawaiian pudding made with coconut cream and arrowroot

Hawaiian salt: Unrefined Hawaiian salt used in purification ceremonies and cooking; also called "'alaea salt"

he'e: Hawaiian name for octopus (*Polypus* sp.)

hoisin sauce: Chinese sauce made with soybeans, flour, sugar, salt, garlic, and chilis and used as a glaze

huli-huli: Hawaiian term meaning "to turn repeatedly"

ika: Japanese name of squid (cephalopod of the order *Teuthida*); widely consumed in Asia and the Pacific

ikura: Salmon eggs

imu: Type of underground oven common in the Pacific and Southeast Asia

'inamona: Hawaiian relish made from candlenuts (*Aleurites moluccana*)

Japanese chilis: Japanese variety of chilis (*Capsicum annuum*) also known as Japone, Hontaka, or Santaka

Japanese eggplant: Type of eggplant (*Solanum melongena*) found in Japan

kabayaki: Japanese technique of grilling fish (such as eel) while basting it with a sweet sauce made of shoyu, mirin, and sugar

kabocha: Japanese pumpkin (*Cucurbita moschata*)

kaffir lime: Citrus widely used in Southeast Asian cuisines

kai choy: Mustard greens (*Braccica juncea*) grown throughout China

kaiware: Young daikon or radish shoots

kalamansi: Type of lime (*Citrofortunella microcarpa*); also spelled "calamansi"

kalo: Hawaiian word for taro (*Colocasia esculenta*)

kālua pig: Hawaiian dish made of pig baked in an underground oven (H. imu)

kamaboko: Japanese fish-paste loaf

kampachi: Amberjack (*Seriola lalandi*); found in both the Atlantic and Pacific Oceans

kanten: Japanese name for agar-agar (*Gelidium amansii*); used to make jellied dishes

kappō: Type of refined Japanese cuisine

kare kare: Filipino stew made with meat (beef, oxtail, or tripe), vegetables, and peanut sauce

katsuobushi: Dried, smoked and mold-cured bonito (J. *katsuo*)

kayu: Japanese porridge made from rice; similar to Chinese congee *kecap manis:* Indonesian sweet soy sauce

kilawin: Filipino-style ceviche made with meat; common in northern Philippines

kinilaw: Filipino-style ceviche made with raw seafood

kinome: Young leaves of a Japanese pepper (*sanshō* [*Zanthoxylum piperitum*])

kombu: Japanese word for kelp (*Laminaria* spp.); used in Japanese cuisine in dried, salted, or fresh form

kudzu starch: Thickening agent made from the *kudzu* vine (*Pueraria lobata*)

kukui: Candlenut tree (*Aleurites moluccana*) whose nuts are made into a relish

kūlolo: Hawaiian pudding made of baked or steamed taro and coconut cream

lamian: Type of Chinese noodle made by stretching by hand; dates from sixteenth century

laulau: Hawaiian dish; pork, beef, fish, or taro tops wrapped in ti or banana leaves and baked, steamed, or broiled

lechon pork: Filipino roasted suckling pig

lemongrass: Type of grass (*Cymbopogon citratus*) widely used in Southeast Asian cuisines

li hing mui: Salted, dried plum made in southern China and popular in Hawaiʻi

liliko'i: Hawaiian name for passion fruit (*Passiflora edulis*)

limu: General Hawaiian name for plants living in either freshwater or seawater; also algae

linguica: Type of Portuguese smoked and cured pork sausage

loco moco: Local dish consisting of a plate of hot short-grain rice, topped with a fried hamburger patty, brown gravy, and a fried egg

lomilomi salmon: Hawaiian dish made with raw salmon mixed with salt and onions

lotus root: Rhizome (*Nelumbo nucifera*) widely used in East Asian cuisines

luau: Hawaiian feast; so named because lūʻau, young taro tops, are always served

lup cheong: Cantonese name of a type of Chinese sausage made of pork and pork liver and duck liver; also spelled "lap cheong"

lychee: Chinese fruit (*Litchi chinensis*) common in south and southeastern China; also spelled "litchi"

mahimahi: Dolphinfish (*Coryphaena hippurus*)

manapua: Hawaiian pidgin rendering of *mea ʻono puaʻu*, Hawaiian for Chinese pork cake; a kind of dim sum

masago: Eggs of the capelin fish (*Mallotus villosus*), a smelt-like fish whose roe is prized in Japan matsutake: Mushroom (*Tricholoma matsutake*) prized in Japan

mentaiko: Japanese name for Alaska pollack roe that has been salted and flavored with chilis

miki: Filipino soup made with chicken stock, rice noodles, shredded chicken, a hard-boiled egg, and chicharron (a dish consisting of fried pork belly or fried pork rinds)

mirin: Type of sweet sake

miso: Japanese paste made from fermented soybeans, barley, or rice

mitsuba: Japanese wild chervil (*Cryptotaenia japonica*)

mizuna: Japanese pot herb mustard (*Brassica campestris* var. *lanciniifolia*)

moano: Hawaiian name for adult goatfish (*Parupeneus multifasciatus*)

mochi: Japanese glutinous-rice cakes

mochigome: Japanese glutinous rice (*Oryza sativa* subsp. *Japonica glutinosa* group)

moi: Hawaiian name for Pacific threadfin (*Polydactylus sexfilis*)

mung bean sprouts: *Phaseolus aureus* or *Vigna radiata*

nagaimo: Japanese name for a type of Chinese yam (*Dioscorea opposita*)

nage: Savory French broth made of wine, vegetables, and herbs; used to poach fish

nam pla: Vietnamese fish sauce made by salting and fermenting anchovies for a long period of time

namasu: Japanese dish of vinegared raw meat, fish, or vegetables that dates from seventh century

natto: Japanese fermented soybeans that are soaked, steamed, and inoculated with *Bacillus subtilis* var. *natto*

nohu: Hawaiian name of scorpion fish (*Scorpaenopsis cacopsis*)

nori: General Japanese name for laver (*Porphyra* spp.) consumed in Japan

nuoc mam: High-grade Vietnamese fish sauce

ogo: Japanese name of a type of seaweed (*Gracilaria* spp.)

onaga: Hawaiian name of long-tail red snapper (*Etelis coruscans*)

ono: Hawaiian name of wahoo (*Acanthocybium solandri*)

'ōpakapaka: Hawaiian name of short-tail pink snapper (*Pristipomoides filamentosus*)

'opihi: Hawaiian name of a type of limpet (*Siphoneria* sp.)

orange peel: Sun-dried orange peel used in spicy Chinese dishes from Hunan and Sichuan

pa'i 'ai: Hawaiian word for undiluted hard poi

pancit: Filipino version of Chinese-style fried noodles

panko: Japanese dried bread crumbs

pao doce: Portuguese sweet bread

papaya: Tropical fruit (*Carica papaya*) brought to Hawaiʻi from Central America

pastele: Puerto Rican version of a tamale; called *patele* in Hawaiʻi

patis: Filipino sauce that is a by-product of the process used to make bagoong

pesto: Genoan sauce made with fresh basil, olive oil, Parmesan cheese, and pine nuts

pho: Vietnamese noodle soup made with beef broth, rice noodles, bean sprouts, and fresh herbs

pinakbet: Stir-fried vegetable dish made with fermented shrimp or fish sauce

pipi kaula: Hawaiian name for salted and sun-dried jerked beef introduced from Mexico

pīpīnola: Hawaiian name for chayote (*Sechium edule*), whose fruit, leaves, and roots are edible

pohā: Hawaiian name for the Cape gooseberry (*Physalis peruviana*)

pohole: Maui name for hōʻiʻo (*Diplazium* [*Athyrium*] *arnottii*), a fiddlehead fern

poi: Chief starch in Hawaiian diet; made of cooked, pounded taro corms and thinned with water

ponzu: Japanese dipping sauce made with soy sauce and citrus juice

pork hash: Cantonese dish made with steamed ground pork, minced ginger, and green onions, garnished with slices of Chinese sausage

quesadilla: Mexican corn or flour tortilla stuffed with cheese, folded, and grilled

ramen: Chinese-style wheat-noodle dish, with many regional variations in Japan

rayu: Japanese name for Chinese red chili oil made by steeping red chili flakes in vegetable or peanut oil

rice paper: Vietnamese rice paper made from white rice flour, tapioca flour, salt, and water

rice wine vinegar: Japanese vinegar made from fermented rice

sablefish: (*Anoplopoma fimbria*); also called "black cod"

saffron: Spice made from the stigmas of crocus flowers (*Crocus sativus*)

saimin: Type of noodle soup served in Hawaiʻi; the word "saimin" is derived from Chinese for "thin noodle"

sambal olek: Southeast Asian spice made by crushing uncooked chilis, citrus juice, and salt

sanshō: Japanese pepper (*Zanthoxylum piperitum*)

sashimi: Japanese dish of sliced raw seafood, either fish or shellfish

sauce bâtarde: French sauce made with butter, flour, salt, egg yolks, cream, and lemon juice

sauce vin blanc: French sauce made with white wine, fish stock, and cream

sea asparagus: Flowering plant (*Salicornia europaea*) native to North America, Europe, South Africa, and South Asia; also called "glasswort," "pickleweed," "picklegrass," and "samphire"

shaoxing: Chinese wine made from glutinous rice; originated in Shaoxing, China

shichimi tōgarashi: Japanese condiment made of red pepper (*Capsicum annuum* var. *conoides*), chilis, mustard, sesame seeds, and seaweed, among other variable ingredients

shiitake: Japanese mushroom (*Lentinus edodes*)

shishito: Japanese name for sweet green pepper (*Capsicum annuum* var. *angulosum*)

shiso: Japanese name for perilla, beefsteak plant (*Perilla frutescens* var. *crispa*)

shoyu: Japanese soy sauce

shutome: Japanese name for broadbill swordfish (*Xiphias gladius*)

Sichuan chili sauce: Sauce made with crushed chilis and salt; common in Sichuan

sinigang: Filipino dish that stews meat or seafood in vinegary sauce

snow peas: Young pea pods (var. *Macrocarpa seringe*) used in Cantonese cooking

somen: Japanese thin white-flour noodles, typically eaten cold in summer, with a dipping sauce

soy sauce: Condiment made by mixing steamed soybeans and roasted, crushed wheat with a fermenting agent (*Aspergillus oryzae* and *Aspergillus soyae*); widely used in Asia

spring roll: Fried Chinese roll filled with minced meat and vegetables; dates from seventeenth century

squid lūʻau: Hawaiian dish made with squid, young taro leaves, and coconut milk

sriracha: Hot sauce made from chilis, distilled vinegar, garlic, sugar, and salt; named for a city in eastern Thailand

star anise: Dried fruit of an evergreen tree (*Illicium verum*) found in China

Surinam cherry: Cherry (*Eugenia uniflora*) found on east coast of South America

tako: Japanese word for octopus (*Octopus vulgaris*.mizudako, madako *Paroctopus dofleini*.iidako *Polypus fangsias*)

tamarind: Fruit from an evergreen tree (*Tamarindus indica*) that is crushed and used in Southeast Asian cuisine tapioca pearls: Clear gelatinous balls made from tapioca flour

tare: Japanese basting sauce made of soy sauce, miso, and sugar or mirin

taro: Root plant (*Colocasia esculenta*) that spread to the Pacific from India or Southeast Asia

tatsoi: Type of Chinese turnip (*Brassica rapa* var. *rosularis*)

teriyaki: Japanese method of grilling with a basting sauce made of soy sauce, sake, mirin, and sugar

Thai ginger: Variety of Thai ginger (*Alpina galanga*); also known as greater galangal

tocino: Filipino dish containing pork cured with sugar and salt

tofu: Asian staple made with soy milk and a coagulant such as calcium sulfate or magnesium chloride and formed into blocks; widely used in Asian cooking

'uala: Hawaiian word for sweet potato (*Ipomoea batatas*); from South America but common in the Pacific

udon: Japanese white-flour noodles, typically served in hot broth

uhu: Hawaiian name for parrot fish (*Scarus perspicillatus*)

'ulu: Hawaiian name for breadfruit (*Artocarpus altilis*)

ume: Prunus mume (*Armeniaca mume*), related to both Chinese plums and Japanese apricots

unagi: Japanese eel (*Anguilla japonica*)

uni: Japanese word for sea urchin (*Echinoidea* var. *genera*), whose ovaries are a delicacy in Japan

vadouvan: French version of garam masala

vinaigrette: French salad dressing made with oil, vinegar, salt, and pepper; also used as a marinade common in Europe

Wagyu: Type of beef raised in Japan; famous for its marbling and unsaturated fat

wakame: Japanese word for type of seaweed (*Undaria pinnitifida*) used in Japanese cuisine

wasabi: Japanese word for a type of horseradish (*Wasabia japonica*)

wonbok: Type of cabbage (*Brassica chinensis*) common in south China

yakitori: Japanese dish made with skewered and grilled pieces of chicken or sparrows

yuba: Soymilk skin

yuzu: Japanese citron (*Citrus junos*), whose juice and peel are used in Japanese cuisine

Notes

CHAPTER 1: ORIGINS

Epigraph: Quoted in Colman Andrews, "Hawaiian Melting Pot: The Diversity of the 50th State's Culture Is Manifest in Its New, Eclectic Cooking," *Los Angeles Times*, February 11, 1990.

1. Some of the chefs at the islands' fine-dining establishments were not trained in Europe. Michel Martin, the founder-owner of Michel's in Waikīkī, was the most famous of those who had no training in classical French cuisine. Although he was raised in France, he learned his craft after he migrated to Hawai'i as a teenager and opened his restaurant in 1942. Another exception was the chefs at the Willows, arguably the most famous fine-dining establishment in the islands from the 1940s until 1980. It opened in July 1944 on land once owned by Hawaiian royalty and initially served only until 7 p.m. because of wartime blackout regulations. Once the war ended, it became a full-fledged restaurant, patronized by the television celebrity Arthur Godfrey of *Hawaii Calls* and Hollywood celebrities such as Dorothy Lamour and Johnny Weissmuller. Yet none of its chefs had formal culinary training: they simply liked to cook (Wanda A. Adams, "Michel Martin, 100, Shared Fine French Cuisine with the Isles," *Honolulu Advertiser*, January 19, 2008; and Adams, "Guide to Good Eating," *Honolulu Star-Bulletin*, April 9, 1961).

2. Arjun Appadurai, "How to Make a National Cuisine," *Comparative Studies in Society and History* 30, no. 1 (1988): 4.

3. Food historian Rachel Laudan has written the definitive study of "local food": *The Food of Paradise: Exploring Hawaii's Culinary Heritage* (Honolulu: University of Hawai'i Press, 1996), 5–9, 16–103. See also Arnold Hiura, *Kau Kau: Cuisine and Culture in the Hawaiian Islands* (Honolulu: Watermark Publishing, 2009), 54–77; and Kathryn Besio and LeeRay Costa, "Eating Hawai'i: Local Foods and Place-Making in Hawai'i Regional Cuisine," *Social & Cultural Geography* 12, no. 8 (2011): 839–854.

4. See Lawrence H. Fuchs, *Hawaii Pono: A Social History* (New York: Harcourt, Brace & World, 1961), 38, 43–46, 59–67; and Stephen Sumida, *And the View from the Shore: Literary Traditions of Hawai'i* (Seattle: University of Washington Press, 1991), xiv–xv. Haunani-Kay Trask argues against the use of the word "local" to describe the

nonindigenous population of the islands; see her "Settlers of Color and 'Immigrant' Hegemony: 'Locals' in Hawai'i," *Amerasia Journal* 26, no. 2 (2000): 2. See also Candace Fujikane and Jonathan Y. Okamura, eds., *Asian Settler Colonialism: From Local Governance to the Habits of Everyday Life in Hawai'i* (Honolulu: University of Hawai'i Press, 2008), 25–29.

5. Judith Kirkendall, "Hawaiian Ethnogastronomy: The Development of a Pidgin-Creole Cuisine" (PhD diss., University of Hawai'i at Mānoa, 1985), 331.

6. See the fine study of the racialization of life in the islands before annexation by historian Gary Okihiro: *Island World: A History of Hawai'i and the United States* (Berkeley: University of California Press, 2009), 98–124.

7. Fuchs, *Hawaii Pono*, 43–47. The Big Five firms, which were established in the nineteenth century and dominated the colony's economic life, are C. Brewer & Co., Castle & Cooke, American Factors, Alexander & Baldwin, and Theo H. Davies. For an account of their history, see ibid., 22, 53–55.

8. English Standard Schools were created in the 1920s and 1930s for Caucasian students whose parents wanted their children to have classmates who spoke standard English and not pidgin English, the local dialect. Entrance to these schools was based on examination, and most of the students were Caucasian, but in later years, the schools reflected a greater ethnic mix, including students of Japanese and Chinese ancestry. English Standard Schools were part of a system of de facto segregation and were abolished in 1947 (ibid., 274–279).

9. David Stannard, *Before the Horror: The Population of Hawai'i on the Eve of Western Contact* (Honolulu: Social Science Research Institute, University of Hawai'i, 1989), 7, 45, 50–75; Sally Engle Merry, *Colonizing Hawai'i: The Cultural Power of Law* (Princeton, NJ: Princeton University Press, 2000), 93–95; Jonathan Kay Kamakawiwo'ole Osorio, *Dismembering Lāhui: A History of the Hawaiian Nation to 1887* (Honolulu: University of Hawai'i Press, 2002), 1–144; Noenoe Silva, *Aloha Betrayed: Native Hawaiian Resistance to American Colonialism* (Durham, NC: Duke University Press, 2004), 39–44; Lilikalā Kame'eleihiwa, "Kualana O'ahu me he 'Āina Momona," in *Food and Power in Hawai'i: Visions of Food Democracy*, ed. Aya Hirata Kimura and Krisnawati Suryanata (Honolulu: University of Hawai'i Press, 2016), 68–72.

10. The overthrow of the monarchy and annexation are described well in Osorio, *Dismembering Lāhui*, 145–249; and Silva, *Aloha Betrayed*, 123–203.

11. Fuchs, *Hawaii Pono*, 68; Consul General Moroi, "Americanizing the Japanese in Hawaii," *Mid-Pacific Magazine*, October 16, 1918; Royal Mead, "Sugar Interests in Hawaii," *San Francisco Chronicle*, July 18, 1910, quoted in Fuchs, *Hawaii Pono*, 49.

12. Fuchs reports that "as many as thirty of the early white residents married Hawaiian women of chiefly rank" (*Hawaii Pono*, 38). See also Osorio, *Dismembering Lāhui*, 27, 70, 82, 87, 140, 153, 242.

13. The Kamehameha School for Boys opened in 1887, and the one for girls opened in 1894; 'Iolani School was founded in 1863 and was affiliated with the Anglican Church of Hawai'i; Mid-Pacific Institute was created in 1908 with the merger of the Kawaiaha'o School for Girls and the Mills Institute for Boys; and the College of St. Louis was founded in 1846 by the Congregation of the Sacred Hearts of Jesus and Mary and was located first in windward O'ahu and then, after 1881, in Honolulu.

14. Fuchs, *Hawaii Pono*, 3, 57–59.

15. *The Friend*, January 1917, 3. By 1940, the number of Caucasians had risen to 25 percent of the colony's population (Fuchs, *Hawaii Pono*, 52).

16. The military presence grew to 17,169 in 1927, increased to 24,952 in 1937, and, after the Pearl Harbor attack, jumped to 135,907 in 1942, peaking at 406,811 in 1944 (Robert C. Schmitt, *Historical Statistics of Hawaii* [Honolulu: University of Hawai'i Press, 1962], 10).

17. W. A. Pickering to CG, Hawaiian Department, Sub: Annual Inspection, Scho-field Barracks, Territory of Hawaii, Fiscal Year 1935, June 30, 1935, Adjutant General's Office Document Number 333.1, National Archives Record Group Inventory Entry Number 11, Record Group 159; and Joseph Y. K. Akana Interview, in Center for Oral History, *Waikīkī, 1900–1985* (Honolulu: Center for Oral History, 1985), 11; and Walter Maciejowski to Brian M. Linn, January 6, 1993, quoted in Brian McAllister Linn, *Guardians of Empire: The U.S. Army and the Pacific, 1902–1940* (Chapel Hill: University of North Carolina Press, 1997), 123, 126.

18. Fuchs, *Hawaii Pono*, 49–52.

19. Arthur Suehiro, *Honolulu Stadium: Where Hawai'i Played* (Honolulu: Watermark Publishing, 1995), 25–117; and Michael Okihiro, *AJA Baseball in Hawaii: Ethnic Pride and Tradition* (Honolulu: Hawaii Hochi, 1999), 7–43.

20. Kirkendall, "Hawaiian Ethnogastronomy," 326, 352–355.

21. Ibid., 124–26. See Woman's Society of Central Union Church, *Hawaiian Cook Book*, 6th ed. (Honolulu: Honolulu Star Bulletin, 1920); and Helen Alexander, *The Helen Alexander Hawaiian Cook Book* (Honolulu: Advertiser Publishing Company, 1938).

22. Woman's Society of Central Union Church, *Hawaiian Cook Book*, 7–9.

23. Elinor Langton, "A Hawaiian Bill of Fare," *Paradise of the Pacific* 16 (April 1903): 11.

24. Stannard adds, "[I]t is now almost certain that Hawaiians in 1778 had life expectancies greater than their European contemporaries" (*Before the Horror*, 60–61).

25. For a detailed account of the immigrants' food and recipes, see Laudan, *The Food of Paradise*, 106–159; and Hiura, *Kau Kau*, 26–53.

26. "What Chinese Eat," *Paradise of the Pacific* 15 (April 1902): 9–10; Franklin Ng, "Food and Culture: Chinese Restaurants in Hawai'i," in *Chinese America: History and Perspectives* (San Francisco: Chinese Historical Society of America with UCLA Asian American Studies Center, 2010), 113; and Hiura, *Kau Kau*, 4–25.

27. Robert C. Schmitt, *Firsts and Almost Firsts in Hawaii*, ed. Ronn Ronck (Honolulu: University of Hawai'i Press, 1995), 115.

28. Ng, "Food and Culture," 114.

29. Ibid., 115; and John Heckathorn, "Dining—The Oldest Restaurant in Hawaii and the Newest," *Honolulu Magazine*, November 1987, 348–352.

30. Center for Oral History, *The Oroku, Okinawan Connection: Local-Style Restaurants in Hawai'i* (Honolulu: Social Science Research Institute, 2004), app. A.

31. Michiko Kodama-Nishimoto, Warren Nishimoto, and Cynthia Oshiro, eds., *Talking Hawai'i's Story: Oral Histories of an Island People* (Honolulu: University of Hawai'i Press, 2009), 164–167.

32. Schmitt, *Firsts and Almost Firsts*, 115.

33. Clarence E. Glick, *Sojourners and Settlers: Chinese Migrants in Hawaii* (Honolulu: Hawaii Chinese History Center, 1977), 80–81.

34. Center for Oral History, *The Oroku*, app. A.

35. "The New Spencecliff," *Sunday Star-Bulletin / Advertiser*, June 7, 1987.

36. Alan Matsuoka, "Lau Yee Chai: Not an Ordinary Chop Suey House," *Honolulu Star-Bulletin*, March 12, 1991.

37. "Clark's Tour No. 8 Menu," Alexander Young Hotel, February 10, 1928; menu, Halekulani Hotel, April 16, 1957; and Center for Oral History, *Waikīkī*, 1726–1727.

38. Fern Tomisato Yoshida, interview by Samuel H. Yamashita, January 12, 2012; Gladys Sato, interview by Samuel H. Yamashita, January 10, 2012; Frank Leake, interview by Samuel H. Yamashita, August 24, 2013.

39. Center for Oral History, *Waikīkī*, 1731.

40. David Kamp, *The United States of Arugula: How We Became a Gourmet Nation* (New York: Broadway Books, 2006), 152.

41. Kirkendall, "Hawaiian Ethnogastronomy, 137; Ng, "Food and Culture," 13; and Kodama-Nishimoto, Nishimoto, and Oshiro, *Talking Hawai'i's Story*, 11, 46–48, 52–55, 72, 74–75, 83, 120, 156–157, 211–213, 225, 249, 271–272, 296–298.

42. Donna R. Gabaccia, *We Are What We Eat: Ethnic Food and the Making of Americans* (Cambridge, MA: Harvard University Press, 1998), 122–148.

43. Stannard, *Before the Horror*, 46–48.

44. Ibid.

45. "The Philippine-American War, 1899–1902," United States Department of State, Office of the Historian, https://history.state.gov/milestones/1899-1913/war.

46. Bernard Cohn, *Colonialism and Its Forms of Knowledge* (Princeton, NJ: Princeton University Press, 1996), 3–4. Cohn was inspired by Edward Said's *Orientalism* (New York: Vintage Books, 1979), but his analysis of British colonialism in South Asia represents a refinement of Said's important but not unflawed approach.

47. Zilkia Janer, "(In)edible Nature: New World Food and Coloniality," *Cultural Studies* 21, no. 3 (April–May 2007): 386–398; Janer, *Latino Food Culture* (Greenwood, CT: Greenwood Press, 2008), 3–6.

48. Janer, "(In)edible Nature," 390–392, 400–402. See also Amy B. Trubek, *Haute Cuisine: How the French Invented the Culinary Profession* (Philadelphia: University of Pennsylvania Press, 2000), 64–68.

49. Bob Dye, "Hawaii's First Celebrity Chef," in *We Go Eat: A Mixed Plate from Hawai'i's Food Culture*, ed. Susan Yim (Honolulu: Hawai'i Council for the Humanities, 2008), 55.

50. Ibid.

51. Bird wrote eleven travelogues during her peripatetic life, including *The Hawaiian Archipelago* (London: J. Murray, 1875).

52. Bob Dye, "Hawaii's First Celebrity Chef," in Yim, *We Go Eat*, 58–59.

53. Rachel Laudan, *Cuisine and Empire: Cooking in World History* (Berkeley: University of California Press, 2015), 280–282.

54. Woman's Society of Central Union Church, *Hawaiian Cook Book*, 113–114, 48–49.

55. Ibid., 5, 35, 109–110.

56. Willa Tanabe, "By the Book: Cookbooks in Hawai'i," in Yim, *We Go Eat*, 62–63.

57. Trubek, *Haute Cuisine*, 2.

58. Sato interview.

59. Center for Oral History, *The Oroku*, 15.

60. Sato interview.

61. Yoshida interview.

62. Sam Choy and Evelyn Cook, *With Sam Choy: Cooking from the Heart* (Honolulu: Mutual Publishing, 1995), 4 (italics in original).

63. Lucy Jokiel, "Food for Thought," *Hawaii Business*, November 1989, 68.

64. Krishnendu Ray, *The Ethnic Restaurateur* (London: Bloomsbury Academic, 2016), 6.

65. Although fourteen chefs attended the meeting on August 27, 1991, two—René Boujet and John Farnsworth—did not attend subsequent meetings. The twelve who did are generally regarded as the founders of Hawai'i Regional Cuisine. They are (in alphabetical order) Sam Choy, Roger Dikon, Mark Ellman, Amy Ferguson, Beverly Gannon, Jean-Marie Josselin, George Mavrothalassitis, Peter Merriman, Philippe Padovani, Gary Strehl, Roy Yamaguchi, and Alan Wong (Alan Wong, interview by Samuel H. Yamashita, March 15, 2009).

66. John Heckathorn, "Delicious Decade," *Honolulu Magazine*, August 2001, 8.

67. Ibid.

68. Janice Wald Henderson, *The New Cuisine of Hawaii: Recipes from the Twelve Celebrated Chefs of Hawaii Regional Cuisine* (New York: Villard Books, 1994), 64; Merriman interview.

69. Henderson, *New Cuisine of Hawaii*, 12; Wong interview; Kamp, *United States of Arugula*, n. 115.

70. Merriman interview.

71. Janice Wald Henderson, "Farm Fresh Takes Root in Hawaii," *Los Angeles Times*, September 22, 1991. Early in 1992, Farnsworth accepted a job heading the kitchen at the new Washington Inn in Connecticut.

72. Kamp, *United States of Arugula*, 239, 259–260.

73. Roy Yamaguchi, interview by Samuel H. Yamashita, July 7, 2009.

74. Merriman interview.

75. Sam Choy, interview by Samuel H. Yamashita, April 5, 2010. See also Sam Choy, *Sam Choy's Cuisine Hawaii: Featuring the Premier Chefs of the Aloha State* (Honolulu: Pleasant Hawaii, 1990), 19.

76. Choy, *Sam Choy's Cuisine Hawaii*, 19.

77. Mark Ellman, interview by Samuel H. Yamashita, October 17, 2009; Beverly Gannon, interview by Samuel H. Yamashita, October 17, 2009; George Mavrothalassitis, interview by Samuel H. Yamashita, March 17, 2009.

78. Ellman interview.

79. Ellman, Gannon, Mavrothalassitis, Wong, and Yamaguchi interviews.

80. Henderson, *New Cuisine of Hawaii*, 12.

81. Ibid., 44.

82. Ibid., 74.

83. Ibid.

84. Ibid., 12.

85. Ibid.

86. Ibid., 96.

87. Merriman interview.

88. Henderson, *New Cuisine of Hawaii*, 84.

89. Janice Wald Henderson, "Farm Fresh Takes Root in Hawaii," *Los Angeles Times*, September 22, 1991.

90. Merriman interview.

91. Ibid.

92. Tane Datta, interview by Samuel H. Yamashita, June 29, 2011.

93. Merriman and Datta interviews.

94. Dean Okimoto, interview by Samuel H. Yamashita, August 9, 2009. For Okimoto's description of his family's farm, see Kimura and Suryanata, *Food and Power*, 207–210.

95. Merriman interview; see also Erin Lee, interview by Samuel H. Yamashita, June 28, 2011.

96. Merriman interview.

97. Ibid.

98. Choy interview.

99. See Kamp, *United States of Arugula*, 132–165, 232–266, 305–306; Lucy M. Long, *Regional American Food Culture* (Westport, CT: Greenwood Press, 2009); Ray, *The Ethnic Restaurateur*, 104.

100. Cory Stieg, "Cooking Local in Paradise," *Pennsylvania Gazette*, July–August 2013; Peter Merriman and Melanie Merriman, *Merriman's Hawaii: The Chef, the Farmers, the Food, the Islands* (Winter Park, FL: Story Farm, 2015), 17.

101. Cory Stieg, "Cooking Local in Paradise," *Pennsylvania Gazette*, July–August 2013.

102. Robert Lindsey, "It's Not Just Steak or Poi Anymore," *New York Times*, January 13, 1991 (italics added).

103. The racialization of haute cuisine has not been widely explored. See Janer, *Latino Food Culture*; Paul Freedman, *Ten Restaurants That Changed America* (New York: Liveright, 2016); and Ray, *The Ethnic Restaurateur*. Ray focuses on the experiences of chefs who were not of European descent and who longed to cook the food they knew.

104. Ray, *The Ethnic Restaurateur*, 82–83, 86.

CHAPTER 2: DEVELOPMENT

1. David Kamp uses the term "food revolution" to describe the changes that occurred in fine dining in the United States in the 1980s and 1990s:

> In truth, the American food revolution has really been more of a food *evolution*, a series of overlapping movements and subtle shifts, punctuated by the occasional seismic jolt. If there's a major difference between now and the sixties and seventies, it's that the scale is so much larger; culinary sophistication is no longer the province of a tiny gourmet elite. The historically unrivaled run of prosperity in the United States in the eighties and nineties, compounded by the culinary advances that had so excited *Time* and *Newsweek* in the previous decades, has led to the creation of an expanded leisure class that treats food as a cultural pastime, something you can follow the way you follow sports or the movies. (Kamp, *United States of Arugula*, xii–xiii)

2. My use of the term "restaurant world" was inspired by Patricia Ferguson's adaptation of sociologist Howard Becker's conception of the "art world." She defines the "restaurant world" as "the network of people whose cooperative activity . . . produces the kind of (culinary) works that (restaurant) world is noted for" (Patricia Parkhurst Ferguson, *Accounting for Taste: The Triumph of French Cuisine* [Chicago: The University of Chicago Press, 2004], 107–108; and Howard Becker, *Art Worlds* [Berkeley: University of California Press, 1982], 1–39, 131–164, 226–350).

3. Honu Seafood & Pizza, https://www.honumaui.com/; and Tom Yoneyama, "Getting Their Just Desserts," *Hawaii Business*, May 1989, 34–36.

4. Roy Yamaguchi and John Harrison, *Roy's Feasts from Hawaii* (Berkeley, CA: Ten Speed Press, 2007), 6.

5. Beverly Gannon with Bonnie Friedman, *The Hali'imaile General Store Cookbook: Home Cooking from Maui* (Berkeley, CA: Ten Speed Press, 2000), xvi.

6. Gannon with Friedman, *Hali'imaile General Store Cookbook*, xvi.

7. Tom Yoneyama, "Getting Their Just Desserts," *Hawaii Business*, May 1989, 38.

8. Waimea had a population of 1,179 in 1980, rising to 5,972 in 1990 ("1990 Census of Population and Housing: Population and Housing Unit Counts, United States," U.S. Department of Commerce, Economics and Statistics Administration, Bureau of the Census, https://www.census.gov/prod/cen1990/cph2/cph-2-1-1.pdf).

9. Susan Hooper, "Cooking Lessons," *Hawaii Business*, November 1990, 74, 78–79.

10. Paul Lasley and Elizabeth Harryman, "Dining in Hawaii: New Waves of Specialty Cuisine Hits Big Island," *Los Angeles Times*, February 5, 1989; Jennifer Lang, "Fresh Horizons in Hawaiian Food," *New York Times*, February 22, 1989.

11. Robert Lindsey, "It's Not Just Steak or Poi Anymore," *New York Times*, January 13, 1991.

12. Hooper, "Cooking Lessons," *Hawaii Business*, November 1990, 78.

13. "Roger Dikon, Maui Prince Exec Chef; Recipes," *Honolulu Advertiser*, June 21, 1989.

14. Although Alice Waters was the best-known advocate of California Cuisine, there were others: in Berkeley, Mark Miller at the Fourth Street Grill and the Santa Fe Bar & Grill; and in Los Angeles, Patrick Terrail at Ma Maison, Michael McCarty at Michael's, Wolfgang Puck at Spago, Susan Feniger and Mary Sue Milliken at City Café, and Mark Peel and Nancy Silverton at Campanile. Advocates of the New American Cuisine included Larry Forgione, who opened An American Place in New York City in 1983; Charlie Palmer, who took over at River Café in New York City in 1984; and Charlie Trotter, who opened Charlie Trotter's in Chicago in 1987 (Kamp, *United States of Arugula*, 132, 137, 140, 152, 157, 161, 168, 183, 243–244, 248, 257, 259–261, 273–278, 281–287, 299–303).

15. Wanda Adams, "Peter Merriman, Chef of Merriman's in Waimea, Big Isle, Featured," *Honolulu Advertiser*, September 12, 1990.

16. Catherine Kekoa Enomoto, "Gary Strehl, Exec. Chef at Hawaii Prince Hotel, Will Take Part in Flavors of Hawaii Dinner to Benefit Hawaii Foodbank," *Honolulu Star-Bulletin*, November 19, 1990.

17. John Heckathorn, "Dining Munching–Maui," *Honolulu Magazine*, April 1991, 87.

18. Ibid., 86. Waters' remark may be found in Colman Andrews, "Hawaiian

Melting Pot: The Diversity of the 50th State's Culture Is Manifest in Its New, Eclectic Cooking," *Los Angeles Times*, February 11, 1990.

19. Lucy Jokiel, "Food for Thought," *Hawaii Business*, November 1989, 64.

20. Vicki Viott, "Welcome to Roy's Kitchen: 'Hawaii Cooks with Roy Yamaguchi' TV Program," *Honolulu Advertiser*, October 8, 1993; and Catherine Kekoa Enomoto, "'Hawaii Cooks with Roy Yamaguchi' on KHET," *Honolulu Star-Bulletin*, October 20, 1993. *Hawaii Cooks with Roy Yamaguchi* aired eight years before *Wolfgang Puck* did (Juliette Rossant, *Super Chef: The Making of the Great Modern Restaurant Empires* [New York: Free Press, 2004], 36).

21. Kathleen Collins, "Ten TV Food-Show Firsts," *Gourmet Live*, October 19, 2011; and Kathleen Collins, *Watching What We Eat: The Evolution of Television Cooking Shows* (London: Bloomsbury Academic, 2009), 31–33. There also were dozens of regional cooking shows that featured local cuisines.

22. "Food: Everyone's in the Kitchen," *Time*, November 25, 1966.

23. In 1993, for example, a leading Japanese food guide offered reviews of 137 French restaurants—99 in Tokyo and 38 in Osaka. See Guruman, *Guide gastronomique pour gourmand: Tōkyō-Kansai furansu ryōriten gaido* (Tokyo: Shinshindō, 1992), 6–13.

24. Colman Andrews, "Best of the West," *Metropolitan Home*, November 1987; John Mariani, "The Best New Bars and Restaurants of 1987," *Esquire*, November 1987.

25. Catherine Kekoa Enomoto, "His Powers with Cuisine Are Princely—Chef Gary Strehl Is on the Verge of National Recognition," *Honolulu Star-Bulletin*, November 19, 1990.

26. Merrill Shindler, "Best of Three Worlds," *Bon Appétit*, June 1988.

27. Janice Wald Henderson, "Roy's," *Bon Appétit*, April 1991.

28. Janice Wald Henderson, "Eating Out: At Last, Honolulu Dining Comes of Age," *Food & Wine*, June 1991.

29. Mimi Sheraton, "2nd Annual Distinguished Restaurant Awards: 50 Worth the Journey," *Condé Nast Traveler*, January 1991; and "Condé Nast Traveler's Third Annual Distinguished Restaurant Awards—Fifty Worth the Journey: Nineteen New Stars Join the Honor Roll," *Condé Nast Traveler*, January 1992.

30. Ruth Reichl, "Did This Man Invent the Modern Restaurant? Michael McCarty Assesses His Place in Restaurant History: The Interview," *Los Angeles Times*, December 31, 1989.

31. Ibid.

32. The term "nouvelle cuisine" was coined by Henri Gault, Christian Millau, and André Gayot to describe what Paul Bocuse and his contemporaries offered at their restaurants in the late 1960s and through the 1970s (André Gayot, "Of Stars and Tripes: The True Story of Nouvelle Cuisine," later published as "Nouvelle Cuisine: The True Story of This Culinary French Revolution," Andre Gayot, "Nouvelle Cuisine: The True Story of the Culinary French Revolution," www.gayot.com/Restaurants/Nouvelle-Cuisine-The-True-Story; and Stephan Mennell, *All Manners of Food: Eating and Taste in England and France from the Middle Ages to the Present* (Urbana, Chicago, and Springfield: University of Illinois Press, 1996), 163–164.

33. Roy Yamaguchi, interview by Samuel H. Yamashita, July 7, 2009; and Yamaguchi and Harrison, *Roy's Feasts from Hawaii*, 5.

34. David Shaw, "And Then Came Roy," *Los Angeles Times*, December 10, 2003.

35. Janice Wald Henderson, "Roy's," *Bon Appétit*, April 1991.

36. Colman Andrews, "Can Rosalie's Succeed Where 385 North Fell on Its Soufflé?" *Los Angeles Times*, December 6, 1987.

37. Wolfgang Puck, *The Wolfgang Puck Cookbook: Recipes from Spago, Chinois and Points East and West* (New York: Random House, 1986), xiv.

38. Ibid.

39. Hayama had been a domain of the ruling shogunal family, the Tokugawas, during the Tokugawa period (1600–1867) and was the site of an imperial villa where Japanese royalty spent the summers during the modern period.

40. Rose Dosti, "Sashimi with a French Accent: Chef Shigefumi Tachibe Combines European, American—and Even Japanese—Food at Chaya Brasserie," *Los Angeles Times Magazine*, November 15, 1987, 36.

41. Kazuto Matsusaka, another Japanese chef, was beginning his career in Los Angeles in the 1980s, first at Ma Maison, next at L'Ermitage, and then at Spago. He had worked with Wolfgang Puck at Ma Maison, and Puck chose him as the chef at Chinois on Main when it opened in 1983. Russ Parsons, "The Master of Fusion," *Los Angeles Times*, March 2, 2005.

42. William Grimes, the food critic for the *New York Times* in the late 1990s, was the exception. When he reviewed the Roy's that opened in New York City, he wrote, "If clowns had a cuisine, this would be it," and he awarded the restaurant no stars, only a "satisfactory" (*New York Times*, May 26, 1999). Around the same time, Grimes famously discredited the New York restaurants of both Charlie Palmer and Daniel Boulud (Rossant, *Super Chef*, 83).

43. Sam Choy, *Sam Choy's Cuisine Hawaii: Featuring the Premier Chefs of the Aloha State* (Honolulu: Pleasant Hawaii, 1990).

44. Jean-Marie Josselin, *A Taste of Hawaii: New Cooking from the Crossroads of the Pacific* (New York: Stewart, Tabori & Chang, 2000), 9.

45. John Heckathorn, "How We Got Our Own Cuisine," *Honolulu Magazine*, August 2001. Gordon played an important part in the emergence of Hawai'i Regional Cuisine.

46. Janice Wald Henderson, *The New Cuisine of Hawaii: Recipes from the Twelve Celebrated Chefs of Hawaii Regional Cuisine* (New York: Villard Books, 1994), xvi.

47. Roy Yamaguchi and Martin Wentzel, *Pacific Bounty: Hawaii Cooks with Roy Yamaguchi* (San Francisco: KQED, 1994), 13–14.

48. *Restaurant Hospitality*, December 24, 1990.

49. *Roy's: New Directions*, November 1, 1991. *Roy's: New Directions* was a newsletter that the Hawaii Kai restaurant began to send out in the fall of 1990, initially to thirty or forty individuals and then, by July 1993, to eight hundred (*Roy's*, July 1993).

50. "Nation Cooks with Local Chef," *Honolulu Star-Bulletin*, March 29, 1994.

51. By 1994, Roy Yamaguchi had achieved two of the things that defined a "celebrity chef": his culinary skills had been recognized, and he had begun to appear on television. Over the next twenty years, he published three more cookbooks, opened more than thirty restaurants in the United States and overseas, had his own line of cookware and culinary products, appeared on every major Food Network program, and was a featured celebrity chef on cruises (Rossant, *Super Chef*, 6).

52. *Roy's*, November 1, 1991.

53. Ibid., February 1, 1991.

54. "Morsels: Ota Costars with Julia Child on TV Series," *Honolulu Star-Bulletin*, August 18, 1994.

55. Joan Clarke, "Notable Neighbor Islanders Open on Oahu," *Honolulu Advertiser*, April 19, 1995.

56. Michael Ruhlman, *The Reach of a Chef: Professional Cooks in the Age of Celebrity* (New York: Penguin, 2006), 214.

57. Joan Clarke, "Alan Wong Leaves Few Culinary Secrets Untold," *Honolulu Advertiser*, May 26, 1999.

58. "Designer Breads," *Honolulu Star-Bulletin*, September 17, 1997; "Vegas Chef Brings Starpower," *Honolulu Star-Bulletin*, June 6, 2007.

59. "Final Touches Put on Padovani's Bistro," *Honolulu Advertiser*, December 23, 1998.

60. "Alan Wong—Owner of Alan Wong's Restaurant, the Pineapple Room, Alan Wong's Hawaii in Tokyo Disneyland, Hualalai Grille by Alan Wong," Greater Good Radio, http://www.greatergoodradio.com/?p=133&trans=133.

61. Ben Wood, "Wood Craft," *Honolulu Star-Bulletin*, January 9, 1999, http://archives.starbulletin.com/1999/01/09/news/wood.html; *Palm Beach Post*, October 13, 2009.

62. Sam Choy and Evelyn Cook, *With Sam Choy: Cooking from the Heart* (Honolulu: Mutual Publishing, 1995); Yamaguchi and Harrison, *Roy's Feasts from Hawaii*.

63. Sam Choy, *The Choy of Cooking: Sam Choy's Island Cuisine* (Honolulu: Mutual Publishing, 1996); Sam Choy, *Sam Choy's Island Flavors* (New York: Hyperion, 1999).

64. Kaui Philpotts, *Great Chefs of Hawaii* (Honolulu: Mutual Publishing, 2003).

65. Beverly Russell, *Women of Taste: Recipes and Profiles of Famous Women Chefs* (New York: Wiley, 1997); Alan Wong and John Harrison, *Alan Wong's New Wave Luau: Recipes from Honolulu's Award-Winning Chef* (Berkeley, CA: Ten Speed Press, 1999).

66. See *Honolulu Magazine*, August 1995, August 1996, August 1997, August 1998, August 1999; and *Honolulu Advertiser*, October 1995, October 1996, October 1997, October 1998, October 1999.

67. Anya Von Bremzen, "America's Top 50 Restaurants," *Travel & Leisure*, April 1999.

68. Russ Lynch, "Continental Enlists Help of Isle Chef," *Honolulu Star-Bulletin*, August 26, 1996; and Betty Shimabukuro, "Chicken? Or Beef? Or Perhaps You'd Like Braised Veal with Chervil Sauce?" *Honolulu Star-Bulletin*, January 19, 2000.

69. Ray, *The Ethnic Restaurateur*, 113–114.

70. Joan Clarke, "California Chefs Give Roy Dinner to Remember," *Honolulu Advertiser*, February 1, 1995.

71. *Honolulu Star-Bulletin*, May 8, 1996.

72. Ibid.

73. Richard Martin, "Maui's Grand Chefs 'Fantasy Camp' to Spawn London Event," *Nation's Restaurant News*, April 14, 1997, 45.

74. Another famous chef came to the islands but for other reasons. In April 1997, André Soltner, chef-owner of Lutèce in New York City, visited Wong, his former mentee, to conduct master classes at Kapi'olani Community College. The visits of extraordinary celebrity chefs like Soltner brought the HRC chefs to the attention of their contemporaries in the restaurant world on the mainland and in the national media.

75. "Hawaii Chefs Net Beard Award Nominations," *Honolulu Advertiser,* March 2, 1995.

76. "Alan Wong," Greater Good Radio, http://www.greatergoodradio/?p=133.

77. John Heckathorn, "How We Got Our Own Cuisine," *Honolulu Magazine,* August 2001, RG, 32.

78. Becker, *Art Worlds,* 158.

79. John Heckathorn, "How We Got Our Own Cuisine," *Honolulu Magazine,* August 2001, RG, 32.

80. "Local Chefs in N.Y.," *Honolulu Advertiser,* October 17, 2001. As representatives of Hawai'i Regional Cuisine, Roy cooked at the James Beard House in 1992 and Roger Dikon cooked there in 1995. Gary Strehl also cooked there in 1996, in a Best Hotel Chefs program.

81. In 2001, Bloomin' Brands opened eight more Roy's restaurants on the mainland, in La Jolla, California; Orlando, Florida; Buckhead, Georgia; Baltimore; Rancho Mirage, California; Philadelphia; Summerlin, Neveda; and Austin, Texas (Lisa Peterson, "Roy Yamaguchi: The King of Roy's Restaurants Rules by Serving Regional Hawaiian Cuisine to Subjects around the Globe," *Nation's Restaurant News,* January 27, 2003).

82. "Ward Centre's A Pacific Café Closes Its Doors," *Honolulu Star-Bulletin,* November 6, 2000; Ruhlman, *The Reach of a Chef,* 224. Jean-Georges Vongerichten opened Prime at the Bellagio Hotel in 1998; Emeril Lagasse opened the Delmonico Steakhouse at the Venetian in November 1999; and Charlie Palmer opened Charlie Palmer Steakhouse at the Four Seasons (Rossant, *Super Chef,* 69–70).

83. "Hawaii Chef Files Chapter 11 for Remaining Restaurants," *Honolulu Advertiser,* August 7, 2001.

84. "Padovani's Restaurant & Wine Bar: French Traditions . . . Tropical Attitude!" Padovani's Restaurant & Wine Bar, http://padovanirestaurants.com/Padovani's %20Press%20Kit.pdf; "Hawaii Chef Likes His San Diego Address," *San Diego Business Journal,* July 28, 2003; "Alan Wong," Greater Good Radio, http://www.greatergoodradio /?p=133.

85. Katherine Nichols, "Tasteful Excellence Sets Padovani's Apart," *Honolulu Star-Bulletin,* May 3, 2006.

86. Padovani's Restaurant & Bar, www.padovanirestaurants.com/Padovani _Restaurants/Portfolio-Philippe.html; and "Vegas Chef Brings Star Power," *Honolulu Star-Bulletin,* June 6, 2007.

87. "Rising Costs Doom Sam Choy's Eatery," *Honolulu Star-Bulletin,* June 28, 2008.

88. The restaurants in Hawai'i were the original Roy's, Roy's Kahana Bar & Grill, Roy's Waikiki, Roy's Poipu Bar & Grill, Roy's Waikoloa Bar & Grill. Those overseas were one each in Guam, Hong Kong, and the Philippines and two in Tokyo.

89. Betty Shimabukuro, "20 Years on a Platter," *Honolulu Star-Bulletin,* September 24, 2008.

90. David Butts, "Japanese Tourists Trickling Back to Local Business," *Honolulu Advertiser,* May 5, 2002.

91. See table 7.04 in State of Hawai'i, Department of Business, Economic Development & Tourism, *State of Hawai'i Data Book* for 2000, 2002, 2003, 2005, 2007, 2008, and 2010.

92. See US Bureau of Labor Statistics, Civilian Unemployment Rate, retrieved from FRED, Federal Reserve Bank of St. Louis, https://fred.stlouisfed.org/series /UNRATE, December 12, 2016; and table 7.04 in State of Hawai'i, Department of Business, Economic Development & Tourism, *State of Hawai'i Data Book* for 2000, 2002, 2003, 2005, 2007, 2008, and 2010.

93. "Local Chef Honored," *Honolulu Advertiser*, May 6, 2003.

94. Erika Engle, "Hawaii Shines among Beard Semifinalists," *Honolulu Star-Bulletin*, February 15 and 19, 2009.

95. "New York Foodies Love Helena's: Helen Chock Takes the Fuss in Stride and Accepts Her Award from the James Beard Foundation, the Restaurant Industry's Oscars," *Honolulu Star-Bulletin*, May 10, 2000.

96. "Alan Wong," Greater Good Radio, http://www.greatergoodradio/?p=133.

97. Ibid.; and "Chew on This: Restaurant Report," *Honolulu Star-Bulletin*, May 19, 2002.

98. "Alan Wong," Greater Good Radio, http://www.greatergoodradio/?p=133; "Chef Mavro Restaurant Wins AAA Five Diamond," *Honolulu Advertiser*, November 14, 2008.

99. "Alan Wong," Greater Good Radio, http://www.greatergoodradio/?p=133.

100. "Top Restaurants," *Honolulu Advertiser*, October 4, 2000.

101. "Alan Wong," Greater Good Radio, http://www.greatergoodradio/?p=133.

102. Ibid. Harvey Steiman, "The Mating Game," *Wine Spectator*, November 30, 2000.

103. "Alan Wong," Greater Good Radio, http://www.greatergoodradio/?p=133.

104. Erika Engle, "The Buzz," *Honolulu Star-Bulletin*, August 22, 2006.

105. "Local Pioneers," *Gourmet*, October 2006, cited in *Honolulu Advertiser*, September 26, 2007.

106. Ibid.

107. Lisa Peterson, "Roy Yamaguchi: The King of Roy's Restaurants Rules by Serving Regional Hawaiian Cuisine to Subjects around the Globe," *Nation's Restaurant News*, January 27, 2003.

108. "Mo Stuffs—Celebrity Chefs Pair Up for Kea Lani Masters," *Honolulu Star-Bulletin*, August 9, 2000.

109. "Cuisines of the Sun," *Honolulu Star-Bulletin*, April 22, 2001.

110. Betty Shimabukuro, "Nobu au Naturale," *Honolulu Star-Bulletin*, September 25, 2002.

111. Shoko Imai, "The Authenticity of Celebrity Chef Nobu: Performance, Taste and Texts" (PhD diss., University of Tokyo, 2016), 105–117.

112. Betty Shimabukuro, "Mr. Zip," *Honolulu Star-Bulletin*, April 14, 2004.

113. Andrew Gomes, "Celebrity Chefs Design Kitchens," *Honolulu Advertiser*, September 19, 2005.

114. "Recipes from Hali'imaile General Store," *Honolulu Advertiser*, December 13, 2000.

115. "Bishop Museum, 'Broken Trust' Wins Book Award," *Honolulu Star-Bulletin*, May 22, 2007.

116. Wanda Adams, "Alan Wong's Repeats Win of 'Ilima's Best Restaurant Honor," *Honolulu Advertiser*, October 10, 2006.

117. Ibid.

118. "Lessons Learned: Bev Gannon," *Hawaii Business*, November 2008.

119. Erika Engle, "Hawaii Regional Cuisine Pleases Palates That Matter," *Honolulu Star-Advertiser*, March 21, 2011.

120. In 2013, this award became Best Chef: West.

CHAPTER 3: CUISINE

1. See Henri Gault, "Nouvelle Cuisine," in *Cooks and Other People: Proceedings of the Oxford Symposium on Food and Cookery 1995*, ed. Harlan Walker (Devon, UK: Prospect Books, 1996), 123–127.

2. Roy Yamaguchi, interview by Samuel H. Yamashita, July 10, 2009.

3. Choy, *Sam Choy's Cuisine Hawaii*, 19.

4. Yamaguchi and Wentzel, *Pacific Bounty*, 15.

5. Ibid., 14.

6. Jacy Youn, "Fruits of Their Labor," *Hawaii Business*, May 2006.

7. Alan Wong, interview by Samuel Yamashita, March 15, 2009.

8. Choy, *Sam Choy's Cuisine Hawaii*, 10.

9. Wong interview.

10. Wanda Adams, "Trailblazer: Discovering Hawaii's Freshest Flavors," *Honolulu Advertiser*, July 8, 1992.

11. Joan Namkoong, "This Little Piggy Went Upscale," *Honolulu Star-Bulletin*, April 28, 2004.

12. Joan Clarke, "Island Chefs Pay Tribute to Mom's Cooking," *Honolulu Advertiser*, May 10, 1995.

13. Susan Hooper, "Cooking Lessons," *Hawaii Business*, November 1990.

14. Vicki Viott, "Welcome to Roy's Kitchen; Hawaii Cooks with Roy Yamaguchi TV Program," *Honolulu Advertiser*, October 18, 1993.

15. Yamaguchi and Wentzel, *Pacific Bounty*, 13.

16. Ibid.

17. Joan Clarke, ". . . For the Love of It," *Honolulu Advertiser*, April 27, 1996.

18. Merriman and Merriman, *Merriman's Hawaii*, 17.

19. Amy Ferguson, interview by Samuel H. Yamashita, June 29, 2011; Tane Datta, interview by Samuel H. Yamashita, June 29, 2011.

20. Yamaguchi interview (italics added). It is interesting that Yamaguchi does not describe HRC cuisine as a "regional cuisine" in Yamaguchi and Wentzel, *Pacific Bounty*, 13–15 (italics added).

21. Yamaguchi interview, italics added.

22. Kamp, *United States of Arugula*, 152, 157.

23. Rossant, *Super Chefs*, 53.

24. "Discovering Hawaii's Freshest Flavors w/ Chef Amy Ferguson-Ota of Ritz-Carlton Mauna Lani," *Honolulu Advertiser*, July 8, 1992.

25. Wanda Adams, "Chef Mavro Discovers Country Freshness," *Honolulu Advertiser*, April 17, 1996.

26. Suzanne Roig, "Roy Yamaguchi Adds More Restaurants," *Honolulu Star-Bulletin*, December 14, 1995.

27. Burl Burlingame, "Hawaii Public TV to Offer New Show 'Hawaii Regional Cuisine' Produced by Melanie Kosaka and Roy Yamaguchi," *Honolulu Star-Bulletin*, November 3, 1992.

28. Yamaguchi and Wentzel, *Pacific Bounty*, 14, 31, 33, 38, 46, 48, 51, 54, 57, 62–63,

74–75, 78–79, 81, 83–86, 96–98, 105, 107–108, 112, 119, 123–124, 128, 134, 140, 142–143, 158, 160, 165, 166–167, 71–73; Joan Clarke, "Notable Neighbor Islanders Open on Oahu," *Honolulu Advertiser*, April 19, 1995; Joan Clarke, "Hawaii on the Hoof . . . ," *Honolulu Advertiser*, September 24, 1997.

29. See Henderson, *New Cuisine of Hawaii*, 76; Yamaguchi and Wentzel, *Pacific Bounty*, 14.

30. Kurt Hirabara and Pam Hirabara, interview by Samuel H. Yamashita, June 28, 2011.

31. David Kamp says that Jeremiah Tower was the first contemporary chef to identify the provenance of the ingredients he used at a dinner he cooked at Chez Panisse on October 7, 1976, and he invoked the precedent of chef Charles Banhofer at Delmonico's in New York City (Kamp, *United States of Arugula*, 161). For the menu, see Jeremiah Tower, *California Dish: What I Saw (and Cooked) at the American Culinary Revolution* (New York: Free Press, 2003), 111.

32. Wanda Adams, "Alan Wong and His Crew Find Culinary Insights," *Honolulu Advertiser*, March 21, 2007.

33. Edward Sakamoto, interview by Samuel H. Yamashita, June 29, 2011.

34. Gannon with Friedman, *Hali'imaile General Store Cookbook*, 92, 136.

35. Joan Clarke, "Hawaii on the Hoof . . . ," *Honolulu Advertiser*, September 24, 1997.

36. Merriman and Merriman, *Merriman's Hawaii*, 20–21; and "Local Pioneers," *Gourmet*, September 26, 2007.

37. Beverly Gannon, interview by Samuel H. Yamashita, October 17, 2009.

38. Derek Paiva, "Recipe for Success," *Hawaii Business*, February 1991.

39. Lisa Peterson, "Roy Yamaguchi: The King of Roy's Restaurants Rules by Serving Regional Hawaiian Cuisine to Subjects across the Globe," *Nation's Restaurant News*, January 27, 2003, 208–209.

40. Janice Wald Henderson, "Roy's," *Bon Appétit*, April 1991.

41. Gannon with Friedman, *Hali'imaile General Store Cookbook*, 5, 11, 21–23, 27–29, 31, 35, 37, 39, 42, 44, 59, 63, 67, 75, 92, 108–109, 112–113, 120, 124, 144, 150, 157, 160, 162, 164, 173; Jean-Marie Josselin, *A Taste of Hawaii: New Cooking from the Crossroads of the Pacific* (New York: Stewart, Tabori & Chang, 1992), 25, 36, 67, 75, 78–79, 90, 92, 101, 142, 149, 167, 178, 186, 204; Wong and Harrison, *Alan Wong's New Wave Luau*, 6, 26, 31, 52–53, 97–98, 103, 116, 135, 137–138, 156–161; Yamaguchi and Wentzel, *Pacific Bounty*, 32–33, 36, 36–37, 38–39, 54, 56–57, 60–61, 68, 70, 73–74, 82–83, 86–87, 97, 108–109, 110, 116–117, 124–125, 133–134, 135, 142–143, 158, 160–161, 172–173.

42. Ray, *The Ethnic Restaurateur*, 156.

43. Yamaguchi interview.

44. Yamaguchi and Wentzel, *Pacific Bounty*, 14.

45. Recall that Yamaguchi claimed to have invented Euro-Asian cuisine in 1980 while he was working in Los Angeles.

46. *Roy's: New Directions*, June 1992.

47. Wanda Adams, "At Avalon, Taste Asia . . . ," *Honolulu Advertiser*, 1990; Susan Hooper, "Cooking Lessons," *Hawaii Business*, November 1990; Yamaguchi and Wentzel, *Pacific Bounty*, 97.

48. Wanda Adams, "At Avalon, Taste Asia . . . ," *Honolulu Advertiser*, 1990.

49. Fern Tomisato Yoshida, interview by Samuel H. Yamashita, January 12, 2012.

50. Joan Clarke, "California Chefs Give Roy Dinner to Remember," *Honolulu Advertiser*, February 1, 1996.

51. Nadine Kam, "The Weekly Eater: Roy Makes a Splash in the Big City," *Honolulu Star-Bulletin*, March 18, 1999.

52. Lisa Peterson, "Roy Yamaguchi," *Nation's Restaurant News*, January 27, 2003.

53. Alan Davidson, *The Oxford Companion to Food* (Oxford: Oxford University Press, 1999), 282; Henderson, *New Cuisine of Hawaii*, 12, 46, 54, 66, 76, 78, 86, 96, 100, 108, 110; and Yamaguchi and Wentzel, *Pacific Bounty*, 31–32, 48–49, 94–96, 104, 108–109, 110, 117–118, 171.

54. Henderson, *New Cuisine of Hawaii*, 71.

55. Ibid., 34, 112.

56. Ibid., 32, 56, 82, 93, 98, 115, 125–126; Yamaguchi and Wentzel, *Pacific Bounty*, 142–143.

57. The best discussion of the global dominance of French cuisine can be found in Trubek, *Haute Cuisine*, 128–134.

58. Amy Ferguson, interview by Samuel H. Yamashita, June 29, 2011.

59. Henderson, *New Cuisine of Hawaii*, 76; Auguste Escoffier, *Escoffier: Le Guide Culinaire*, trans. H. L. Cracknell and R. J. Kaufmann, 3rd ed. (New York: Wiley, 2011). 20.

60. Yamaguchi and Wentzel, *Pacific Bounty*, 94–96.

61. *Kappō* cuisine is slightly less formal than kaiseki cuisine, the haute cuisine that emerged together with the tea ceremony in seventeenth-century Japan, but more formal than typical home cooking, whether urban or rural. As at the best small sushi shops, at a *kappō* restaurant, the chef decides what to serve each day based on what he or she could obtain at the local fish shop and greengrocer's.

62. See Roy Yamaguchi and John Harrison, *Roy's Fish and Seafood: Recipes from the Pacific Rim* (Berkeley, CA: Ten Speed Press, 2005), 13.

63. Yamaguchi and Harrison, *Roy's Feasts from Hawaii*, 108; Yamaguchi and Harrison, *Roy's Fish and Seafood*, 13.

64. Gannon with Friedman, *Hali'imaile General Store Cookbook*, 117.

65. Merriman and Merriman, *Merriman's Hawaii*, 212. Although namasu can be dated in Japan from the seventh century, it also can be traced back to the *Analects of Confucius*, which dates from the fifth century BCE. See Shinoda Osamu and Kawakami Kōzō, eds., *Zusetsu edo jidai shokuseikatsu jiten, shinsō-han* (Tokyo: Yūsankaku, 1997), 297; and Matsushita Sachiko, *Zusetsu edo ryōri jiten* (Tokyo: Kashiwa shobō, 2009), 96.

66. Gannon with Friedman, *Hali'imaile General Store Cookbook*, 153; Merriman and Merriman, *Merriman's Hawaii*, 141.

67. Merriman and Merriman, *Merriman's Hawaii*, 201.

68. See ibid., 220–221. Ramen has become very popular in the United States, thanks to David Chang's Momofuku restaurant and its many spin-offs.

69. Joan Namkoong, "Beard House behind the Scenes," *Honolulu Star-Bulletin*, June 16, 2004.

70. Beverly Gannon with Joan Namkoong, *Family-Style Meals at the Hali'imaile General Store* (Berkeley, CA: Ten Speed Press, 2009), 85.

71. Ibid., 97–98.

72. Ibid., 77.

73. Merriman and Merriman, *Merriman's Hawaii*, 249; Irma S. Rombauer, *The Joy of Cooking: A Compilation of Reliable Recipes with an Occasional Culinary Chat* (Indianapolis: Bobbs-Merrill, 1931), 559.

74. Rombauer, *The Joy of Cooking*, 143–144.

75. Wong and Harrison, *Alan Wong's New Wave Luau*, 96. Japanese mothers often make *kayu*, a rice gruel, for their sick children.

76. Joan Clarke, "Mom's Cooking," *Honolulu Advertiser*, May 10, 1995.

77. Ibid.

78. Joan Clarke, "Chef Alan Wong Creates His Own Version of Spam," *Honolulu Advertiser*, July 29, 1998.

79. Matthew Gray, "Wong Menu Has Creative Flavor," *Honolulu Advertiser*, October 22, 1999.

80. Joan Clarke, "Chef Alan Wong Creates His Own Version of Spam," *Honolulu Advertiser*, July 29, 1998.

81. Matthew Gray, "Wong Menu Has Creative Flavor," *Honolulu Advertiser*, October 22, 1999.

82. James Kelly, "Loco Moco," *Social Process* 30 (1983): 59–64.

83. Joan Clarke, "Chef Alan Wong Creates His Own Version of Spam," *Honolulu Advertiser*, July 29, 1998.

84. Joan Clarke, "Alan Wong Putting Finishing Touches on Pineapple Room," *Honolulu Advertiser*, September 15, 1999.

85. Matthew Gray, "Wong Menu Has Creative Flavor," *Honolulu Advertiser*, October 22, 1999.

86. Janice Wald Henderson, "Roy's," *Bon Appétit*, April 1991.

87. Wanda Adams, "At Avalon, Taste Asia . . . ," *Honolulu Advertiser*, 1990; Susan Hooper, "Cooking Lessons," *Hawaii Business*, November 1990.

88. Yamaguchi and Wentzel, *Pacific Bounty*, 140–141.

89. Brett Thorn, "Roy Yamaguchi," *Nation's Restaurant News*, September 13, 1999.

90. Yamaguchi interview.

91. In his 2003 cookbook, Yamaguchi uses the term "Hawaiian fusion cuisine." See Roy Yamaguchi and Joan Namkoong, *Hawaii Cooks: Flavors from Roy's Pacific Rim Kitchen* (Berkeley, CA: Ten Speed Press, 2003), 1.

92. Yamaguchi interview.

93. *Roy's*, June 1992.

94. George Mavrothalassitis, interview by Samuel H. Yamashita, March 17, 2009.

95. Joan Namkoong, "Beard House behind the Scenes," *Honolulu Advertiser*, June 16, 2004.

96. Mavrothalassitis interview.

97. Wanda Adams, "Bread, Sweat and Fears," *Honolulu Star-Bulletin*, June 16, 2004.

98. Ginger-Crusted Onaga has been on Wong's menu for a very long time, and he tried "taking it off the menu but so many people requested it . . . [I] decided to keep it on the menu" (Wong interview).

99. Wong interview.

100. Wong and Harrison, *Alan Wong's New Wave Luau*, 89.

101. To a seasoned local palate, the first thing that comes to mind is the fabled pork hash served at a particular restaurant in Honolulu's Chinatown, Tin Tin Chop Suey (1110B Maunakea Street), which no longer exists.

102. Aron Vinegar and Michael J. Golec, *Relearning from Las Vegas* (Minneapolis: University of Minnesota Press, 2008), 22.

103. Nelson Goodman, "How Buildings Mean," *Critical Inquiry* 11, no. 4 (June 1985): 648.

104. Vinegar and Golec, *Relearning from Las Vegas*, 22–23.

105. Ray, *The Ethnic Restaurateur*, 156.

CHAPTER 4: SUCCESSORS

1. Ed Kenney, interview by Samuel H. Yamashita, July 26, 2015.

2. Ibid.

3. Ibid.

4. Michelle Karr-Ueoka, interview by Samuel H. Yamashita, July 30, 2015.

5. Wade Ueoka, interview by Samuel H. Yamashita, July 30, 2015.

6. Karr-Ueoka and Ueoka interviews.

7. The Regency Club closed in 2011.

8. Kevin Chong, interview by Samuel H. Yamashita, July 28, 2015. For reviews of Splichal's restaurants, see Ruth Reichl, "Max Covers All of the Angles," *Los Angeles Times*, March 10, 1985; Ruth Reichl, "A Patina of Success: A Year Later, Joachim Splichal's Melrose Avenue Restaurant Has Finally Found Its Footing . . . Paris, Look Out," *Los Angeles Times*, July 15, 1990; and Charles Perry, "Patina Gets a Shine," *Los Angeles Times*, October 25, 2000.

9. Chong interview.

10. It was founded in 1846.

11. Andrew Le, interview by Samuel H. Yamashita, August 26, 2015.

12. Hank's Haute Dogs is owned by Hank Adaniya, who had owned Trio, a famous Chicago restaurant where chefs like Grant Achatz, Gale Gand, Shawn McClain, and Dale Levitski once cooked.

13. Evan and Sarah Rich are the chef-owners of Rich Table, a well-regarded eatery that is the epitome of the new smart-casual type of restaurant popular in the United States since the first decade of the 2000s. For a full discussion of the "smart-casual" restaurant style, see Alison Pearlman, *Smart Casual: The Transformation of Gourmet Restaurant Style in America* (Chicago: The University of Chicago Press, 2013), 1, 12–15; and Patricia Ferguson, *Word of Mouth: What We Talk about When We Talk about Food* (Berkeley: University of California Press, 2014), 170–196.

14. Le interview.

15. Sheldon Simeon, interview by Samuel H. Yamashita, July 29, 2015.

16. Peter Lindberg, "Where to Eat Now in 18 American Cities," *Gourmet*, October 2005.

17. Erika Engle, "New Restaurant in Kaimuki Gets National Ink," *Honolulu Star-Bulletin*, April 20, 2006.

18. "Smart casual" is Alison Pearlman's term, and "haute food" is Patricia Ferguson's. See Pearlman, *Smart Casual*, 12–32; and Ferguson, *Word of Mouth*, 170–196.

19. Peter Merriman and Beverly Gannon also were semifinalists for the same Beard award in 2009. In fact, Gannon was a semifinalist again in 2010 and has the distinction of being the last member of the original HRC group to be nominated for this award.

20. Nicholas Rummell, "2012 Hawaii Rising Star Chef Andrew Le," StarChefs,

November 2012, http://www.starchefs.com/cook/chefs/rising-stars/2012/hawaii/ andrew-le; Antoinette Bruno, "Rising Star Chef Sheldon Simeon of Star Noodle— Biography," StarChefs, November 2012, http://www.starchefs.com/cook/chefs/bio /sheldon-simeon.

21. "2012's People's Best New Chef," *Food & Wine*, April 2014. Simeon was one of nine regional winners chosen from a list of one hundred chefs.

22. Chong interview.

23. Kenney interview.

24. Rich Newman, "America's Most Profitable Malls," *U.S. News & World Report*, June 26, 2009.

25. Chong interview.

26. Ibid.

27. Simeon interview.

28. Kenney interview.

29. Ibid.

30. Simeon interview.

31. Conrad Nonaka, interview by Samuel H. Yamashita, January 11, 2012.

32. John Morton, interview by Samuel H. Yamashita, January 13, 2012.

33. Chong left ʻAmaʻAma in 2016 and now works in Florida.

34. Chong interview.

35. Martha Cheng, "Dining: The Boys Are Back in Town," *Honolulu Magazine*, June 2010.

36. Lesa Griffith, "First Time: Ama Ama at Disney Aulani," *Honolulu Magazine*, 2015.

37. Carolyn Jung, "Look Past the Pupu Platter for the Next Level of Hawaiian Cuisine," *Plate Magazine*, July 6, 2015.

38. Karr-Ueoka interview.

39. Karr-Ueoka and Ueoka interviews.

40. For Ueoka's oxtail soup recipe, see "Oxtail 'Soup': Oxtail and Corned Beef Roulade, Boiled Peanuts, and Shiitake Mushroom," StarChefs, https://www.starchefs. com/cook/recipe/oxtail-corned-beef-roulade-risotto.

41. Alan Wong and Arnold Hiura, *Blue Tomato: The Inspirations behind the Cuisine of Alan Wong* (Honolulu: Watermark Publishing, 2010), 172–174, 204–207.

42. Kenneth Frampton, "Towards a Critical Regionalism: Six Points for an Architecture of Resistance," in *Anti-Aesthetic: Essays on Postmodern Culture*, ed. Hal Foster (Seattle: Bay Press, 1983), 16–30. Frampton defines the *"arrière-garde* position" as "one which distances itself equally from the Enlightenment myth of progress and from a reactionary, unrealistic impulse to return to the architectonic forms of the preindustrial past" (ibid., 20).

43. Derek Walcott, *What the Twilight Says—Essays* (New York: Farrar, Straus & Giroux, 1998), 40–41.

44. Martha Cheng, "Review: MW Restaurant," *Honolulu Magazine*, February 2014.

45. Martha Cheng, "Best of Honolulu 2015: Food," *Honolulu Magazine*, July 2015.

46. Joan Clarke, "Chefs Peer into the Millennium," *Honolulu Advertiser*, November 1999.

47. Wong and Harrison, *Alan Wong's New Wave Luau*, 89.

48. "Mode of inflection" is Derek Walcott's term; see Walcott, *What the Twilight Says*, 15.

49. "America's Top Restaurants," *Gourmet*, October 2005; Joan Namkoong, "Taste the World: They Came from Different Countries and Backgrounds, but These Honolulu Restaurateurs Now Share the Same Passions: Good Food, Fresh Ingredients, and Feeding a Legion of Happy Customers," *Honolulu Magazine*, January 2007.

50. Kenney interview.

51. Ibid.

52. Ed Kenney (as told to Jennifer Flowers), "How to Eat Like a Local," *Afar*, May/June 2016.

53. Kenney interview.

54. Ibid.

55. Nicholas Rummell, "Paʻiʻai: Hawaii's Link to the Past and Glimpse at Its Future," StarChefs, October 2012, https://www.starchefs.com/cook/savory/product/paiai.

56. Mahina & Sun's menu, August 20, 2016.

57. On June 14, 2011, Governor Neil Abercrombie signed Act 107, which "required the Department of Health to adopt rules in order to recognize the preparation of poi and paʻi ʻai using traditional Hawaiian cultural food preparation practices." State of Hawaiʻi, Office of the Auditor, *Hawaiʻi 2050 Sustainability Plan—Ten Year Measurement Update* (Honolulu: State of Hawaiʻi, 2018), 49.

58. Brett Martin, "The Perfect Night Out: GQ's Best New Restaurants of 2016," *Gentlemen's Quarterly*, May 24, 2016.

59. Kenney interview.

60. Nicholas Rummell, "Interview with 2012 Hawaii Rising Star Chef Andrew Le," StarChefs, November 2012, http://www.starchefs.com/cook/chefs/rising-stars/2012/hawaii/andrew-le.

61. Jody Eddy, "Chef to Watch 2015: Andrew Le, The Pig & The Lady, Honolulu, Hawaii," *Plate Magazine*, September 29, 2015.

62. Jeff Mull, "When Pigs Fly: The Pig and The Lady," *Flux Hawaii*, August 22, 2013.

63. Ibid.

64. Tejet Rao, "Why You Must Eat Vietnamese Food in Honolulu," *Bloomberg*, November 25, 2015.

65. Le interview.

66. "The Pig and the Lady at Lemongrass Café!" Pacific Gateway Center, https://www.pacificgatewaycenter.org/the-pig-and-the-lady.

67. Le interview.

68. Ibid.

69. Jody Eddy, "Chef to Watch 2015: Andrew Le, The Pig & The Lady, Honolulu, Hawaii," *Plate Magazine*, September 29, 2015.

70. Amy Ferguson, interview by Samuel H. Yamashita, June 29, 2011.

71. Ray, *The Ethnic Restaurateur*, 155–156.

72. Simeon interview.

73. Martha Cheng, "Sheldon Simeon of Star Noodle and Leoda's Pie and Kitchen Shop Makes Top Chef," *Honolulu Magazine*, October 2012.

74. Ibid.

75. Erika Engle, "Culinary Awards Notice Two Chefs and a Restaurant," *Honolulu Star-Advertiser*, March 4, 2011.

76. *Food & Wine*, July 2012.

77. Martha Cheng, "Shelton Simeon on Top Chef: Any Regrets?" *Honolulu Magazine*, February 22, 2013; Pati Poblete, "Rising Chef Sheldon Simeon," *SFGate*, updated March 7, 2014, https://www.sfgate.com/style/article/Rising-chef-Sheldon-Simeon-of -Migrant-Maui-5295836.php.

78. Celeste Flores, "Sheldon Simeon May Have Lost Top Chef but Makes Filipino Cuisine the Winner," March 2, 2013, *Inquirer.net*, https://lifestyle.inquirer.net/92057 /sheldon-simeon-exits-top-chef-but-makes-filipino-cuisine-a-winner/.

79. Ibid.

80. Catherine Toth Fox, "Q & A with Hawaii's 'Top Chef' Sheldon Simeon," *The Cat Dish*, February 27, 2013, www.thecatdish.com/food/qa-with-hawaiis-top-chef --sheldon-simeon.

81. Pati Poblete, "Rising Chef Sheldon Simeon," *SFGate*, updated March 7, 2014, https://www.sfgate.com/style/article/Rising-chef-Sheldon-Simeon-of-Migrant-Maui -5295836.php.

82. Heidi Pool, "Talk Story with Chef Sheldon Simeon," *Maui Concierge*, January 2012.

83. Mari Taketa, "First Look: Sheldon Simeon's Migrant," *Frolic Hawaii*, March 10, 2014.

84. Pati Poblete, "Rising Chef Sheldon Simeon," *SFGate*, updated March 7, 2014, https://www.sfgate.com/style/article/Rising-chef-Sheldon-Simeon-of-Migrant-Maui -5295836.php.

85. Joleen Oshiro, "Simeon Named Best New Chef in Pacific Region," *Honolulu Star-Advertiser*, April 10, 2014.

86. Carolyn Jung, "Look Past the Pupu Platter for the Next Level of Hawaiian Cuisine," *Plate Magazine*, July 6, 2015.

87. Kenney interview.

88. John Heckathorn, "Present at the Revolution," *Honolulu Magazine*, October 2011.

89. These terms are from Ray, *The Ethnic Restaurateur*, 111–115.

90. "Taste of place" is Amy Trubek's felicitous term; see Trubek, *The Taste of Place: A Cultural Journey into Terroir* (Berkeley: University of California Press, 2008), 104.

91. Walcott, *What the Twilight Says*, 40, 42, 50, 53, 61.

Chapter 5: Legacy

1. In 2011, Roy Yamaguchi was chef-owner of six Roy's restaurants in the islands, a joint-venture partner in twenty-two restaurants on the mainland, and the franchiser of three others in Pebble Beach, California; Tamuning, Guam; and Tokyo. (Erika Engle, "Changing Flavors in Hawaii," *Honolulu Advertiser*, February 27, 2011).

2. Roy Yamaguchi, interview by Samuel H. Yamashita, July 7, 2009.

3. John Morton, personal communication, August 31, 2017.

4. The number of sugar and pineapple plantations dropped from fifty-six in 1948 to zero in 2016 (Jeffrey Melrose, Ryan Perroy, and Sylvana Cares, "Statewide Agriculture Land Use Baseline 2015" [Honolulu: Department of Agriculture, 2016], 18).

5. George Ariyoshi, "Leadership Lessons," and "Diversified Agriculture, Land Use and Agrofood Networks in Hawaii," both in *Hawaii Business*, November 1, 2003.

6. "Questions & Answers—Sandra Lee Kunimoto," *Hawaii Business Special Report*, 2003.

7. State of Hawai'i, Office of Planning, Department of Business, Economic Development & Tourism, in Cooperation with the Department of Agriculture, *Increased Food Security and Food Self-Sufficiency Strategy* (Honolulu: Office of Planning, 2012), 9–12.

8. "Hawai'i Seals of Quality Program Launches," State of Hawai'i, Department of Agriculture, Agricultural Development Division, http://hdoa.hawaii.gov/add/md/seals-of-quality/soq-program-history/news-release-soq-program-launch/.

9. Gayle Kaleilehua Greco, "From Seed to Soul: North Kohala's Eat Locally Grown Community Initiative," *Ke Ola*, https://keolamagazine.com/food/eat-locally-grown-initiative (accessed August 17, 2017).

10. State of Hawai'i, Office of Planning, *Increased Food Security*, 11–12

11. The location of the first farmers' market near both a tony suburb and Waikīkī explains its distinctive demographic.

12. Monique Mironesco, "Farmers' Markets in Hawaii," in Kimura and Suryanata, *Food and Power in Hawai'i*, 90, 93.

13. Pierre Desrochers and Hiroko Shimizu, *The Locavore's Dilemma* (New York: Public Affairs, 2012), 48–52.

14. Peter Merriman, interview by Samuel H. Yamashita, July 18, 2010.

15. Wanda Adams, "Flavor That's Made in Hawai'i," *Honolulu Advertiser*, May 13, 2009.

16. Peter Merriman, "All Can Play a Role in Protecting Bottomfish," *Honolulu Advertiser*, December 26, 2006.

17. State of Hawai'i, Department of Business, Economic Development & Tourism, *State of Hawaii Data Book*, 1998, 2003, 2006. The following table represents the commercial landings of 'ōpakapaka and onaga between 1985 and 2006 (ibid., 1985, 1990, 1995, 2000, 2005, 2006):

Year	'Ōpakapaka	Onaga
1985	357,531	177,807
1990	214,954	145,666
1995	330,419	119,773
2000	229,246	192,033
2005	138,563	158,076
2006	92,965	99,814

18. Peter Merriman, "All Can Play a Role in Protecting Bottomfish," *Honolulu Advertiser*, December 26, 2006.

19. See State of Hawai'i, Department of Business, Economic Development & Tourism, *State of Hawaii Data Book*, 2007, 2010, 2013, 2014.

20. C. Cruz, "Economies of Scale," *Hawaii Business*, October 2001. Seafood consumption in the islands was said to be three times higher than that on the mainland.

21. J. McCulley, "Boom Times Again," *Hawaii Business*, March 1998.

22. C. DeSilva, "Something Fishy Going On," *Hawaii Business*, February 2000.

23. State of Hawai'i, Department of Business, Economic Development & Tourism, *State of Hawaii Data Book*, 1991, 1999, 2009. The following table represents the number of aquaculture businesses and their sales between 1991 and 1999 (ibid., 2015):

Year	Number	Sales (millions)
1991	71	$6.884
1999	100	$18.102
2009	70	$32.330
2012	70	$55.740

24. J. McCulley, "Boom Times Again," *Hawaii Business*, March 1998. The case of moi is illustrative. Moi was especially attractive because production costs were low ($3.50 per fish in 1998) and demand from restaurants was high. Beginning in the 1990s, the production of moi increased dramatically when it first appeared on the menus of HRC restaurants. For example, 17,000 pounds of moi were raised in 1996 and 70,000 in 1997. Marine biologist Anthony Ostrowski called moi "one of the most amenable species we have . . . [and] it's the marine fish of the future" (Peter Wagner, "Promise from the Past," *Honolulu Star-Bulletin*, August 27, 1998).

25. In 1885, there were 221 man-made fishponds in the islands, each producing 300 to 500 pounds of fish a year. Careful management by the *konohiki* (water managers) enabled their productivity (Kame'eleihiwa, "Kaulana O'ahu me he 'Āina Momona," 64–68).

26. J. McCulley, "Boom Times Again," *Hawaii Business*, March 1998.

27. Mari N. Jensen, "A Side of Algae? Hawaiian Farmers Sell Seaweed by the Seashore," *UA News*, https://uanews.arizona.edu/story/side-algae-hawaiian-farmers-sell-seaweed-seashore, accessed August 24, 2017.

28. State of Hawai'i, Department of Business, Economic Development & Tourism, *State of Hawaii Data Book*, 1972, 1991, 1992, 2003, 2014.

29. Joan Namkoong, "Bully on Beef," *Honolulu Star-Bulletin*, March 28, 2007.

30. University of Hawai'i at Hilo, Spatial Data Analysis and Visualization Lab, *Statewide Agricultural Land Use Baseline Project 2015* (Honolulu: Hawai'i Department of Agriculture, 2015), 36.

31. Joan Namkoong, "Ranchers Face Up to Obstacles," *Honolulu Star-Bulletin*, March 28, 2007.

32. Alan Wong, interview by Samuel H. Yamashita, March 15, 2009.

33. Allison Schaefers, "Vet's Hobby Attracts Family," *Honolulu Star-Bulletin*, August 8, 2004.

34. Wong interview.

35. Beverly Gannon, interview by Samuel H. Yamashita, October 17, 2009.

36. Joan Namkoong, "Bully on Beef," *Honolulu Star-Bulletin*, March 28, 2007.

37. Dave Donnelly, "Hawaii," *Honolulu Star-Bulletin*, September 10, 1996.

38. Joan Namkoong, "Bully on Beef," *Honolulu Star-Bulletin*, March 28, 2007.

39. University of Hawai'i at Hilo, *Statewide Agricultural Land Use*, 83.

40. Kame'eleihiwa, "Kaulana O'ahu me he 'Āina Momona," 55.

41. University of Hawai'i at Hilo, *Statewide Agricultural Land Use*, 12.

42. State of Hawai'i, Office of Planning, *Increased Food Security*, ii.

43. State of Hawai'i, Hawai'i 2050 Sustainability Task Force, *Hawai'i 2050 Sustainability Plan: Charting a Course for Hawai'i's Sustainable Future* (Honolulu: Hawai'i 2050 Sustainability Task Force, January 2008), 5.

44. Ibid., 15–16, 19–61, 63–67.

45. Billy Mason, "The Future of Sustainability in Hawaii," *HuffPost*, http://www.huffingtonpost.com/billy-mason/the-future-of-sustainability_b_4311008.

46. "New UH Sustainability Policy Aims for Carbon Neutrality by 2050," *University of Hawai'i News*, February 26, 2015.

47. Ibid., 8.

48. See "Subsistence Hunting in Alaska," Alaska Department of Fish and Game, www.adfg.alaska.gov/index.cfm?adfg=subsistence.hunting; and David Wilkins and K. Tsianina Lomawaima, *Uneven Ground: American Indian Sovereignty and Federal Law* (Norman: University of Oklahoma Press, 2001), 117–142, 180, 208, 237–245.

49. State of Hawai'i, Office of Planning, *Increased Food Security*, ii; Patricia Yollin, "Aloha Spam," *California Magazine*, Winter 2011.

50. State of Hawai'i, Hawai'i 2050 Sustainability Task Force, *Hawai'i 2050 Sustainability Plan*, 67.

51. Patricia Yollin, "Aloha Spam," *California Magazine*, Winter 2011.

52. State of Hawai'i, Hawai'i 2050 Sustainability Task Force, *Hawai'i 2050 Sustainability Plan*, 4.

53. For an update on the sustainability issue in the islands, see Dennis Hollier, "Can Hawaii Feed Itself?" *Hawaii Business*, November 2014.

54. State of Hawai'i, Hawai'i 2050 Sustainability Task Force, *Hawai'i 2050 Sustainability Plan*, 4.

55. Amy Ferguson, interview by Samuel H. Yamashita, June 29, 2011; Gannon interview.

56. Peter Merriman, "Sustainable Farming Vital for Health Issues; Support for Produce Cultivated in Hawai'i Benefits Economy," *Honolulu Advertiser*, December 26, 2006; Peter Merriman, "Support Local Farmers, Boost Sustainability; Consumers Can Make a Difference," *Honolulu Advertiser*, May 27, 2008; Patricia Yollin, "Aloha Spam," *California Magazine*, Winter 2011.

57. Joleen Oshiro, "Whole Hog," *Honolulu Star-Advertiser*, April 13, 2011.

58. Merriman interview.

59. Shinsato Farm was sold to Floor Technologies of Hawaii Inc. in 2016. Duane Shimogawa, "Shinsato Pig Farm to Close after Being Sold to Construction Company," *Pacific Business News*, August 25, 2016.

60. Joleen Oshiro, "Whole Hog," *Honolulu Star-Advertiser*, April 13, 2011.

61. Ed Kenney, interview by Samuel H. Yamashita, July 26, 2015; Michelle Karr-Ueoka, interview by Samuel H. Yamashita, July 30, 2015.

Selected Bibliography

Documents

State of Hawaiʻi, Department of Business, Economic Development & Tourism. *State of Hawaiʻi Data Book*. Honolulu: State of Hawaiʻi, published annually.

State of Hawaiʻi, Hawaiʻi 2050 Sustainability Task Force. *Hawaiʻi 2050 Sustainability Plan: Charting a Course for Hawaiʻi's Sustainable Future*. Honolulu: Hawaiʻi 2050 Sustainability Task Force, 2008.

State of Hawaiʻi, Office of Planning, Department of Business, Economic Development & Tourism, in Cooperation with the Department of Agriculture. *Increased Food Security and Food Self-Sufficiency Strategy*. Honolulu: Office of Planning, 2012.

State of Hawaiʻi, Office of the Auditor. *Hawaiʻi 2050 Sustainability Plan—Ten Year Measurement Update*. Honolulu: State of Hawaiʻi, 2018.

University of Hawaiʻi at Hilo, Spatial Data Analysis and Visualization Lab. *Statewide Agricultural Land Use Baseline 2015*. Honolulu: Hawaiʻi Department of Agriculture, 2015.

Interviews

Wanda Adams (food writer)
Kevin Chong (chef)
Sam Choy (chef)
Tane Datta (farmer)
Mark Ellman (chef)
Amy Ferguson (chef)
Hiroshi Fukui (chef)
Beverly Gannon (chef)
John Heckathorn (food writer)
Kurt Hirabara (farmer)
Pam Hirabara (farmer)
Edward Kenney (chef)
Derek Kurisu (businessman)

Andrew Le (chef)
Frank Leake (educator)
Erin Lee (farmer)
Gary Maunakea-Forth (farmer)
George Mavrothalassitis (chef)
Peter Merriman (chef)
John Morton (educator)
Dan Nakasone (rancher)
Joan Namkoong (food writer)
Conrad Nonaka (educator)
Dean Okimoto (farmer)
Edward Sakamoto (farmer)
Gladys Sato (educator)
Sheldon Simeon (chef)
Russell Siu (chef)
David Sumida (farmer)
Joe Wilson (aquaculturist)
Alan Wong (chef)
Roy Yamaguchi (chef)
Fern Tomisato Yoshida (educator)

MAGAZINES

Bon Appétit
Condé Nast Traveler
Esquire
Food & Wine
The Friend
Gourmet
Hawaii Business
Honolulu Magazine
National Restaurant News
Pacific Business News
Paradise of the Pacific
The Pennsylvania Gazette
Restaurant Business Magazine
Restaurant Hospitality
Saveur
Travel & Leisure
Wine Spectator

NEWSPAPERS

Chicago Tribune
Honolulu Advertiser

Honolulu Star-Bulletin
Los Angeles Times
The Maui News
The New York Times
Palm Beach Post
San Diego Business Journal
San Francisco Chronicle
Tampa Bay Times

COOKBOOKS

Alejandro, Reynaldo G. *The Philippine Cookbook*. New York: Perigree Books, 1985.
Alexander, Helen. *The Helen Alexander Hawaiian Cook Book*. Honolulu: Advertiser Publishing Company, 1938.
Choy, Sam. *Aloha Cuisine*. Honolulu: Mutual Publishing, 2006.
———. *The Choy of Cooking: Sam Choy's Island Cuisine*. Honolulu: Mutual Publishing, 1996.
———. *Hawai'i Cuisine: A Sampler of Favorite Island Recipes by Chef Sam Choy*. Honolulu: Mutual Publishing, 2000.
———. *Poke: Hawai'i's Food*. Honolulu: Mutual Publishing, 2009.
———. *Sam Choy & the Mākaha Sons' A Hawaiian Lū'au*. Honolulu: Mutual Publishing, 2003.
———. *Sam Choy's Cuisine Hawaii: Featuring the Premier Chefs of the Aloha State*. Honolulu: Pleasant Hawaii, 1990.
———. *Sam Choy's Island Flavors*. Los Angeles: Hyperion, 1999.
———. *Sam Choy's Little Hawaiian Cookbook for Big Appetites*. Honolulu: Mutual Publishing, 2003.
———. *Sam Choy's Poke: Hawaii's Soul Food*. Honolulu: Mutual Publishing, 1999.
———. *Sam Choy's Polynesian Kitchen: More Than 150 Authentic Dishes from One of the World's Most Delicious and Overlooked Cuisines*. Los Angeles: Hyperion, 2002.
———. *Sam Choy's Sampler: Hawai'i's Favorite Recipes*. Honolulu: Mutual Publishing, 2000.
Choy, Sam, and Evelyn Cook. *With Sam Choy: Cooking from the Heart*. Honolulu: Mutual Publishing, 1995.
Choy, Sam, and Lynn Cook. *Sam Choy Woks the Wok: Stir Fry Cooking at Its Island Best*. Honolulu: Mutual Publishing, 2001.
Choy, Sam, and Joannie Dobbs. *Sam Choy's Kitchen: Cooking Doesn't Get Any Easier Than This*. Honolulu: Mutual Publishing, 1999.
Choy, Sam, and Catherine K. Enomoto. *Sam Choy's Cooking: Island Cuisine at Its Best*. Honolulu: Mutual Publishing, 2000.
Choy, Sam, U'i Goldsberry, and Steven Goldsberry. *The Choy of Seafood: Sam Choy's Pacific Harvest*. Honolulu: Mutual Publishing, 1998.
Escoffier, Auguste. *Escoffier: Le Guide Culinaire*. Translated by H. L. Cracknell and R. J. Kaufmann. 3rd ed. New York: Wiley, 2011.

Gannon, Beverly, and Bonnie Friedman. *The Hali'imaile General Store Cookbook: Home Cooking from Maui.* Berkeley, CA: Ten Speed Press, 2000.

Gannon, Beverly, and Joan Namkoong. *Family-Style Meals at the Hali'imaile General Store.* Berkeley, CA: Ten Speed Press, 2009.

Henderson, Janice Wald. *The New Cuisine of Hawaii: Recipes from the Twelve Celebrated Chefs of Hawaii Regional Cuisine.* New York: Villard Books, 1994.

Jaffrey, Madhur. *A Taste of India.* New York: Atheneum, 1985.

Josselin, Jean-Marie. *A Taste of Hawaii: New Cooking from the Crossroads of the Pacific.* New York: Stewart, Tabori & Chang, 1992.

Kuo, Irene. *The Key to Chinese Cooking.* New York: Knopf, 1977.

Matsuhisa, Nobuyuki. Translated by Laura Holland. *Nobu: The Cookbook.* New York: Kodansha USA, 2013.

Meahl, Elizabeth, and Joanne Fujita. *Sam Choy's Little Hawaiian Poke Cookbook.* Honolulu: Mutual Publishing, 2004.

Merriman, Peter, and Melanie Merriman. *Merriman's Hawai'i: The Chef, the Farmers, the Food, the Islands.* Winter Park, FL: Story Farm, 2015.

Phan, Charles. *Vietnamese Home Cooking.* Berkeley, CA: Ten Speed Press, 2012.

Philpotts, Kaui. *Great Chefs of Hawaii.* Honolulu: Mutual Publishing, 2003.

Puck, Wolfgang. *The Wolfgang Puck Cookbook: Recipes from Spago, Chinois and Points East and West.* New York: Random House, 1986.

Rombauer, Irma von Starkloff. *The Joy of Cooking: A Compilation of Reliable Recipes with an Occasional Culinary Chat.* New York: Bobbs-Merrill, 1931.

Siu, Russell W. J., and Arnold Hiura. *On the Rise: New Traditions Cooking with Russell Siu.* Honolulu: Booklines, 1996.

So, Yan-Kit. *Classic Food of China.* New York: Macmillan, 1992.

Tsuji, Shizuo. *Japanese Cooking: A Simple Art.* New York: Kodansha USA, 1980.

Woman's Society of Central Union Church. *Hawaiian Cook Book.* 6th ed. Honolulu: Honolulu Star-Bulletin, 1920.

Wong, Alan, and John Harrison. *Alan Wong's New Wave Luau: Recipes from Honolulu's Award-Winning Chef.* Berkeley, CA: Ten Speed Press, 1999.

Wong, Alan, and Arnold Hiura. *Blue Tomato: The Inspirations behind the Cuisine of Alan Wong.* Honolulu: Watermark Publishing, 2010.

Yamaguchi, Roy, and John Harrison. *Roy's Feasts from Hawaii.* Berkeley, CA: Ten Speed Press, 2007.

Yamaguchi, Roy, and John Harrison. *Roy's Fish and Seafood: Recipes from the Pacific Rim.* Berkeley, CA: Ten Speed Press, 2005.

Yamaguchi, Roy, and Joan Namkoong. *Hawaii Cooks: Flavors from Roy's Pacific Rim Kitchen.* Berkeley, CA: Ten Speed Press, 2003.

Yamaguchi, Roy, and Martin Wentzel. *Pacific Bounty: Hawaii Cooks with Roy Yamaguchi.* San Francisco: KQED, 1994.

NEWSLETTER

Roy's: New Directions

SECONDARY SOURCES

Anderson, E. N. *Food of China*. New Haven, CT: Yale University Press, 1990.

Appadurai, Arjun. "How to Make a National Cuisine." *Comparative Studies in Society and Culture* 30, no. 1 (1988): 3–24.

Ashcroft, Bill, Gareth Griffiths, and Helen Tiffin. *The Empire Writes Back: Theory and Practice in Postcolonial Literatures*. 2nd ed. London: Routledge, 2002.

Becker, Howard. *Art Worlds*. Berkeley: University of California Press, 1982.

Besio, Kathryn, and LeeRay Costa. "Eating Hawai'i: Local Foods and Place-Making in Hawai'i Regional Cuisine." *Social & Cultural Geography* 12, no. 8 (2011): 839–854.

Bhatt, Ritu. "Aesthetic or Anaesthetic: A Nelson Goodman Reading of the Las Vegas Strip." In *Relearning from Las Vegas*, edited by Aron Vinegar and Michael J. Golec, 19–30. Minneapolis: University of Minnesota Press, 2008.

Bird, Isabel. *The Hawaiian Archipelago*. London: J. Murray, 1875.

Burroughs, W. Jeffrey. "Mahimahi Musubi: Cosmopolitanizing Strategies in Hawaiian Regional Cuisine." *Pacific Studies* 37, no. 3 (2014): 147–171.

Center for Oral History. *The Oroku, Okinawan Connection: Local-Style Restaurants in Hawai'i*. Honolulu: Social Sciences Research Institute, 2004.

———. *Waikīkī, 1910–1985*. Honolulu: Center for Oral History, 1985.

Cohn, Bernard. *Colonialism and Its Forms of Knowledge*. Princeton, NJ: Princeton University Press, 1996.

Collins, Karen. *Watching What We Eat: The Evolution of Television Cooking Shows*. London: Bloomsbury Academic, 2010.

Counihan, Carole, and Penny Van Esterik, eds. *Food and Culture: A Reader*. 3rd ed. New York: Routledge, 2013.

Davidson, Alan. *The Oxford Companion to Food*. Oxford: Oxford University Press, 1999.

Desrochers, Pierre, and Hiroko Shimizu. *The Locavore's Dilemma*. New York: Public Affairs, 2012.

Douglas, Mary. "How to Decipher a Meal." *Daedalus* (Winter 1972): 61–82.

Ferguson, Patricia Parkhurst. *Accounting for Taste: The Triumph of French Cuisine*. Chicago: The University of Chicago Press, 2004.

———. *Word of Mouth: What We Talk about When We Talk about Food*. Berkeley: University of California Press, 2014.

Frampton, Kenneth. "Towards a Critical Regionalism: Six Points for an Architecture of Resistance." In *Anti-Aesthetic: Essays on Postmodern Culture*, edited by Hal Foster, 16–30. Seattle: Bay Press, 1983.

Freedman, Paul. *Ten Restaurants That Changed America*. New York: Liveright, 2016.

Freedman, Paul, Joyce E. Chaplin, and Ken Albala, eds. *Food in Time and Place: The American Historical Association Companion to Food History*. Berkeley: University of California Press, 2014.

Fuchs, Lawrence. *Hawaii Pono: A Social History*. New York: Harcourt, Brace & World, 1961.

Fujikane, Candace, and Jonathan Okamura, eds. *Asian Settler Colonialism: From*

Local Governance to the Habits of Everyday Life in Hawai'i. Honolulu: University of Hawai'i Press, 2008.

Gabaccia, Donna R. *We Are What We Eat: Ethnic Food and the Making of Americans*. Cambridge, MA: Harvard University Press, 1998.

Gault, Henri. "Nouvelle Cuisine." In *Cooks and Other People: Proceedings of the Oxford Symposium on Food and Cooking*, edited by Harlan Walker, 123–127. Devon, UK: Prospect Books, 1996.

Glick, Clarence E. *Sojourners and Settlers: Chinese Migrants in Hawaii*. Honolulu: Hawai'i Chinese History Center, 1977.

Goodman, Nelson. "How Buildings Mean." *Critical Inquiry* 11, no. 4 (1985): 642–653.

Goody, Jack. *Cooking, Cuisine and Class: A Study in Comparative Sociology*. Cambridge: Cambridge University Press, 1982.

Guruman. *Guide gastronomique pour gourmand: Tōkyō-Kansai furansu ryōriten gaido*. Tokyo: Shinshindō, 1992.

Hiura, Arnold. *Kau Kau: Cuisine and Culture in the Hawaiian Islands*. Honolulu: Watermark Publishing, 2009.

Hosking, Richard. *A Dictionary of Japanese Food: Ingredients and Culture*. North Clarendon, VT: Tuttle, 2002.

Hu, Shiu-ying. *Food Plants of China*. Hong Kong: Chinese University Press, 2005.

Imai, Shoko. "The Authenticity of Celebrity Chef Nobu: Performance, Taste, and Texts." PhD diss., University of Tokyo, 2016.

Janer, Zilkia. "(In)edible Nature: New World Food and Coloniality." *Cultural Studies* 21, no. 3 (April–May 2007): 385–405.

———. *Latino Food Culture*. Greenwood, CT: Greenwood Press, 2008.

Jayaraman, Saru. *Beyond the Kitchen Door*. Ithaca, NY: Cornell University Press, 2014.

Kame'eleihiwa, Lilikalā. "Kualana O'ahu me he 'Āina Momona." In *Food and Power in Hawai'i*, edited by Aya Hirata Kimura and Krisnawati Suryanata, 54–80. Honolulu: University of Hawai'i Press, 2016.

Kamp, David. *The United States of Arugula: How We Became a Gourmet Nation*. New York: Broadway Books, 2006.

Kelly, James. "Loco Moco: A Folk Dish in the Making." *Social Process* 30 (1983): 59–64.

Kimura, Aya Hirata, and Krisnawati Suryanata, eds. *Food and Power in Hawai'i: Visions of Food Democracy*. Honolulu: University of Hawai'i Press, 2016.

Kirkendall, Judith. "Hawaiian Ethnogastronomy: The Development of a Pidgin-Creole Cuisine." PhD diss., University of Hawai'i at Mānoa, 1985.

Kodama-Nishimoto, Michiko, Warren Nishimoto, and Cynthia Oshiro, eds. *Talking Hawai'i's Story: Oral Histories of an Island People*. Honolulu: University of Hawai'i Press, 2009.

Ku, Robert Ji-Song, Martin Malansan IV, and Anita Mannur, eds. *Eating Asian America: A Food Studies Reader*. New York: New York University Press, 2013.

Laudan, Rachel. *Cuisine and Empire: Cooking in World History*. Berkeley: University of California Press, 2015.

———. *The Food of Paradise: Exploring Hawaii's Culinary Heritage*. Honolulu: University of Hawai'i Press, 1996.

Lefaivre, Liane, and Alexander Tzonis. *Architecture of Regionalism in the Age of Globalisation: Peaks and Valleys in the Flat World*. New York: Routledge, 2011.

———. *Critical Regionalism and Identity in a Globalised World*. London: Prestel Publishing, 2003.

Linn, Brian McAllister. *Guardians of Empire: The U.S. Army and the Pacific, 1902–1940*. Chapel Hill: University of North Carolina Press, 1997.

Long, Lucy. "Culinary Tourism." In *The Oxford Handbook of Food History*, edited by Jeffrey Pilcher, 389–402. Oxford: Oxford University Press, 2012.

———. *Regional American Food Culture*. Westport, CT: Greenwood Press, 2009.

Matsushita Sachiko. *Zusetsu edo ryōri jiten*. Tokyo: Kashiwa shobō, 2009.

Mennell, Stephen. *All Manners of Food: Eating and Taste in England and France from the Middle Ages to the Present*. Urbana-Champaign: University of Illinois Press, 1996.

Merry, Sally Engle. *Colonializing Hawai'i: The Cultural Power of Law*. Princeton, NJ: Princeton University Press, 2000.

Mintz, Sidney. *Sweetness and Power: The Place of Sugar in Modern History*. New York: Penguin, 1986.

Mumford, Lewis. "Report on Honolulu." In Lewis Mumford, *City Development: Studies in Disintegration and Renewal* (New York: Harcourt Brace and Company, 1945), 84–153.

Namkoong, Joan. *Food Lover's Guide to Honolulu*. Honolulu: Bess Press, 2005.

Ng, Franklin. "Food and Culture: Chinese Restaurants in Hawai'i." In *Chinese America: History and Perspectives*. San Francisco: Chinese Historical Society of America, with UCLA Asian American Studies Center, 2010.

Okihiro, Gary. *Island World: A History of Hawai'i and the United States*. Berkeley: University of California Press, 2009.

Okihiro, Michael. *AJA Baseball in Hawaii: Ethnic Pride and Tradition*. Honolulu: Hawaii Hochi, 1999.

Osorio, Jonathan Kay Kamakawiwo'ole. *Dismembering Lāhui: A History of the Hawaiian Nation to 1887*. Honolulu: University of Hawai'i Press, 2002.

Pearlman, Alison. *Smart Casual: The Transformation of Gourmet Restaurant Style in America*. Chicago: The University of Chicago Press, 2013.

Pilcher, Jeffrey M., ed. *The Oxford Handbook of Food History*. Oxford: Oxford University Press, 2012.

Pukui, Mary Kawena, and Samuel H. Elbert. *Hawaiian Dictionary: Hawaiian-English English-Hawaiian*. Rev. and enlarged ed. Honolulu: University of Hawai'i Press, 1986.

Pukui, Mary Kawena, Samuel H. Elbert, and Esther T. Mookini. *Place Names of Hawai'i*. Rev. and expanded ed. Honolulu: University of Hawai'i Press, 1974.

Ray, Krishnendu. *The Ethnic Restaurateur*. London: Bloomsbury Academic, 2016.

———. "Migration, Transnational Cuisines and Invisible Ethnics." In *Food in Time and Place: The American Historical Association Companion to Food History*, edited by Paul Freedman et al., 209–229. Berkeley: University of California Press, 2014.

Rossant, Juliette. *Super Chefs: The Making of the Great Modern Restaurant Empires.* New York: Free Press, 2004.

Ruhlman, Michael. *The Reach of a Chef: Professional Cooks in the Age of Celebrity.* New York: Penguin, 2006.

Russell, Beverly. *Women of Taste: Recipes and Profiles of Famous Women Chefs.* New York: Wiley, 1997.

Said, Edward. *Orientalism.* New York: Vintage Books, 1979.

Schmitt, Robert C. *Firsts and Almost Firsts in Hawaiʻi.* Edited by Ron Ronck. Honolulu: University of Hawaiʻi Press, 1995.

———. *Historical Statistics of Hawaiʻi.* Honolulu: University of Hawaiʻi Press, 1962.

Shinoda Osamu and Kawakami Kōzō, eds. *Zusetsu edo jidai shokuseikatsu jiten, shinsō-han.* Tokyo: Yūsankaku, 1997.

Silva, Noenoe. *Aloha Betrayed: Native Hawaiian Resistance to American Colonialism.* Durham, NC: Duke University Press, 2004.

Simoons, Frederick. *Food in China: A Cultural and Historical Inquiry.* Boca Raton, FL: CRC Press, 2000.

Stannard, David. *Before the Horror: The Population of Hawaiʻi on the Eve of Western Contact.* Honolulu: Social Science Research Institute, University of Hawaiʻi, 1989.

Suehiro, Arthur. *Honolulu Stadium: Where Hawaiʻi Played.* Honolulu: Watermark Publishing, 1995.

Sumida, Stephen. *And the View from the Shore: Literary Traditions of Hawaiʻi.* Seattle: University of Washington Press, 1991.

Tompkins, Kyla. *Racial Indigestion: Eating Bodies in the 19th Century.* New York: New York University Press, 2012.

Tower, Jeremiah. *California Dish: What I Saw (and Cooked) at the American Culinary Revolution.* New York: Free Press, 2003.

Trask, Haunani-Kay. "Settlers of Color and 'Immigrant' Hegemony: 'Locals' in Hawaiʻi." *Amerasia Journal* 26, no. 2 (2000): 1–24.

Trubek, Amy B. *Haute Cuisine: How the French Invented the Culinary Profession.* Philadelphia: University of Pennsylvania Press, 2000.

———. *The Taste of Place: A Cultural Journey into Terroir.* Berkeley: University of California Press, 2008.

Venturi, Robert, Denise Scott Brown, and Steven Izenour. *Learning from Las Vegas, Revised Edition: The Forgotten Symbolism of Architectural Form.* Cambridge, MA: MIT Press, 1977.

Vester, Katharina. *A Taste of Power: Food and American Identities.* Berkeley: University of California Press, 2015.

Vinegar, Aron, and Michael J. Golec. *Relearning from Las Vegas.* Minneapolis: University of Minnesota Press, 2008.

Walcott, Derek. *What the Twilight Says—Essays.* New York: Farrar, Straus & Giroux, 1998.

Walker, Harlan, ed. *Cooks and Other People: Proceedings of the Oxford Symposium on Food and Cookery 1995.* Devon, UK: Prospect Books, 1996.

Wheaton, Barbara Ketcham. "Cookbooks as Social History Resources." In *Food in Time and Place: The American Historical Association Companion to Food History*, edited by Paul Freedman et al., 276–299. Berkeley: University of California Press, 2014.

Wilkins, David E., and K. Tsianina Lomawaima. *Uneven Ground: American Indian Sovereignty and Federal Law*. Norman: University of Oklahoma Press, 2001.

Yamashita, Samuel Hideo. "The Post-colonial Significance of Hawai'i Regional Cuisine." In *Eating Asian America*, edited by Robert Ku et al., 98–122. New York: New York University Press, 2013.

Yim, Susan. *We Go Eat: A Mixed Plate from Hawai'i's Food Culture*. Honolulu: Hawai'i Council for the Humanities, 2008.

Index

Adams, Wanda. *See* food writers.
airlines: Aloha, 43; Continental, 43; United, 43
Alexander, Helen, *Helen Alexander's Hawaiian Cook Book*, 12
Aloha Mixed Plate. *See* restaurants (Hawai'i).
American regional cuisine. *See* regional cuisine.
Anthony, David, 108
Ariyoshi, George, 119
Armstrong Produce, 22
arrière-garde position, 104, 108, 111, 115, 156n42. *See* also Kenneth Frampton.
awards and honors: Bertolli Sous Chef Award, 50; Best New Chef, People's Choice, 96, 112; Five Diamond Award, 50; Hale 'Aina awards, 42, 54; 'Ilima Award, 42, 54; James Beard Foundation awards (*see* James Beard Foundation); Médialle de Mérite for Outstanding Service to the Chaîne des Rôtisseurs, 50; Small Business Person of the Year, 54

Becker, Howard, 46
Bertranou, Jean. *See* chefs.
Bhatt, Ritu, 81–82
Big Five, 2
Bird, Isabella, 11
Blanchet, Michel. *See* chefs.
Boulud, Daniel. *See* chefs.

California cuisine. *See* regional cuisine.
CanoeHouse. *See* restaurants (Hawai'i).
celebrity chefs, 23–24, 33, 38–40, 42–46, 51–52, 56, 117
Central Union Church, 4, 12
chefs: Adaniya, Hank, 155n12; Ariel, Steve, 50; Banhofer, Charles, 152n31; Barker, Ben, 51; Barker, Karen, 51; Batali, Mario, 45; Benno, Jonathan, 52; Bertranou, Jean, 16, 34, 77; Blanchet, Michel, 34; Boulud, David, 38–40; Bowien, Danny, 116; Caldiero, Dave, 88; Centeno, Josef, 116; Chang, David, 112, 114, 116; Child, Julia, 31–33, 40; Chock, Helen, 50; Choi, Roy, 116; Chong, Pang Yat, 6; Clarke, Sally, 34; Colicchio, Tom, 46, 112; DiCataldo, Andrew, 52; Doumani, Lissa, 51; Farnsworth, John, 16, 19, 25, 143n71; Fearing, Dean, 39, 44; Foley, Michael, 44; Forgione, Larry, 43; Fox, Jeremy, 116; Frank, Ken, 34; Fujita, Sakazo, 6; Fukui, Hiroshi, ix; Germon, George, 51; Hefter, Lee, 51; Hirabayashi, Wayne, 104; Kajioka, Christopher, 96; Keller, Thomas, 43, 45, 57, 89, 103; Killeen, Johanne, 51; Kosaka, Lance, 50; Lagasse, Emeril, 40, 43–44, 51; Le, Loan, 109–110; Lomonaco, Michael, 51; Loperfido, Donato, 48; Martin, Michel, 139n1; Matsuhisa, Nobuyuki,

chefs *(Cont.)*

35, 38, 43–44, 52, 69, 71; Matsukata,
Kazuto, 38, 147n41; Maxim, Jacques,
91; McCarthy, Michael, 16, 34–35;
MacPherson, Grant, 51; Meyer, Danny,
112; Morrone, George, 43, 51, 69;
Murphy, Neil, 50; Ogden, Bradley, 45;
Palmer, Charlie, 63; Peel, Mark, 34;
Phan, Charles, 49, 52; Prudhomme,
Paul, 52; Puck, Wolfgang, 35, 61, 69,
147n41; Rich, Evan and Sarah, 155n13;
Richard, Michel, 40; Röckenwagner,
Hans, 44; Rodrigues, Douglas, 44–45;
Salgado, Carlos, 116; Schwarznegger,
Arnold, 39; Silverton, Nancy, 34; Siu,
Russell, ix, 45, 52; Soltner, Andre, 40,
148n74; Sone, Hiroki, 51; Splichal,
Joachim, 38–39, 91–92; Stange,
Barbara, 43; Streng, Göran, 52; Tachibe,
Shigefumi, 35, 69; Takara, Wallace,
12, 14; Tanaka, Makoto, 43, 69; Tariga,
Enrique, 49; Tommasi, Antonio, 38;
Tosi, Christina, 112; Tower, Jeremiah,
63, 152n31; Trotter, Charlie, 38–40;
Tsai, Ming, 51–52; Vergé, Roger, 38–39,
97; von Oehlhoffen, Robert, 11; Wakiya,
Yūji, 52; Waters, Alice, 1, 23, 30–31, 35,
40, 61; Waxman, Jonathan, 34; White,
Jasper, 38
Child, Julia, 32, 40
Chinatown, 19, 80–81, 93–94, 98, 125
Chock, Helen, 50
Chong, Kevin: ix; career, 87, 91–92, 101–
102; cuisine, 102–103, 114; culinary
training, 87, 91–92, 102; early life, 87,
91; honors, 96; restaurants, 97–98
Choy, Sam: ix; career, 14, 23, 31, 44, 84,
118; cookbooks, 36, 42, 54; cuisine, 16,
22–23, 58, 68, 84–85; culinary training,
84, 87; early life, 14, 22, 60, 84–85;
honors, 45, 49; restaurants, 25–26, 48;
service, 48, 51–52, 111
Christiansen, Elwood, 6
colleges and universities: College of
Tropical Agriculture and Human
Resources, 119, 127; community
college, 102; Guilford College, 20;
Kapiʻolani Community College, 80, 87,
89, 101–102, 120; Leeward Community
College, 54; Lewis & Clark College, 88;
University of Colorado, 87; University
of Hawaiʻi–Mānoa, 3, 30, 88–89, 93,
102, 127; University of Pennsylvania,
15; University of Redlands, 20
Cooking Channel, 32
Corbin, John, 122
cuisines: American, 5–6, 12, 72, 74,
76, 84, 103, 118, 129; Asian, 65–68,
71, 73, 76–79, 84–85, 108–109, 111,
113–114, 129; Cajun, 76; California-
Mediterranean, 88; Chinese, 5–6, 32,
52, 60, 65, 67, 71–72, 74, 79–81, 104,
108–109; Chinese-American, 74, 118;
Continental, 1–2, 56, 68, 80, 84–85,
108, 129; ethnic cuisine, 116; Euro-
American, 12; Euro-Asian, 33–35, 38,
55, 68–70, 72, 74, 77, 85, 101, 111, 114;
Euro-Asian / Local, 103, 105; Euro-
Asian / Local-American, 74–75, 85,
118; Euro-Asian / Pacific-Local, 72;
Euro-Asian / Pacific-Local-American,
74, 118; European, 14, 68; Filipino, 60,
65, 67, 78, 96, 104, 112–115; French:
cuisine classique, 1–2, 10–12, 32, 34,
56, 67–71, 74, 76–81, 84–85, 87, 91, 95,
100, 103–105, 108, 110–111, 115, 118,
129; fusion, 35, 77; haute cuisine, 80,
104, 108, 111, 118; Hawaiian, 5–6, 12,
50, 60, 65–67, 74, 76, 84–85, 105–108,
116; indigenous, 10; Italian, 32, 35,
105, 113; Japanese, 23, 32, 35, 56, 60,
65, 67, 71–72, 74, 79–80, 85, 108–109,
115; *kappō*, 71, 153n61; Korean, 76;
"local," 2, 8, 14–15, 23, 75–76, 79–80,
85, 104, 108, 111, 115–116, 118, 120, 129;
nouvelle cuisine, 23, 34–35, 38–39, 57,
77–78, 97, 146n32; Pacific, 65–67, 76,
84–85; Portuguese, 72, 108; Spanish,
10; Tex-Mex, 74, 118; Thai, 76–77;
Vietnamese, 65, 67, 76, 93, 108–111,
115–116
culinary awards. *See* awards and honors.
culinary schools: Culinary Institute of
America, 16, 58, 89, 91–92, 94, 96,

101–104, 108–110; Culinary Institute of the Pacific, 102; Greenbrier Cooking School, 80, 102; Kapiʻolani Community College, 80, 87, 89–90, 101–102, 118, 120, 148n74; Kyushu Culinary Academy, 35; Leeward Community College, 94, 101, 111; Maui Culinary Academy, 94, 100–101, 118
culinary technique: 68, 76–77, 79, 81–85, 113, 115; baking, 74; boiling, 113; deep frying, 76, 80, 107; grilling, 107; pounding, 107; sautéing, 107; simmering, 79; steaming, 81

Datta, Tane. *See* HRC food producers.
Dikon, Roger: career, 15, 84; cuisine, 29–30, 61, 63, 68, 84; culinary training, 58, 61; honors, 42; restaurants, 15, 25, 41; service, 39

Ellman, Judy, 25
Ellman, Mark: ix; career, 44, 84; cookbooks, 54; cuisine, 30–31, 61, 68, 76, 84; culinary training, 18, 84; early life, 18, 84; honors, 46; restaurants, 25, 30–31, 97; service, 39, 52
Enomoto, Catherine. *See* food writers.
Escoffier, Auguste: 69–70, 76–78, 80; *Le Guide Culinaire*, 69–70, 78, 80
ethnicity, 3–4, 12, 14, 23, 86–87, 111, 116, 118

Farmer Series Dinner, 53
farmers' market, 86, 91, 120, 159n11
Farnsworth, John, 16, 19, 25, 143n71
Ferguson, Amy: ix; career, 18, 25, 40, 84, 118; cuisine, 18, 61–63, 70–71, 84, 118, 128; early life, 18, 84; honors, 33, 40, 42–43, 45; restaurants, 33, 41, 43, 58
Ferguson, Patricia: restaurant world, definition of, 145n2
Food Network, 32–33
"food revolution," 22–23, 36–38, 45, 114–115, 129, 144n1
food television: 24, 32–33, 102, 117; programs (food-related): *A Taste of Hawaii with Jean-Marie Josselin*, 52;

CBS Early Show, 51; *CBS Morning*, 51; *Chef Milani*, 32; *Cooking with Master Chefs*, 40; *Elsie Presents James Beard in "I Love to Eat,"* 32; *Emeril Live*, 51; *Epicurious*, 51; *Essence of Emeril*, 43, 51; *Fishing Tales*, 101; *French Chef*, 31–33; *Frugal Gourmet*, 32; *Galloping Gourmet*, 32; *Good Morning America*, 51; *Good Morning, Hawaii*, 42; *Great Chefs of Hawaii*, 42; *Hawaii Cooks with Roy Yamaguchi*, 31–33, 36, 38, 50–51; *iVillage*, 51; *Iron Chef (Ryōri no tetsujin)*, 32–33; *Iron Chef USA*, 50; *Joyce Chen Cooks*, 32; *Let's Go Fishing*, 101; *Live with Regis and Kelley*, 51; *My Country, My Kitchen*, 50; *Queen Was in the Kitchen*, 32; *Sam Choy's Kitchen*, 101; *To the Queen's Taste*, 32; *Today*, 51; *Top Chef*, 32, 51, 96, 112–113; *What's Cooking*, 32
food writers, 24–25, 33–34, 40, 94, 117; Adams, Wanda, ix, 30, 78; California Restaurant Writers Association, 33; Cheng, Martha, 104, 112; Clarke, Joan, 74–75; Enomoto, Catherine, 30; Gray, Matthew, 75; Heckathorn, John, ix–x, 30, 45–46, 114; Henderson, Janice Wald, 33, 36, 46, 65, 67, 70, 76, 100; Lindberg, Peter, 95; Namkoong, Joan, ix, 120, 144; Peterson, Lisa, 68; Philpotts, Kaui, 42; Reichl, Ruth, 34; Richman, Alan, 106; Shaw, David, 34; Sheraton, Mimi, 33
Frampton, Kenneth: *arrière-garde* position, definition of, 156n42

Gallery Restaurant. *See* restaurants (Hawaiʻi).
Gannon, Beverly: ix; career, 42, 44, 84, 118; cookbooks, 54, 67; cuisine, 31, 61, 65, 68–74, 76, 84–85, 118; early life, 72, 74, 84; honors, 42, 46, 49; restaurants, 25–28, 31; service, 39
Gault, Henri, 57
Gayot Guide, 38
gender. *See* women.
genocide, 9–10

Goodman, Nelson, 81
Gordon, Shep, 36, 97
grass-fed beef, 124–126

Hawai'i: agriculture, 19–22, 119–120; aquaculture, 122–123; fishing, 22, 120–122; fishponds, 123; overfishing, 120, 159n17; ranching, 21–22, 123–126; self-sufficiency, 127; sustainability, 126–129
Hawai'i Farm Bureau Federation, 41, 52, 119–120
Hawai'i food: butter, 30; canned goods, 8, 18, 126; cheese, 30, 64, 118, 120; coffee, 65, 118; eggs, 118, 126, 129; fish, 4–6, 18–19, 64, 106, 108, 118, 120, 129; fowl, 4, 8; frozen food, 6–7, 18, 22–23; fruit, 4–5, 8, 18–19, 30, 64, 106, 108, 127, 129; imports, 4, 6, 8, 18, 20, 61, 126–127; meat, 4, 8, 18–19, 21–22, 30, 64, 118, 120, 123–126, 129; milk, 4, 125; seaweed, 5, 60, 123; shellfish, 4, 64, 106, 118, 120; sustainability, 126–129; vegetables, 4–5, 8, 18–21, 30, 36–37, 64, 106, 127, 129
Hawai'i food events: Big Island Bounty, 43; Cuisines of the Sun, 43–44, 51; Grand Chefs on Tour, 44; Kapalua Wine & Food Symposium, 43; Kea Lani Food & Wine Festival, 51; Winter Wine Escape, 43
Hawai'i history: annexation, 2, 12; colony, 1–2, 4, 9, 11–12, 14–15, 85–86; kingdom, 1; republic, 1, 11–12; state, 1, 86, 107–108, 119, 126–127, 157n57
Hawai'i population: Caucasian, 2–5, 8; Chinese, 2–3, 5; Filipino, 2, 5, 112–113; Hawaiian, 2–3, 106–108; Japanese, 2–3; locals, 2–3, 5, 8; Okinawan, 6, 12, 14; part-Hawaiian, 3; Portuguese, 2–3, 5, 72; Puerto Rican, 2–3, 72; Spanish, 2–3
Hawai'i Regional Cuisine (HRC): brand, 23, 57, 97, 117; community, 1, 27; cuisine, 36, 57–58, 60–74, 76, 79, 84, 86, 118; development, 24–25, 33–42, 45–46, 48, 52, 55–56; ethnicity, 1, 4, 12, 14, 23, 56; experimentation, 68–74, 76–78, 118; humor, 70, 74–75, 80, 84,

118; impact, 102–105, 115; innovation, 68, 74–76, 84, 86, 118; legacy, 117–123, 126–129; memory, 58–61, 77; origins, 1, 15, 22–23; successors, 86, 97, 100–103, 105–106, 108, 114–116
HRC benefit dinners: A Taste of Oregon, 42; Big Brothers / Big Sisters, 41, 51; Chopsticks and Wine, 52; culinary programs in Hawai'i, 52; Easter Seal Society of Hawai'i, 41–42; Farm Bureau Benefit Dinner, 41, 52; Farmer Series Dinner, 120; Hale 'Aina Ohana, 52; Hawaii Restaurant Association's Chefs of Aloha, 52; Hurricane Katrina and Kaua'i, 52; 'Iolani School, 52; Leeward Community College Culinary Arts Gala, 54; O'ahu Art Center, 52; Save a Child's Life, 51; Taste of the Stars, 52
HRC food producers (aquaculturists, cheese makers, farmers, fishermen/women, ranchers): 19, 38, 63–65, 81–84, 102, 114, 117–120, 122–124, 127, 129, 160n24; Anthony, David, 108; Datta, Maureen, 20; Datta, Tane, ix, 20, 46, 64; Ha, Kimo, 65; Ha, Richard, 64; Hamakua Mushroom Farm, 53, 65; Hamakua Springs Country Farm, 64; Hawaii Island Goat Dairy, 64; Hirabara, Kurt, ix–x, 64–65; Hirabara, Pam, ix, 64–65; Jardine, Alex, 65; Kahuā Ranch, 64; Lee, Erin, ix, 21, 64–65; MA'O Farms, 108; Maui Cattle Company, 55; Okimoto, Dean, ix, 20–21, 64, 120; Pacific Gateway Foundation Farm, 108; Paniolo Cattle Company, 125; Parker Ranch, 125; Petersons' Upland Egg Farm, 55; Richards, Herbert Montague "Monty," Jr., 21, 64–65; Sakamoto, Edward, ix, 65; Shinsato Farm, 128; Stanga, Bob, 65; Sumida Watercress Farm, 55; Trefall, Heather, 65; Troutlodge Marine Farm, 53; Ulupono Initiative, 125
HRC restaurants: 808 La Jolla, 46; A Pacific Bakery & Grill, 41; A Pacific Café, 15, 25–26, 33, 40–42, 46, 48; Alan Wong's, x, 40–42, 45, 50, 52,

54–55, 61, 75–76, 78–79, 82–84, 88–91, 94, 101; Alan Wong's Hualalai Grill, 47–48; Avalon, 25–26, 30–31; Cassis, 47–48; Chef Mavro, 41, 50, 54–55, 92–94, 101, 103, 108–109; Diamond Head Restaurant, 41, 48, 52, 54; Elua Restaurant & Wine Bar, 48; Hali'imaile General Store, 25–28, 30–31, 71; Merriman's, 26, 28–29, 42, 54; Merriman's Market Café, 47; Oodles of Noodles, 41, 43, 48; Padovani's Bar & Grill, 50; Padovani's Bistro & Wine Bar, 41, 51; Padovani's Restaurant & Wine Bar, 46, 47, 51; Pineapple Room, 41, 61, 75, 125; Roy's Hawaii Kai, 15–16, 25–26, 33, 38, 40–43, 52, 54, 67, 69, 76, 87, 101; Roy's Ko Olina, 52; Roy's New China Max, 41; Roy's Pebble Beach, 40; Roy's Poipu Bar & Grill, 40; Roy's Waikoloa Bar & Grill, 41; Sam Choy's Diner, 25–26; Sam Choy's Kaloko, 25, 49
Hawaii Restaurant Association, 52
Hawai'i secondary schools: English Standard schools, 2, 140n8; Hilo High School, 94; 'Iolani School, 3, 52, 140n13; Kamehameha Schools, 3, 102, 140n13; McKinley High School, 91; Mid-Pacific Institute, 3, 89, 140n13; Oahu College, 2; private schools, 3, 52, 87–89, 93, 118; Punahou, 2–3, 87–88, 140n13; St. Louis School, 3, 93, 140n13
Hawai'i Visitors Bureau, 105–106
"Hawaiian Sense of Plate," 105
Hawaiians: agriculture, 126; ahupua'a, 127; ali'i, 3; cuisine (*see* cuisine); diet, 5; ethnicity, 14, 22, 36; fishponds, 123; genocide, 2–3; Kanaka Maoli, 127; opposition to annexation, 2–3; population, 2, 9; precontact, 5, 126; self-sufficiency, 126
Heckathorn, John. *See* food writers.
Henderson, Janice Wald. *See* food writers.
Higa, Francis, 40
Hirabara, Kurt. *See* HRC food producers.
Hirabara, Pam. *See* HRC food producers.
Home Shopping Network, 51
hotels: Alexander Young Hotel, 6; Bellagio Hotel and Casino, 51; Caesar's Palace,

46; Coco Palms Hotel, 25; Disney Aulani Resort, 97, 100, 103; DoubleTree Alana, 41; Four Seasons (Maui), 41; Greenbrier, 80, 102; Hakata Prince Hotel, 35; Halekulani Hotel, 6, 25–26, 100; Hapuna Beach Prince, 43; Hawaii Prince Hotel, 25–26; Hawaiian Hotel, 11; Highlands Inn, 38–39; Hilton Hawaiian Village Beach Resort & Spa; 51; Hotel Hana Maui, 18, 25, 118; Hualalai Resort, 47; Kahala Mandarin Oriental Hotel, 104; Kapalua Bay Hotel, 18; Kona Hilton Beach and Tennis Club, 14; Kona Village Resort, 18; Lodge at Koele, 16, 25, 43; Manele Bay Hotel, 16, 25; Maui Prince Hotel, 15–16, 18, 25–26, 29–30; Mauna Kea Beach Hotel, 43; Mauna Lani Bay Hotel, 15, 43; Mauna Lani Hotel, 18, 25; Mauna Lani Resort, ix, 22, 25; Ritz-Carlton Mauna Lani, 25–26, 43, 118; Royal Hawaiian Hotel, 12, 14; Sheraton Plaza La Reina, 16; Sheraton Waikiki, 52; Surfjack Hotel, 97, 100, 107; Waikoloa Beach Resort, 47; Wailea Beach Marriott Resort, 97, 100

immigration, 5–6, 12, 58, 91, 93–94, 102, 109, 115
'Iolani Palace, 4, 11

James Beard Foundation awards and honors: America's Classics, 49–50; Best Chef: California, 49; Best Chef: Midwest, 39; Best Chef: New York City, 39, 112; Best Chef: Northeast, 39; Best Chef: Pacific Northwest, 38–39, 45, 49, 90, 96; Best Chef: Southwest, 44; Best Chef: West, 91, 96; Best Chef in America, 39, 49; Best Hotel Chefs of America, 42; Best New Restaurant, 52, 96, 112; Hawaii Regional Cuisine Dinners, 46, 72, 149n80; James Beard House, 42, 49, 55, 149n80; Outstanding Chef, 43; Outstanding Pastry Chef, 96; Rising Star Chef of the Year. 96, 112
Janer, Zilkia, 10

Josselin, Jean-Marie: career, 25, 41, 46, 48, 52, 58, 84; cookbooks, 36; cuisine, 18, 65, 68, 84, 127–128; early life, 84; honors, 33, 38–39, 45, 49; restaurants, 25, 41, 46, 48; service, 41–42

Kalākaua, David, 11
Kamehameha V, 11
Kamp, David, 7, 16, 63, 152n31
Ka Palapala Poʻokela Book awards, 54
Kapiʻolani Community College. *See* colleges and universities.
Karr-Ueoka, Michele: ix; career, 87–89; cuisine, 100, 102–104, 114–115; culinary training, 87–89; early life, 87–88, 103, 115; honors, 96; restaurants, 98, 100
Ke Kuaʻaina Hanauna Hou, 123
Kenney, Edward: ix; career, 87, 101; cuisine, 100, 105–108, 114–115; culinary training, 87–88, 101; early life, 87–88, 97–98, 115; "Hawaiian Sense of Plate," 105; honors, 87, 95–96; restaurants, 87–88, 94, 96–97, 100
Kimball, Richard, 6
Knapp, George, 6
Kojima, Hari, 101
Kosaka, Melanie, 31–32
Kunimoto, Sandra Lee, 119

La Mer, 19, 25–26, 41, 100
Laudan, Rachel, 11, 139n3
Le, Andrew: ix; career, 86–87, 93; cuisine, 108–111, 114–116; culinary training, 9, 87, 101–102; early life, 87, 93, 111; honors, 96–98; restaurants, 94, 98
Le, Loan, 109–110
Lee, Erin. *See* HRC food producers.
Le Guide Culinaire. See Escoffier, Auguste.
Leoda's Kitchen and Pie Shop. *See* restaurants (Hawaiʻi).
Lingle, Linda, 119
locavorism: 24, 35–37; 57, 61, 63–65, 68, 76, 79, 82, 84, 86, 102, 108, 117–120, 127–128; Buy Local, It Matters, 119; Growing Agricultural Tourism in North Kohala, 119; Grown on Maui, 119, 127; Hawaiʻi Seals of Quality, 119;

Kauai Made, 119, 127; Keep Kohala, Kohala, 119; North Kohala Eat Locally Grown, 119
loco moco, 75–76, 80–81
luau, 12, 54, 61, 72
Lum, Calvin, 125

Makaha Sons, 54
Maori, 9
Mavrothalassitis, George: ix; career, 25, 48, 84; cuisine, 62–64, 68, 70, 72, 77–78, 84, 103; culinary training, 58, 84; early life, 84; honors, 49–50, 96; restaurants, 41, 92, 94, 108–109; service, 42, 52
McDonald, Marie, 120
mediated reference, 80–84, 114
Merriman, Peter: ix; career, 15, 120–122, 128; cookbooks, 74; cuisine, 18, 20–22, 61–62, 64–65, 68, 72, 74, 84; culinary training, 58, 84; early life, 74, 84; honors, 42, 49–50, 54; restaurants, 20, 25, 28–29, 46–48; service, 39, 120–122
Merriman, Vicki, 20
Michelin star, 38, 52, 62
migration. *See* immigration.
Millaut, Christian, 57
Momofuku, 112
Mondavi, Robert, 43
Monsef, Stanley, 28
Morton, John, ix, 102
multiculturalism, 115

Namkoong, Joan. *See* food writers.
Native Americans, 127
New American Cuisine. *See* regional cuisine.
new casual. *See* smart casual.
nouvelle cuisine. See cuisine.

Obama, Barack and Michele, 54
Okimoto, Dean. *See* HRC food producers.
Okinawa, 6, 12, 14
Opelo Plaza, 28

Pacific Gateway Foundation, 98
Padovani, Philippe: career, 18–19, 25, 51, 84; cuisine, 18–19, 61, 64, 68, 70–71, 84;

culinary training, 58, 84; early life, 84; restaurants, 41, 46–48; service, 52
Philippines, 94, 112–114
plantations, 58–60, 86, 94, 112–115, 119, 123, 158n4
Plantation Village, 53
post-HRC chefs: 86–87, 97, 100, 102, 105, 110, 113–118; *arrière-garde* position, 102, 104, 108, 111, 115; community, 114; culture, 102–104, 106–108, 110, 112–114; ethnicity, 86–87, 111, 116, 118; family: 102, 105, 109–111, 113, 115–116, 118; innovation, 102, 115, 118; local, 116; memory, 105, 110–111, 113, 115; nostalgia, 115; place, 100, 102, 105, 115–116, 118; "taste of place," 116
post-HRC chefs' restaurants: Downtown, 97–98; Kaimuki Superette, 97–99; Lanikea YWCA Café, 87; Mahina & Sun's, 97, 100, 107–108; Migrant Maui, 97, 100, 113–114; Mud Hen Water, 97–100; MW, 91, 97–98, 100, 104, 115; The Pig and the Lady, 94, 97–98, 110–111, 115; Town, 87, 94–95, 98, 100, 105–106
Prince Court. *See* restaurants (Hawai'i).
professional organizations: American Culinary Federation, 12; Professional Chefs of Hawaii, 14

racism, 2–4, 8, 12, 14, 23, 84–85, 91–92, 118, 140n8, 144n103
Ray, Krishnendu: 14, 23, 43, 56, 68, 84–85, 111, 116; celebrity chef network, 24, 43; embodied experience, 68, 84–85, 111; ethnic, 23, 56, 85, 111, 116, 118; ethnic cuisine, 32, 56, 85; *The Ethnic Restaurateur*, 84–85; expert, 84–85, 111, 116, 118; foreign cuisine, 23, 32, 56, 85; taste, 56, 116
recession, 48
regional cuisine: 1, 22, 24, 29–30, 38–39, 62, 85, 117–118; American regional cuisine, 1, 85; California Cuisine, 16, 30, 34–35, 63, 85, 88, 145n14; Hawai'i Regional Cuisine (*see* HRC (Hawai'i Regional Cuisine)); New American

Cuisine, 30, 34, 39, 63, 85, 145n14; Southwestern Cuisine, 39, 44, 62, 85
restaurants (Asia): Alan Wong's Hawaii (Tokyo, Japan), 41; La Marée de Chaya (Hayama, Japan), 35; Roy's New China Max (Hong Kong), 41; Turandot (Yokohama, Japan), 52
restaurants (Central America): Le Cirque (Mexico City), 92
restaurants (France): Chanticleer (Nice), 91; La Bonne Auberge (Nouzerines), 91; La Pyramide (Vienne), 1; Moulin de Mougin (Mougin), 38
restaurants (Hawai'i): Alexander Young Hotel, 6; Aloha Mixed Plate, 94–95, 111; 'Ama'Ama, 97, 103; American Café, 6; Butler's Coffee House, 5; Canlis, 6; CanoeHouse, ix, 25, 40, 60; Diamond Ice Cream Parlor, 6; Donato's, 87; Duc's Bistro, 93; Fishermen's Wharf, 6; Gallery Restaurant, 22; Garden House, 93; Hank's Hot Dogs, 94, 155n12; Helena's Hawaiian Foods, 50; Hew's Store and Restaurant, 5; Indigo, 87; Jurison's Inn, 45; L'Uraku, 91; Lau Yee Chai, 6–8; Lemongrass, 98; Leoda's Kitchen and Pie Shop, 94; Longhi's, 18; Michel's, 6; Po Hee Hong's, 5; Prince Court, 25; Seascape Ma'alaea Restaurant, 49; Shipley's, 87; Side Street Inn, 45; Star Noodle, 95, 111–112; Sun Yun Woo, 6; Swanky Franky, 6; Tango, 52; Taste, 91; Tin Tin Chop Suey, 154n101; Tsunami, 91; Unique Lunch Room, 6; Warren House, 5; Willows, 139n1; Wo Fat, 6; Zippy's, 40, 89, 104
restaurants (mainland U.S.): 385 North, 16, 33, 35, 58, 69; Al Forno, 51; Alex, 90; An American Place, 43; Aqua, 43, 69; Baby Routh's, 33, 58; Blue Ginger, 51; Charlie Trotter's, 38; Chaya Brasserie, 35, 69; Chez Panisse, 30, 40, 61, 63, 152n31; Chinois on Main, 35, 38, 69; Citrus, 40; Condotierre, 34; Daniel, 50; Daniel Boulud, 50; Disney World, 94; Emeril's, 40; Fifth Floor, 51; French

restaurants (mainland U.S.) *(Cont.)*
Laundry, 43, 89–90, 103; Jasper's, 38;
Jean-Louis, 43; L'Ermitage, 16, 34, 77;
L'Escoffier, 16, 34; La Côte Basque, 1,
63; La Petite Marmite, 63; La Serene,
34, 77; Le Chantilly, 63; Le Cirque,
38, 91–92, 103; Le Gourmet, 16, 34; Le
Petite Chaya, 35, 69; Locanda Veneta,
38; Lutèce, 15, 40, 80, 148n74; Magnolia
Grill, 51; Mako's, 43; Matsuhisa, 35, 38,
43, 69; Max au Triangle, 91; Michael's,
16, 34; Momofuku Noodle Bar, 112;
Park Café, 41; Patina, 38; Patria, 52;
Per Se, 52, 96, 103; Pinot Bistro, 91–92;
Regency Club, 91; Rich Table, 94,
155n13; Schatzi on Main, 39; Seventh
Street Bistro, 91; Slanted Door, 49;
Spago, 51, 61, 69; Terra, 51
restaurant world, definition of, 22, 24, 33,
38, 40, 42–43, 45, 56, 95, 101, 111–112,
116–118, 129; 145n2. *See also* Patricia
Ferguson.
Richards, Herbert Montague "Monty," Jr.
See HRC food producers.
Rombauer, Irma, 74
Ruhlman, Michael, 40
Russell, Beverly, 42

Sakamoto, Edward. *See* HRC food
producers.
Sakamoto, Mike, 101
Santos, Barbara, 54
Sato, Gladys, ix, 14
Schuster, Robert, 36
semiotics, 79–84, 114
Simeon, Sheldon: ix; career, 87, 94–95,
100–101, 111–114; cuisine, 111–116;
culinary training, 87, 94–95, 101; early
life, 87, 94; honors, 96–113; restaurants,
97, 100
smart casual style, definition of, 96; 94,
96–97, 116, 129, 155n13
Southwestern Cuisine. *See* regional
cuisine.
Spencecliff restaurants, 6
Stannard, David, 9
Star Noodle. *See* restaurants (Hawai'i).

State of Hawai'i: Aquaculture
Development Program, 107; Clean
Energy Initiative, 127; Department
of Agriculture, 119; Department of
Energy, 127; Department of Health,
107–108, 157n57; *Hawai'i 2050
Sustainability Plan*, 126–127
Strehl, Gary: career, 18, 25, 41, 44, 84;
cuisine, 18, 61, 68, 70, 84; culinary
training, 58, 84; early life, 84; honors,
33, 42; restaurants, 18, 25
Suisan Company, 22
Sumida Watercress Farm. *See* HRC food
producers.
sustainability. *See* Hawai'i food.

Takara, Wallace, 12, 14
Tanabe, Willa, 12
Tokyo Disneyland, 41
tourism: 25–26, 29, 41, 48, 98, 100, 108;
Japan, 48; West Coast, 48
Tsunoda family, 35, 69
Tuzon, Patricia, 72

Ueoka, Wade: ix; career, 87, 89–91;
cuisine, 100, 102–105; culinary
training, 87, 89–90, 101; early life, 87,
89, 103; honors, 96; restaurants, 91,
97–98
Ulupono Initiative, 125
United States of America: Alaska, 165n48;
Minnesota, 127; National Maritime
Fisheries Service, 122; Supreme Court,
127; Washington, 127
URBANo, 112

Venturi, Robert, 81; *Learning from Las
Vegas*, 81
Vietnam, 93, 98, 109–111
Villard Books, 36

Walcott, Derek, 86, 104–105, 116
Weaver, Clifton, 6
Weaver, Spencer, 6
WGBH, 32
Whole Foods, 108

Woman's Society of Central Union
Church, *Hawaiian Cook Book*, 12
women, 12, 23, 118, 128
Wong, Alan: ix; career, 15, 23, 25,
44, 45, 48, 51, 84–85, 101–102, 118;
cookbooks, 42, 67, 100; cuisine, 15,
55–56, 58–61, 65, 68, 70, 74–76, 78–84,
103–105, 109, 114–115, 125; culinary
training, 15, 80, 84, 101–102; early
life, 60–61, 84–85; honors, 42, 45, 50,
54–56; restaurants, 25, 46–47, 40–41,
45, 48, 55–56, 88–90, 94, 101–102, 125;
service, 42, 51–53, 120

Yamaguchi, Roy: ix; career, 15–16, 20–21,
23; 31–32, 36–39, 48, 50–53, 64, 84–85,
101, 117–118, 147n51; cookbooks, 36,
42, 54, 67, 76; cuisine, 27, 34–35, 57–58,
60–64, 67–69, 76–78, 84, 100–101, 109,
114, 117, 120; culinary training, 51, 77,
84; early life, 61, 67, 77, 84–85; honors,
33, 38–39, 42–43, 54; restaurants, 15,
25, 27, 40–42, 46, 48, 58, 67; service, 41,
52–54, 120
Yoshida, Fern Tomisato, ix, 14, 68

Zippy's. *See* restaurants (Hawai'i).

About the Author

Samuel Hideo Yamashita grew up in Kailua, a beach town in Hawai'i, and studied history in college. A Woodrow Wilson Fellowship led to graduate work in history at the University of Michigan and a postdoctoral year at Harvard University. He is currently the Henry E. Sheffield Professor of History at Pomona College, where he has taught since 1983. Long fascinated with food as a historical subject, he has been gathering material for a history of Japanese food since 2009 and has given lectures on the origins and evolution of Japanese cuisine and the "Japanese turn" in fine dining in the United States. *Hawai'i Regional Cuisine: The Food Movement That Changed the Way Hawai'i Eats* is his first book-length foray into food studies and part of a larger exploration of fusion cuisines along the Pacific Rim.